TOO FEW
TO MATTER

Institutional Inertia in the Prisoning of Women in Canada and Québec

TOO FEW TO MATTER

Institutional Inertia in the Prisoning of Women in Canada and Québec

JOANE MARTEL

Presses de
l'Université Laval

Financé par le gouvernement du Canada
Funded by the Government of Canada | Canadä

Nous remercions le Conseil des arts du Canada de son soutien.
We acknowledge the support of the Canada Council for the Arts.

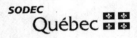

Conseil des arts   Canada Council
du Canada   for the Arts

Each year, Presses de l'Université Laval receives financial support from the Société de développement des entreprises culturelles du Québec for their publishing programs.

SODEC
Québec

Bibliothèque et Archives nationales du Québec and Library and Archives Canada Cataloguing in Publication

Title: Too few to matter : institutional inertia in the prisoning of women in Canada and Québec / Joane Martel.

Names: Martel, Joane, 1962- author.

Description: Includes bibliographical references.

Identifiers: Canadiana (print) 20230071376 | Canadiana (ebook) 20230071384 | ISBN 9782766300914 | ISBN 9782766300921 (PDF)

Subjects: LCSH: Reformatories for women—Canada—History. | LCSH: Reformatories for women—Québec (Province)—History. | LCSH: Women prisoners. | LCSH: Imprisonment—Canada. | LCSH: Imprisonment—Québec (Province) | LCSH: Alternatives to imprisonment.

Classification: LCC HV8738.M37 2023 | DDC 365/.430971—dc23

Linguistic revision: Linda Arui
Page layout: Diane Trottier
Cover design: Laurie Patry

Legal Deposit 4th Quarter 2023
ISBN : 978-2-7663-0091-4
ISBN PDF : 9782766300921

Les Presses de l'Université Laval
www.pulaval.com

Foreword

This book focuses on the imprisonment of women in Canada and Québec. It is interested, more specifically, in prisons' tenacity through time and space. The reflection developed in this book took shape in my mind when, in 2016, the Québec government decided to shut down Maison Tanguay, its main prison designated for women, for reasons of dilapidation, and to move the women prisoners to a former federal penitentiary for men that the federal government had closed a few years earlier for the same reasons. Are incarcerated women forever destined to occupy decrepit spaces that men no longer want or need? How could this still be happening in 2016 despite the notable number of critical analyses, historical and contemporary, of women's treatment in prison? Thirty years of academic research on a variety of issues faced by incarcerated women have taught me that imprisonment, as a penal device, is surprisingly tenacious. Nearing the end of my scholarly career, I felt it was important to look straight into this tenacity and to shed light on its contours using a novel theoretical perspective. I hope that this book will be useful to scholars in carceral sociology, to correctional decision-makers and, above all, to the community organizations that, every day, deliver crucial services to incarcerated or released women who often struggle to forge a pathway for themselves through the opaque twists and turns of prison or the adversities of their own community resettlement upon their prison release.

I would like to express my eternal appreciation to the women with lived experience of incarceration who collaborated in this research and without whom this book would have remained an intangible idea. Their selfless involvement in this study is a testament to their human strength, courage, and extraordinary resilience in the face of adversity, of which imprisonment is not the least. I hope that this book is a witness to their unrelenting resistance to their own and other women's dehumanization in prison. This book is dedicated to them.

Warm thanks, also, to my research assistants Caroline Pelletier and Daniel Benson for their highly contributive work in data collection and coding; to my research assistant Simon Bélanger who collated media stories on the 2016 Leclerc transfer and the subsequent prison conditions; to Karine Lacoste and Kathy Jaworski for their verbatim transcriptions of the women's interviews and to Jean-François Gaudreault, the graphic artist who designed the timeline that synthesizes the main argumentation supported in this book. I would like to thank the Société Elizabeth Fry du Québec as well as Québec City's Community Chaplaincy, which collaborated generously and made this study possible.

Loving thanks to my spouse, Yves, who not only prepared every evening meal during the last months of the preparation of this book so that I could extend writing days beyond the usual and remain focused and dedicated to writing, but also took time out of his busy professor's work schedule to provide a linguistic review of the manuscript. Without his loving support, the book would have taken much longer to come to fruition. Thank you to my strong and beautiful daughters, Séverine and Pénélope Fuxia, who have brought sunshine into my life for the past 20 years and supported the completion of this book either by enthusiastically enquiring about its development, or by turning the music down while mommy was writing in the next room. Séverine directed me to the stimulating work of cultural theorist Lauren Berlant, and I thank her for the wonderful read that complemented one of my arguments.

Within the Presses de l'Université Laval, Denis Dion, then Director of Publishing, and Marie-Hélène Boucher, Executive Director, were instrumental in the publication of this book. They initially welcomed the idea behind the book. Warm thanks to publisher Cynthia Boutillier and her wonderful team of professionals at the Presses de l'Université Laval for their expertise, openness, and patience. They read and commented on versions of the manuscript, and provided linguistic editing in both French and English. I am forever grateful for their interest and support in my work. Many thanks must be directed also to the two anonymous reviewers of the book who gracefully agreed to read and comment on the manuscript and provided thoughtful comments and complementary analytical leads. Warm thanks to my colleague, Kelly Struthers Montford from Toronto Metropolitan University, who read and commented on an unfinished version of the book. Many of her thoughtful insights have been included in the book's final shape.

This monograph is supported with funding from the Social Sciences and Humanities Research Council of Canada (grant # 890-2014-0034), as well as with internal funding by Université Laval.

The royalties from this book will be donated to community organizations that deliver much needed services to women with lived experiences in prison.

Table of contents

Introduction

> The prison itself was a significant reform—one
> that repeatedly failed, only to be replaced,
> through reform, by a new iteration of itself.
> (Rubin, 2019b:152)

Hoping to save tens of millions of dollars, in April 2010, the Canadian federal correctional authorities[1] announced the closure of two of their most decrepit penitentiaries. The first was the 178-year-old Kingston maximum security penitentiary designated for men (known locally as KP), which opened on June 1, 1835, in Kingston, Ontario, and closed on September 30, 2013. It employed approximately 460 workers and kept between 350 and 500 prisoners plus another 120 prisoners at the Regional Treatment Centre, a forensic psychiatric facility enclosed within Kingston Penitentiary's perimeter (TVA Nouvelles, 2012; Hennessy, 1999). At the time of its closure, Kingston Penitentiary held the sad record of being one of the oldest prisons in continuous use in the world. The second dilapidated penitentiary to be decommissioned by the federal government was the Leclerc medium security penitentiary also designated for men. It originally opened in 1961 in Laval, Québec, and also closed at the end of September 2013. It housed up to 481 men prisoners and employed 350 workers who learned of the closure during the Minister Vic Toews' press conference,

---

1. In Canada, prison sentences of two years or more are reserved for serious crimes and are served in federal institutions managed by the federal government, while sentences of less than two years are given for minor crimes and are served in provincial prisons which are under the purview of provincial governments (Alberta, Manitoba, Ontario, Québec, Newfoundland, etc.).

at the same time as all Canadians (TVA Nouvelles, 2012). In the meantime, and at a time of significant prison overcrowding in provincial prisons for men in the early 2010s, the Québec government commissioned the construction of four new men's prisons. The Roberval prison opened in the fall of 2015, the prisons in Sept-Îles and Sorel-Tracy in 2017 and the prison of Amos in 2018. Roberval was a new construction, while Amos, Sept-Îles and Sorel-Tracy replaced smaller decommissioned prisons.[2] While awaiting the completion of these four new prisons, and to attend to overcrowding in men's provincial prisons, the Québec government undertakes to rent the closed Leclerc penitentiary in a ten-year lease (2014-2024) with a possible lease extension of five supplemental years not excluding a conceivable purchase of the infrastructure. As a result, approximately 250 provincial men prisoners are transferred to the decommissioned Leclerc in the Fall of 2014.

On September 24, 2015, in a unilateral, unexpected decision, Québec's Ministry of Public Safety announced the upcoming closure of the decaying Tanguay institution, its sole provincial prison designated for women,[3] and the women's swift transfer to the same Leclerc prison that federal correctional authorities had shut down because of its own state of dilapidation.

Since the government of Québec's original decision to rent the old Leclerc was to provide quick relief for the overcrowding in men's prisons, its subsequent decision to transfer women to the Leclerc prison goes against this very objective. Several months later, the women's transfer to the Leclerc prison was undertaken in February 2016, shortly after the hasty transfer of approximately 160 men to make room for the 248 women being relocated from the decrepit Tanguay prison. Eighty-four men remained at Leclerc in a unit separated from the

---

2.   https://www.securitepublique.gouv.qc.ca/services-correctionnels/milieu-carceral/
     etablissements-detention.html, accessed February 16, 2021.

3.   I understand that prisons for women are built on a particular social construction of
     the category "woman," and that persons who do not self-identify as women may be
     incarcerated in such prisons, while persons who do self-identify may be incarcerated in "men's prisons." Nevertheless, the term "women" is used in this book, since
     correctional services, both federal and provincial, continue to favour this term to
     differentiate between prisons where individuals of one of these two groups (men and
     women) are housed in a sex-segregated prison system. To recognize that "women's
     prisons" incarcerate cisgender women, transgender men, and non-binary and Two-
     spirit persons, the expression "prisons designated for women" will be favoured.

women's living areas before allegations of bullying, suggestive looks, and rubbing eventually forced the government to transfer out the remaining men (Fortier, 2016). Meanwhile, imposed gender diversity and other dehumanizing conditions such as the absence of shower curtains, the lack of clean underwear and feminine hygiene products (Nadeau, 2016d) under which the women's transfer to Leclerc was undertaken were condemned by scholars, advocacy groups, and the media as violations of basic human rights and as a deficit of governmental transparency. On May 10, 2016, three months after the women's transfer to Leclerc, Québec's Women's Federation and Civil Liberties Union, supported by nine organizations and legal professional associations, requested that the Ministry of Public Safety authorize an independent observation mission by the Federation and the Union into Leclerc to document prison conditions. On May 27, 2016, the Ministry refused, invoking security concerns and improvements that had been implemented at the prison (Alter-Justice, 2016; Lévesque, 2016). The Ministry also refused access to journalists from *Le Devoir*, a well-respected independent and large-circulation Québec-based media outlet (Nadeau, 2016a and g).

Since then, reports continue to abound about the ill treatment of women at the Leclerc prison.[4] Yet, since the middle of the 19th century, scholarly literature on women's imprisonment and governmental inquiries of all sorts have documented the dire situation and the specific needs of imprisoned women in Canada. Historically, correctional services surfaced as a result of societies' "need" for protection against "criminals," most of whom were men. Societies reacted by sequestering these men in prisons away from the rest of the community. When studies in criminology began to document that education and professional training could facilitate successful social reintegration following imprisonment, correctional programs began to appear in prisons and were developed based on men prisoners' needs. For their part, feminist scholars and advocacy groups have maintained a constant reform narrative toward either the implementation of women-centred prison

---

4. Aubin, 2020; Dauphin-Johnson, 2018; Drainville, 2020; Feith, 2018; Figarol and Descoteaux, 2022; Groguhé, 2018 and 2019; Hébert, 2019; La Presse canadienne, 2019; Nadeau 2018, 2019, 2021a and b; Plante, 2019; Québec Ombudsman, 2020; Radio-Canada, 2019; TVA Nouvelles, 2018.

programming or decarceration.[5] However, the prison conditions at Leclerc in 2016, as well as in subsequent years, suggest that the prison is resisting formidably to significant change.

This book offers a critical rereading of the history of women's prisoning in Canada, explaining its unfolding and expansion while drawing on the rich conceptual apparatus borne from political science and criminal justice reform literature on path dependence—the propensity of institutions or professional practices to bolster a given set of arrangements increasing, over time, the toll of changing them. I then use this theoretical foundation to contextualize the transfer of Québec's provincially sentenced women to Leclerc prison. The book's focus is therefore on the stability or persistence of women's prisoning despite repeated calls for humane reform. My analysis does not aim primarily to contribute to theory building of path dependence. Rather, in the hope of stimulating reflection and discussion, the book uses women's penal history as a theory illustrative case providing an analytical application of several path dependence concepts that may deepen scholarly appreciation of the mechanisms that enable the process of prisoning to stay the course despite calls for reform. Through this illustration, I seek to provide some sense of the persistence of the prison that many scholars have observed aptly in the last few decades (e.g., McMahon, 1992; Piché, 2012) but have infrequently engaged analytically with the conditions of possibility surrounding institutional and organizational stability.

Simple observation of the prison's durability is not surprising per se. It becomes interesting when it tells a tale of something gone wrong. I seek to address the problem of women's prisoning from a different angle, a less threaded analytical path in criminal justice which holds

---

5.   For example, Adelberg and Currie, 1987; Balfour and Comack, 2014; Bertrand, 1979 and 1998; Berzins and Collette-Carrière, 1979; Boritch, 2001; Cadieux, 2003; Canada 1921, 1977a and b, 1978a and b, 1990; Canadian Human Rights Commission, 2003; Comack, 2018; Commission des droits de la personne du Québec, 1985; Cooper, 1987; Correctional Investigator Canada, 2010, 2014, 2019, 2020; Canadian Association of Elizabeth Fry Societies; Frigon, 2001, 2002; Hannah-Moffat, 1999, 2001; Hannah-Moffat and Shaw, 2000a and b; Hayman, 2000, 2006; Laplante, 1991; Marques and Monchalin, 2020; Martel, 2006; Martel and Brassard, 2008; McLean, 1995; McMahon, 1992; Nova Scotia, 1992; Ontario, 1995; Piché, 2012; Pollack, 2005; Société Elizabeth Fry du Québec, 2011; Turnbull, Martel, Parkes and Moore, 2018.

the potential to challenge conventional wisdom and assumptions about women's imprisonment in Canada and elsewhere. I articulate my discussion around four analytical components. The first chapter discusses relevant theoretical underpinnings of path dependence and its main uses in the criminal justice reform literature. This is followed by a brief methodological account. A third chapter brings to the fore the historical prisoning of women at the federal level by identifying important periods of stability, as well as points of critical junctures and path bifurcations. In a fourth chapter, the same is accomplished for Québec, with highlights from the media, as well as experiential data from women documenting the conditions of their transfer to Leclerc. It will be argued that women's prisoning in Québec, and in Canada in general, follows a persistent institutional path that is useful in understanding what happened at Leclerc during and following the women's transfer in 2016.

The issues discussed in this book have relevance, since women's incarceration rates have been rising in Québec (Chéné, 2020; Québec, 2020a), in Canada (Correctional Investigator Canada, 2019; Marques and Monchalin, 2020) as well as in several parts of the world (Jeffries and Newbold, 2016; McIvor, 2010; Van Hout and Wessels, 2022), often faster than those of men. Further, since geopolitical territories of the Global North commonly encounter the issue of women's prisoning, the processes discussed in the book have an empirical foundation and theoretical and policy relevance, that reach beyond the geopolitical territory within which they were studied. In France, for example, women accounted for 3.1% of the total prison population in 2022, which is equivalent to an average low of 2219 and an average high of 2282 imprisoned women (Ministère de la justice, 2022). Apart from a short but higher peak from January to March 2020 (approximately 3250 women), the number of imprisoned women rose in 2021 in France (peaked at 3050 women) as well as in 2022 (peaked at 3150 women). Such averages and peaks indicate trends that are akin to women's increasing rates of incarceration in Canada and in several other countries.

In 2016, only the Rennes penitentiary complex—opened in 1878—housed women exclusively. It is the largest women's prison in Europe, and includes one prison for sentenced women, a remand ward, a nursery, a private family unit, and a halfway house. Apart from the Rennes penitentiary, one remand centre also housed solely women, the *maison d'arrêt* in Versailles. Approximately 15 other penitentiary complexes housed men with dedicated wards for women, such as *maisons d'arrêt*, detention centres and progressive release wards (Observatoire international des prisons, n.d.; Ministère de la Justice, 2016). Within these mixed prisons, women are isolated from men and suffer from reduced access to collective premises used notably for work, schooling, sociocultural/sports activities, and health care. According to sociologist Corinne Rostaing (2017), women's prisoning in France is based on greater moral control than the prisoning of men, whereby a significant component of the prisoning process tends to reproduce social roles traditionally attributed to women, such as maternity and the domestic sphere. Thus, women's prisoning in France follows a similar decision-making corridor as the one adopted in Canada.

For their part, territories of the Global South have different political, cultural, and prisoning contexts, varying incarceration rates and assorted prisoner profiles. Nonetheless, they face issues related to the prisoning of women like those documented in Canada and France, as well as in other countries of the Global North (e.g., Di Corleto, 2015, for South America; Chen, Lai, and Lin, 2013, for Taiwan; Van Hout and Wessels, 2022, for South Africa). One compelling example are the mandates often placed on transitioning democracies to implement criminal justice procedures and practices that endorse the rule of law based on exclusionary models of the Global North, of which the prison is a central constituent (Drake, 2018). Growing scholarship notes the spread of Western "best practices" as a hegemonic imaginary on how to manage prisons (i.e., Jefferson, 2005; Martin, Jefferson, and Bandyopadhyay, 2014). As such, geopolitical territories of the Global South may find potential resonance in this book in terms of theoretical significance and policy relevance.

From the outset, this book was motivated by a concern for human rights violations against incarcerated women in Canada in both federal and provincial correction systems. The final product, however, is not so much about women's direct experiences of prison as it is about prison practices, policies, and decisions often incapable of threading off the beaten track.

CHAPTER 1

How to Think Women's Prisoning

1.1 THE ECONOMIC ORIGINS OF PATH DEPENDENCE IDEAS

P ath dependence scholars are part of the neo-institutionalist movement, a heterogeneous set of perspectives that contributed to the
revitalization of the economic analysis of institutions in the 1970s.
Oliver E. Williamson is considered to have coined the term "new
institutional economics" in 1975 (Williamson, 1975; Klein, 1999). The
neo-institutionalist movement is an interdisciplinary endeavour
blending economics, law, organization theory, political science, sociology, and anthropology to understand the social, political, and
commercial institutions that regulate everyday life. This group of
perspectives seeks to "explain what institutions are, how they arise,
what purposes they serve, how they change and how they may be
reformed" (Klein, 1999:456). Within the realm of economics, neo-
institutional economics, specifically, came about as a critique of the
assumptions carried by neoclassical economics, which assumed that
linear market mechanisms were at work in non-market institutions such
as political and social institutions (like interest groups and the media),
and thus that economic efficiency would prevail in such non-market
institutions. A contrario, neo-institutional economics assumes that,
within non-market institutions, the most economically efficient of two

or more alternatives does not necessarily prevail. Although neo-institutional economics appreciates corporate culture, organizational memory, and other such meso-social phenomena, proponents couch institutional explanations in terms of the aims, strategies, beliefs, and actions of individuals embedded in institutions (Klein, 1999).

Path dependence[1] approaches were fostered primarily by economic historian Paul David (1985), who is said to have coined the concept of path dependence. They were further advanced by economist Douglass North (1990, 2005), who placed great emphasis on related path dependence arguments in his analysis of the development of modern capitalism for which he was awarded the Nobel Prize for Economics in 1993.[2] These approaches describe "how the reinforcement of a given set of arrangements [in social processes] over time raises the cost of changing them" (Prado and Trebilcock, 2009: 350). In other words, institutional frameworks create incentives or constraints on contemporary organizational behavior in a way that a feature of the economy (e.g., a technical standard, a pattern of economic development) may become affected by the path it has traced in the past, by an acceptance of past actions as the norm.

An institution is thus said to be on a path dependent process when it becomes locked into a trajectory from which it can only depart with the involvement of **exogenous forces** or shocks such as major changes in the global economy, depression, or war. The COVID-19 pandemic may be such an exogenous shock forcing corporations to review traditional in-person work standards and contemplate teleworking, an organizational model toward which these corporations have been apathetic before.

In the economics literature, the development of a path dependence is a process that may become locked in. The **lock-in** concept usually refers to being "locked out of something better," of some existing superior standard or product whose switching costs are not horrendously high (Liebowitz and Margolis, 1999: 982). This lock-in process stems, notably, from "**positive feedback mechanisms**" such as

---

1. A glossary of path dependence terms is included at the end of the book to support readers' confident navigation in the subsequent analytical chapters.
2. https://www.nobelprize.org/prizes/economic-sciences/1993/summary/, accessed February 25, 2021.

network or bandwagon effects that can entrench a particular standard into manufacturer choices and consumer habits and insulate them from change. An example of a network effect is the geographical congregation of similar industries (e.g., Silicon Valley, textile manufacturers in northern Italy) which attracts skilled workers who, in turn, attract, like a magnet, more key businesses seeking skilled workers, thus forming industrial clusters, even though the location may face rising local costs (Arthur, 1994; Wolfe and Lucas, 2005). Another example suggested by Ebbinghaus (2005) is the use of emails; the more people are already using this mode of communication, the greater the benefit for others to embrace it also.

An example of a bandwagon effect is the switching to VHS production, since VCR manufacturers expected this videotape format to win the standards battle over the Betamax format (Liebowitz and Margolis, 1999).

Hence, the more a choice is made the bigger its benefit, and the more difficult it becomes to thread away from this choice as the toll of reversal (switching to some other plausible alternative) becomes increasingly costly. Progressively, the selected path will stabilize.

Pioneering economist and business mathematician W. Brian Arthur (1989) called this key insight "**increasing returns**," whereby the benefits of engaging in certain economic activities grow rather than decline over time "as more and more people invest in a given way of doing things. As these investments—of time, money, skills, and expectations—add up, the relative cost of exploring alternatives steadily rises" (Prado and Trebilcock, 2009: 351). Increasing returns is the economic term for "**self-reinforcing processes**," that is, "social mechanisms that are responsible for one alternative to take a lead over others" (Ebbinghaus, 2005: 9). They lead to self-reinforcing institutional patterns which are forces that sustain the decision to stay the course, despite contemporary know-how showing such patterns to be less adapted or inefficient.

According to Arthur (1994), four key characteristics of an activity or an environment contribute to this build-up effect and produce self-reinforcement: 1) large set-up or fixed costs which create incentives to "stick with" the preferred activity or environment; 2) **learning effects**, which increase gains as the familiarity with that activity itself augments;

3) the above-mentioned network effects, whereby more people derive benefits as the cluster of adherents to an activity or environment grows; and 4) **adaptive expectations**, whereby individuals adapt their actions so that they will converge toward economic or political options that are expected to generate broad acceptance. As such, they tend to engage in a "pick the right horse" gamble (Pierson, 2000: 254).

In this regard, Douglass North, in his 1993 Nobel Prize lecture (1993: section III), observed that, because individuals and organizations adapt to existing institutions, "if the institutional framework rewards piracy, then piratical organizations will come into existence," and people will invest in becoming good pirates. Later, Ebbinghaus (2005) adjoined the following self-reinforcing mechanisms: vested interest, institutional complementarities (systems effects), and internalization (taking practices for granted).

In economic arrangements, inferior standards may persist in part because the probability of further steps along the same path increases with each action/decision down that path, rendering the path more and more attractive as its effects begin to accumulate and generate powerful circles of self-reinforcing activity, or simply said, because of the legacy these economic arrangements have built up. As a result, paths may become largely inflexible the further we are into the process, to a point where a path may eventually lock in on one product solution, industrial standard, or economic practice (Arthur, 1994: 112).

The forces that can alter such institutional trajectories are called "**critical junctures**," (Collier and Collier, 1991) choice points (Levi, 1997: 28), triggering events (Pierson, 2000: 263) or tipping points (Ebbinghaus, 2005: 24). Within economics, they refer to random or accidental events that occur when new conditions disrupt or overwhelm the ongoing trajectory and may either initiate a locked-in path or a bifurcation toward a different path. Critical junctures are the short-term periods of institutional flux that sporadically disturb long phases of path dependent institutional stability. Such institutional instability increases the range of possible actions and decisions for key actors and intensifies their imaginable long-term impact. During critical junctures, more dramatic change becomes possible, change that may place institutional arrangements on substitute trajectories. Yet, path dependence may prevail, since deviation from a taken-for-granted journey often remains difficult to achieve.

Since the events that constitute critical junctures are accidental, it becomes impossible to identify in advance which activities will be adopted in the long run (Prado and Trebilcock, 2009). These chance events do not cancel out over time. They cannot be ignored as "noise" (Pierson, 2000: 253). Rather, they are reminisced, they build on each other, and may feed back into future choices. This means that not only big events can have big consequences, but small ones also can have major outcomes over time (such as the locking into a suboptimal, lower payoff outcome) if they happen at the right time. As a result, self-reinforcing processes may lock in a particular option even though it occurred by accident. They may also lock in a specific option even if the components undergirding the earlier advantage of that option have long since vanished.

On a wide array of research topics ranging from the spatial location of production to the rise of technologies, economists have prevalently embraced and developed path dependence ideas. In so doing, they offered precious insights into the dynamics of locking processes and recognized self-reinforcing processes as key incentives toward path dependence. The pioneering works of Paul David (1985) and W. Brian Arthur (1989, 1994) are powerful examples in this regard. However, most essentially focused on technological innovation.

1.2 THE EXPORTATION OF PATH DEPENDENCE IDEAS IN POLITICAL SCIENCE, SOCIOLOGY AND ORGANIZATIONAL STUDIES

Debates exist between economics scholars, who tend to consider path dependence as a theory, and political scientists such as Paul Pierson (2000), public policy scholars such as Adrian Kay (2003), and sociologists such as Bernhard Ebbinghaus (2005) who consider it to be much more of a concept than a theory since they believe it has difficulty explaining how or why systems may develop in a path dependent way. In particular, the concept of path dependence has thrived in the context of the revitalization of institutional theories in economics, political science, and sociology, especially since the 1990s (Ebbinghaus, 2005). Amid this impulse, in the early 2000, political scientists such as Paul Pierson imported path dependence arguments from the neo-economics literature to document how institutions materialize and adopt shapes through self-reinforcing mechanisms, and why it becomes arduous to alter them. In contrast to the economic version of path dependence, political scientists and sociologists enlarged the concept as developed in economics to be less limiting and deterministic by suggesting that path dependence essentially aims at explaining institutional persistence and not institutional change. They also gave greater conceptual importance to the notion of critical juncture. Common to many social scientists using historical approaches, critical junctures are not the result of chance events; they stem from political conflict and power relations, whereby collective actors institute new rules during a window of opportunity for action (Ebbinghaus, 2005).

Following this train of thought, Pierson (2000) argued that Arthur's (1994) four key features of an economic activity or context that produce self-reinforcement (discussed earlier) are also present in emerging or established organizations and institutions other than those of the economic variety. Such organizations or institutions entail start-up costs; they (and their employees) learn by doing; their activities are often more beneficial if they are coordinated with those of other individuals or organizations; and they adapt their actions in ways that contribute to making expectations come true.

In this line of thought, Douglass North's (1990) application of path dependence ideas to his own reinterpretation of economic history—via institutional emergence, persistence, and change—is perhaps most significant to political scientists (Pierson, 2000). According to North (1990: 95), an interesting feature of path dependence is that the concept allows for a sophisticated understanding of "the interdependent web of an institutional matrix," which tends to produce colossal increasing returns as the web induces complementary configurations of organizations and institutions.

Pierson (2000) explains that there are four key facets of politics that make this ambit of social life favourable to increasing returns processes. The first is the prevalence of collective action within politics, in the sense that political action habitually requires coordination. In politics, the consequences of one's actions are highly dependent on the actions of others, on one's confidence that many others will do the same, be it in developing a political coalition, funding interest groups, or promoting incarceration. Confidence that others will do the same thus generates efforts toward collective action or behaviour coordination. In return, behaviour coordination creates forces that sustain expectations about the contemporary and future actions or behaviours of other actors. These expectations about others' actions, decisions, or behaviours become adaptive, in that actors tend to adjust their own "proper" action, decision, or behaviour on the basis of trial and error, themselves highly dependent on the actions of others. Therefore, political actors' actions, decisions, and behaviours tend to mimic those of other similar political actors. According to Pierson (2000), adaptive expectations are not only prevalent in politics, but they are also conducive to self-reinforcing processes which, ultimately, generate remarkable organizational stabilities. Hence, "self-reinforcing dynamics associated with collective action processes mean that organizations have a strong tendency to persist once they are institutionalized" (Pierson, 2000: 259).

The second facet of politics is its institutional density. Efforts toward action coordination also require the construction of formal institutions which, once launched, generate pervasive institutional restraints that are applicable to all, and are often backed up by authority, even force. This is the case, for example, with constitutional arrangements, which are legally binding rules that govern social action and are exorbitantly costly to change. Relevant to my overarching argument, Pierson (1993) also argues that, although they may be more easily altered than the organic rules of formal institutions, public policies (such as incarceration) are similarly prominent constraining and durable features of the political landscape, and their structure shapes patterns of political change. "Policies grounded in law and backed by the coercive power of the state, signal to actors what has to be done and what cannot be done, and they establish many of the rewards and penalties associated with particular activities" (Pierson, 2000: 259). Hence, since formal institutions and public policies have co-evolved over long periods of time, coordination effects are ubiquitous, and such interconnected webs create conditions highly susceptible to extensive self-reinforcing processes, and therefore to substantial resilience and inertia. Nonetheless, institutions are capable of speedy change, in many different directions, as the swift decline and transformation in post-war social institutions suggests (Karstedt, 2010).

Another interconnected facet that makes politics auspicious to self-reinforcing processes is that, over time, these mechanisms will amplify power asymmetries and render power relations inconspicuous. When actors are capable of imposing rules covertly on others, the employment of power may be self-reinforcing, since political actors may use political authority to generate (or hinder) changes in the rules to enhance their power. Such amplification of power asymmetries may craft a vein for path dependence.

The fourth and last facet identified by Pierson (2000) is politics' intrinsic opaque environment compared with the economic realm, which is believed to use an array of observable, unambiguous, and transparent indicators[3] and other metrics to account for and adjust economic performance. Although complications certainly may arise in the economic realm, these tools—as well as others such as competition and learning—are thought to enable economic actors to rectify errors over time. It is believed that, in a market economy, competitive pressures mean that new, more efficient organizations grow and eventually replace suboptimal ones. Learning means that organizations that face unanticipated consequences will learn from them and understand them, which, in turn, will generate anticipation and the subsequent modification of the organizational design.

Pierson argues that it is much more difficult to correct mistakes in politics, since 1) it lacks clear-cut and transparent measuring rods; 2) political actors, especially politicians, have short time horizons as well as rapid turnover rates; 3) formal institutions and public policies are designed to be change resistant and difficult to overturn (the persistence of penalization comes to mind); and 4) actors who operate in social contexts of high complexity and opacity like politics tend to incorporate confirming information and filter out disconfirming information from their mental maps and, as a result, learning becomes arduous. In turn, mental maps become shared with other political or social actors and generate network effects as well as adaptive expectations which, over time, generate "communities of discourse" that replicate and institutionalize similar ideological paths (Pierson, 2000:

---

3. Economists such as Diane Coyle (2014) and sociologists such as Theodore Porter (1995) have argued that economic indicators are far from transparent and unambiguous.

260). Following Pierson (2000) and Ebbinghaus (2005: 10), I adopt the view that path dependence is often the outcome of "multi-actor collective interaction." As a result of the above dimensions of politics, it becomes more difficult to reverse course in politics, since this realm is "unusually prone to increasing returns" (Pierson, 2000: 262). Furthermore, the high complexity of the goals of politics "as well as the loose and diffuse links between actions and outcomes render politics inherently ambiguous" (Pierson, 2000: 260).

Apart from their successful importation into political science, path dependence ideas have also been adapted into sociology and organizational theory. Historical sociologists, such as James Mahoney (2000, 2002: 7), have emphasized the importance of willful actors' agency and choices in shaping outcomes "in a more voluntaristic fashion than normal circumstances permit" during critical junctures. For their part, scholars in organizational processes have used path dependence ideas predominantly to explain the persistence and rigidification, or narrowing down, of organizational routines. According to Schreyögg and Sydow (2011), an emerging theory of organizational path dependence has received sustained attention in organization and management studies since the beginning of the 2010s.

Schreyögg and Sydow (2011) offer a three-stage organizational process of becoming path dependent. The first is the "**preformation phase**," where the scope of organizational action is not restricted significantly albeit by the organization's heritage of rules and culture. It is a period of open access to a wide range of possible actions/alternatives.

Stage two is the "**formation phase**" which begins when a decision has been made, or an action has been taken in stage one. It begins with a critical juncture. Unlike original economic path dependence thought, organizational analysts argue that "[a]s organizations are social systems and not natural entities, triggering events in organizations are likely to prove not so innocent, random, and small" (Schreyögg and Sydow, 2011: 324). According to other scholars in organizational analysis such as Garud, Kumaraswany and Karnoe (2010), serendipity needs not, in fact, be accidental or non-purposive. Rather, it can be nurtured by embedded actors making meaning out of what they come upon. Notwithstanding their size, actors' initial decisions or actions may not be considered causal determinants of path dependence, since they are essentially fortuitous, and the result cannot be identified before the path dependent process has taken shape. This happens in stage two (formation phase), where a dominant action pattern begins to emerge, and an initially unspecified logic begins to take on a trailblazer role as alternative patterns have increasing difficulty attracting notice and approval, thus furthering the irreversible character of the process. At this stage, though, decisions made by embedded actors are still contingent; not accidental and not yet predictable. They try to navigate their way through a birthing process (Garud, Kumaraswany and Karnoe, 2010). With time, a process becomes patterned and is reproduced over a certain timespan through increasing returns processes and positive feedback mechanisms (e.g., coordination effects, network effects, bandwagon effects, adaptive expectations effects).

Stage three is the "lock-in phase," which involves a further contraction of the dominant pattern which will eventually crystallize. As a result, "when faced by more efficient alternatives or critical changes in the system's environment, decision processes and established practices tend to continue to reproduce this and only this particular outcome" (Schreyögg and Sydow, 2011: 325).

The organizational approach to path dependence is less restrictive than that developed in economics. Organizational path approaches use a modified conception of lock-in, one that is less quasi-deterministic, since organizational processes are social in nature, more complex and ambiguous. Their conception of the lock-in leaves a corridor of possible variations. Contrary to a deterministic vision of the lock-in that rejects individual actors' self-determination and discounts the prospective for change, organizational and sociological views of lock-in do not rule out ongoing adjustments of an institution to the very environment that may be indispensable for its enduring survival. Nonetheless, organizations engaged in locked-in institutional arrangements run the risk of losing some of their flexibility because they lose the ability to adapt to better alternatives, and thus remain enclosed in existing paths that may reproduce ineffective, perhaps inhumane, solutions.

Support for organizational path dependence has been offered by several authors. Baron, Hannan and Burton's (1999) analyses of managerial intensity within young technology start-up companies in California's Silicon Valley found that firms whose founders adopted a bureaucratic model later showed more intensive managing than firms whose founders privileged a commitment model. Such findings support notions of path dependence in the growth of organizational structures based on certain conditions that were present at the time of foundation, such as the original gender-mix within the embryonic firms, and the founders' employment model. A few years later, still interested in the underlying logics of bureaucratic organization in start-up firms, Baron et al. (2007) looked at employment systems and found that employment patterns, once espoused in nascent firms, have strong lasting effects on successive labour force arrangements within these firms: "initial differences in founding [employment] blueprints shaped the extent to which women were integrated into core technical roles as the firms evolved" (p. 59).

In relation to the dynamics of gender relations, still, Kronsell (2016) studied masculinities within military institutions, with a particular focus on how gender is incorporated into the formal and informal dimensions of the European Union's Security and Defence Policy. She confirmed path dependency in the persistence and resilience of historical gender war roles within the military, whereby a "hierarchical military masculinity" (p. 311) still dominates and is still accompanied by a "combat heterosexual masculinity" (p. 321) and a "protector masculinity" (p. 317), notably via the promotion of values such as heroism, chivalry, and virtue. For its part, through everyday acts such as the application of norms, the reproduction of practices, the recurrence of routines and the design of training programs, femininity is constructed via a "protector/protection binary" (p. 320) undergirded by stereotypical gender images of "beautiful souls" (Elshtain, 1995: 140, cited on p. 320) that are too good for the conflict-ridden world and need shielding from it. According to Kronsell (2016), shaping masculinities and femininities in accordance with historically instituted gender war roles is a form of **gender path dependence** within military organizations.

1.3 PATH DEPENDENCE INSIGHTS IN CRIMINOLOGY AND LAW & SOCIETY SCHOLARSHIP

For their part, criminology and law and society scholarship have been strongholds of institutional analysis. Indeed, their interest in the production of laws and the reactions to law violations implies the systematic analytical undertaking of the setting, the structure, and the functioning of law or criminal justice agencies. It is particularly in this line of thought that path dependence arguments have found their way into research concerned with criminal justice reform. Notably, they have informed studies of incarceration especially as the prison has grown to be a central institution in modern society.

Larason Schneider (2006), among a few other scholars, took an interest in annual incarceration rates in the United States using propositions derived from path dependence perspectives. She statistically showed that, between 1927 and 2003, the incarceration rates in multifarious types of states progressed simultaneously in the same direction even though these rates have various origins. Indeed, incarceration rates are produced at the state level by a wide variety of governors, judges, prosecutors, parole boards, and probation officers working in institution-bound settings, as well as state-bound economic, political, and cultural environments. She also showed that, apart from the increasing returns and bandwagon effects often associated with the progressive lock into a path dependent process, the social construction of the target populations of penal policy accounts for differences in institutions' susceptibility to path dependence processes. Thus, imagining criminalized individuals with little power as being dangerous and deviant (especially the ubiquity of this image) is more likely to generate increasing returns—in the form of reduced political risk, for example—as well as path dependent growths in imprisonment.

Larason Schneider (2006) finally showed that, although all states experienced several phases of prolonged path dependence preceded or followed by lengthy intervals of increases and decreases in incarceration rates, a major critical juncture occurred in the late 1960s and early 1970s, when a striking spate of imprisonment rates emerged across the board. This critical juncture has been likened by Larason Schneider (2006) to the progressively punitive public antipathy toward criminalized individuals, which reached uncommonly high degrees of public consensus in that period. Regarding criminalized or imprisoned women, Martel (1991) noted, in the same period, a reactionary effect within Québec media resulting from the protest movements of the 1960s and 1970s, especially the second wave feminist movement. Journalistic accounts of women became sarcastic and sexist and showed an increase in prejudice against women. Québec media was suddenly showing a conservatism worthy of the Victorian era. Drawing from Larason Schneider's insights (2006), I argue that such media conservatism toward criminalized or imprisoned women sustained a consensus in public opinion which, by ricochet, generated increasing returns toward the persistence and even growth of women's prisoning as per the opening, in 1964, of a prison for provincially sentenced women in Montréal. Sarcastic and sexist media may have also contributed to a negative **"cognitive stickiness"** (Larason Schneider, 2006: 466) amid correctional cultures and among decision-makers. *Sticky* modes of thinking consist of reasoning, or lines of thought, from which it is laborious to disengage (van Vugt and Broers, 2016). They tend to drive decisions in the same direction across many, even decentralized, institutional settings.

Beckett et al. (2016; 2018) took up where Larason Schneider left off and attempted to explain recent drops in incarceration rates in the United States between 2000 and 2013. It had been observed elsewhere that such drops were the result of the demise of prior political consensus in favour of getting tough on crime, a kind of critical juncture, at which point a paradigmatic shift emerged promoting, instead, prison down-sizing. Informed by institutional studies of path dependence, Beckett, Reosti and Knaphus (2016) argued that, in addition to institutional and political obstacles that may thwart the achievement of criminal justice reform (such as decarceration policies), cultural barriers may also prevent a comprehensive reform in that neither policy-makers or reform advocates appear to be willing to make the case for comprehensive sentencing reform embedded in arguments highlighting the human costs of mass incarceration.

They, as well as the media, adopted a bifurcated reform narrative largely embedded in a fiscal rather than a human cost argumentative schema. On the one hand, the reform narrative supports progressive legislative enactments toward decarceration for non-violent drug offences and technical parole violations but, on the other hand, it promotes the maintenance, even intensification, of imprisonment for violent, property and public order offences. According to Beckett, Reosti and Knaphus (2016), the latter is based on "law and order" and public safety arguments, as well as on a long-established rhetoric of deserving/undeserving offenders, echoing Larason Schneider's (2006) argument about the importance of sympathetic/antipathic public and organizational sentiments about the groups targeted by penal policy.

To broaden this discussion still, in 2018, Beckett et al. showed the importance of focusing analysis on the outcomes of on-the-ground case processing in discussions about mass incarceration policies and practices. In explaining the modest decline of incarceration rates while crime rates had been plummeting in the United States, Beckett et al. showed that legislative measures to reduce imprisonment outnumbered those enacted to increase prison use since the 2007 peak in the United States' incarceration rates. However, measures to reduce imprisonment were limited to drug and property offences and did not encompass the repeal of punitive sentencing laws that participated in mass incarceration (Beckett et al., 2018). Furthermore, they identified that trends in case processing are not consistent with the decarcerative legislative enactments for non-violent and drug offences, but are more coherent with path dependence approaches as the system's reaction to property crimes and all types of drug arrests intensified in recent years. They argued that, consistent with path dependence literature, substantial institutional developments like mass incarceration boost the ability and incentive of organizational actors to safeguard jobs, resources, long-established expertise, and newly expanded political and economic interest groups by cognitively "sticking" to traditional rhetoric, policies, and practices which perpetuate current institutional arrangements and sustain penal status quo. Such self-reinforcing processes (Pierson, 2000:810) that enhance institutional capacity and create vested interests in turn impede efforts to change routes, since the costs of reversal would be too significant.

In a similar fashion, Rubin (2019a) used formal penal change such as punishment intentions, practices, policies, and organizations (in other words, law in action) to clarify the actual significance of legal change on the books. Drawing on neo-institutional theory from organizational sociology, Rubin (2019a) proposed a "theory of formal legal change," which argues that it is insufficient for novel structural models of punishment to be authorized and reproduced to the point of becoming significant signals of penal change. One such novel structural model of punishment was the Walnut Street jail of 1776.[4] Originally a city jail located at the corner of Sixth and Walnut streets in Philadelphia, Pennsylvania, the Walnut Street prison housed vagrants, debtors, and the like while waiting their official punishment, corporeal chastisement, or execution. It was under the lax management of the local sheriff and

---

4.   The first prisoners were admitted in January 1776 (Skidmore, 1948). Skidmore is believed to have coined the term "Walnut Street jail" (p. 167).

court officials. At the time, contemplations to create a statewide penal system—complete with a centralized and consolidated penal administration—in Pennsylvania were initiated by state leaders and Quaker reformers. The Walnut Street prison became the cradle of this new statewide penal system and changed vocation in 1790 to become a prison dedicated to the actual punishment of prisoners. It played an important role in developing the solitary confinement of prisoners and harboured several other penal reforms and innovations, such as the creation of an overseeing board of inspectors, a school, increased granting of pardons, religious services (and Bibles in individual cells), and industrial employment that generated profit for government: "industry, health, reformation and rehabilitation were the ideals sponsored in this jail—particularly during the years 1789 to 1799" (Skidmore, 1948: 167). To embody such ideals, a "penitentiary house" was built in the jail yard to house "the more hardened offenders from all the counties in the state," where they would be punished by being held in "unremitted" solitary confinement, forced into "laborious employment" (Skidmore, 1948:168) and fed diminished portions (p. 174). This "penitentiary house" is the forefather of the segregation units one still finds in contemporary prisons in many countries around the world.

Between 1790 and 1835, national and international decision-makers and reformers visited the Walnut Street prison, observed its operations, made notes, and replicated the model elsewhere in the United States and abroad. Although the pioneering prison model was reproduced domestically and on an international level, it is insufficient, according to Rubin (2019a), for novel structural models of punishment such as the Walnut Street model to be authorized and reproduced to the point of becoming significant signals of penal change. The Walnut Street prison needed to become institutionalized and widely diffused through time and space to generate long-lasting changes in society's expectations about punishment: "prisons pioneered by northern penal reformers eventually spread throughout the entire [United States], despite distinct local needs and preferences, eventually becoming taken for granted" (Rubin, 2019a: 547). In other words, the Walnut Street prison needed to become a social convention notably by repeated use and by marshalling wide societal acceptance to a point where the possibility of people diverting from its prisoning model progressively waned and "more and more people orient their decisions based on the perception that a sufficient number of other people have already done so" (Ebbinghaus, 2005: 8). Once a widely adopted prison model emerges, it becomes expedient for any latecomer to adopt the shared social convention. This accepted way of doing things, in turn, shapes anticipations about what punishment is supposed to look like and hampers citizens' critical imagination about novel forms of punishing, or even about punishing at all. Hence, according to Rubin (2019a), the institutionalization of structural models of punishment may have long-term consequences for ideas about punishment. This is so because these models tend to circumscribe the rhetoric and efforts of future penal reformers who will have preserved substantial components of the old hegemonic model of punishment, even if this model eventually fails.

It is obvious that global contexts always matter, that larger social, political, and cultural movements, as well as colonialist and racialized arrangements, produce and reify prisoning policies and practices. It is obvious also that scholarly attention must continue to be directed toward geographical and contextual differences when documenting women's prisoning processes. However, without minimizing the crucial importance of the overall context, this book offers a perspective on organizational pathways whereby path dependence theory provides meaningful analytical guidance into an alternative understanding of prisons' sad track record in terms of human rights safeguard, and failure to espouse significant historical and contemporary changes. As with all research, this one began with an empirical journey that I depict in the following chapter.

CHAPTER 2

What Matters in Women's Prisoning

This book stems from data collected as part of a large government funded multi-year Canadian partnership development study (2015-2019; #890-2014-0034) entitled the Prison Transparency Project (PTP). The research team—comprised of six Canadian scholars cumulating decades of expertise in carceral sociology from six different universities—drew upon participatory action-based methodologies with persons with lived experience of incarceration to document human rights violations and conditions of confinement in Canadian prisons. Such methodologies recognize that producing knowledge from the viewpoint of the researcher is not a guarantee of academic rigour or objectivity. Thus, the team prioritized a participatory action research methodology (PAR) that adopts a partnership approach to research involving community organization representatives as well as community members. In this study, "community members" comprised essentially former prisoners. Although the term "former prisoner" may be read as a negative master status, it is used here in accordance with the preferences of several of our co-researchers who have lived experience of the prison. The term may be read also as compelling the acknowledgment of invaluable experiential expertise. It also forces the recognition of the human suppleness, abilities, and dignity needed along the difficult route from the prisoner stigma toward community resettlement following incarceration.

The Prison Transparency Project set out with four aims: to develop a PAR approach with formerly incarcerated persons; to build a documentation method for lived experience of prison conditions inside provincial jails/prisons and federal penitentiaries in Canada; to develop strategies to help strengthen institutional transparency and accountability; and to begin the process of establishing a national critical prison scholarship network. This network comprises prison scholars from six Canadian universities and multiple community organizations and advocacy groups across Canada, including the Canadian Civil Liberties Association, the Canadian Association of Elizabeth Fry Societies, the John Howard Society of Canada, Aboriginal Legal Services of Toronto, No One Is Illegal (migrant justice organization), the Elizabeth Fry Societies of Ottawa and Québec, the Association des services de réhabilitation sociale du Québec, and the John Howard Society of Manitoba. Recently, the Prison Transparency Project's network has developed internationally with university partners from Spain (Universidade da Coruña) and Argentina (Universidad de Buenos Aires; Universidad Nacional José C. Paz; Universidad Nacional del Litoral), as well as Argentina's federal government (Comité nacional para la prevención de la Tortura), the provincial governments of Andalusia (Asociación Pro Derechos Humanos de Andalucia) and of Catalonia in Spain (Associacio Irídia – Centre per a la Defensa dels Drets Humans), as well as five private non-profit organizations in Argentina and Canada.

The research team selected four Canadian sites of data collection to substantiate lived experiences of the prison, common features, and regional specificities. The sites were selected based on three criteria: 1) the location of the prisons; 2) researchers' established connections with local prisoner communities; and 3) the variety of prison cultures (jurisdictions, populations, usage, etc.). Data collection was then undertaken in Vancouver, the Greater Toronto Area, Ottawa and Montréal. I was the principal investigator for the Québec research site. As a result of these methodological choices, ethical clearance had to be obtained from the research ethics boards of the six different universities with which the six main researchers were affiliated. This opened the door to the possibility of encountering many local interpretations of the federal ethical guidelines for scientific research. Researchers completed approximately 40 semi-directed interviews in each of the four sites with women and men formerly incarcerated in provincial or federal prisons in Canada. At the Québec research site, interviews were conducted either in French or in English.

Because the rate of over-incarceration of Indigenous peoples[1] is astounding in Canada as in many colonizing countries, their involvement could not be overlooked in the study. Although First Nations, Métis and Inuit peoples represented approximately 5% of the overall Canadian population according to the 2021 Canadian census (Statistics Canada, 2022), prison population data shows that their incarceration rate has been mounting steadily for years, reaching "a new historic high surpassing the 30% mark" of the federal prison population (Correctional Investigator, 2020: 20). In provincial prisons, Indigenous adults represent approximately 25% of prisoner populations (Reitano, 2017). For their part, Indigenous women are the fastest growing proportion of prisoners in Canada, now representing 42% of federally sentenced women (Correctional Investigator, 2020: 20). In such a colonialist setting, critical prison research must attend to the lived experience of imprisonment of men and women of Indigenous descent. Hence, persons of Indigenous ancestry comprised a sizable portion of the interviewees across Canada. However, no such person was interviewed in Québec. This peculiar situation resulted from what Balfour and Martel (2018: 225) documented as being an "overly cautious interpretation of federal ethical guidelines" by Université Laval's Research Ethics Board, leading to the exclusion of Indigenous peoples from the Québec portion of the project. Balfour and Martel (2018: 241) explain that:

> While the [research ethics boards] of the other five universities involved in the project considered that the provisions designed into the project covered adequately the ethical requirements of research involving First Nations, Métis and Inuit peoples, University E [located in Québec] required additional forms of approval, notably by local, regional, or national representatives of Indigenous communities or political bodies. It was strongly

---

1. As colleagues and I have clarified elsewhere: "Expressions such as 'Native', 'Indian', 'Amérindien' (French form) or 'Aboriginal' originate from 'outside-naming' (Chartrand, 1991)—a process whereby settler people attach settler (often derogatory) names to describe the descendants of the original inhabitants of what is now Canada. As a constant source of confusion to commentators, labels used in reference to first peoples have garnered valuable discussions (e.g., Paci, 2002; Lawrence, 2004). While acknowledging the sensitivity of identities to outside manipulations, [I] adopt the term 'Indigenous' as it appears to be associated with an emerging emancipation of ancient societies from social domination as well as from outside naming (Chartrand, 1991)" (Martel, Brassard and Jaccoud, 2011: 235).

suggested by this [research ethics board] that we minimally obtain the written support of at least one such organization within research site 4 [Québec]. Discussions with a well-known scholar cumulating over ten years of experience in research by and for First Nations, Métis, and Inuit peoples, led to the conclusion that, in this particular research site, approval by regional or provincial representatives was increasingly lengthy and arduous to obtain and that it had to abide by each organization's own ethical guidelines. Hence, an approval dossier would have had to be submitted by the research team to Assembly of First Nations of [Québec] in accordance with its own research protocol which specifies, for example, that ownership and control of the data and publication of the data are to remain in the hands of Indigenous partners or Indigenous national bodies (e.g., Haggerty 2004). Along similar lines, the team would have had to submit another approval dossier to [Québec] Native Women Inc. also in accordance with its own research guidelines comprising a series of terms and conditions with which researchers must comply such as the justification that the research must be based on local needs and priorities and that scholars must have experience in Indigenous research. Moreover, it was also suggested that we seek approval from the political body representing Inuit peoples in research site 4 as it is deemed to be a major landing point of Northern Inuit peoples into provincial prisons. Both the Chair of University *E*'s [Research Ethics Board] and the expert scholar (who sits on a national committee on Indigenous research) admit to the increasing difficulty in doing research in partnership with Indigenous bodies in the province.

Whether the Research Ethics Board's decision was the result of a narrow reading of federal ethical guidelines for scientific research involving Indigenous communities, or whether it was framed as a safe-guard procedure on the part of a risk-averse university, two important consequences ensued. First, the most overrepresented racialized group of prisoners in Canada was suppressed from data collection in one entire research site. Second, this group's lack of contribution engendered a void in the co-construction of documented evidence on prison conditions, even though Indigenous peoples remain the most over-represented set of prisoners in federal penitentiaries and provincial prisons in Canada.

We used a time range of imprisonment within the last five years prior to the interview to ensure the contemporaneity of lived experiences. Since interviews took place during 2016–2017, we were able to document prison experiences that occurred between 2011 and 2016–2017. The verbatim and anonymized transcriptions of all interviews were uploaded onto a secured *NVivo for Teams* platform, a virtual simulta-neous multi-user access infrastructure. Coding was completed at each site by research team members using a master consensual coding template (27 parent nodes and 12 child nodes) developed by the team, which included persons with lived experience of the prison.

Overall, the research team then constituted a significant databank of over 180 interviews of raw data with former Canadian prisoners.[2] The arguments developed in this book stem from the analysis of governmental task forces, reports, inquiries, media data from 2010 to 2022, and the 21 interviews conducted in French or in English with women at the Québec research site. More than half of these women (15 out of 21) experienced either the actual transfer to the Leclerc prison formerly designated for men, or the prison conditions that persisted at Leclerc for months after the transfer.

This experiential data is supplemented by additional data from mainstream news media coverage stemming from approximately 100 media stories and editorials that appeared in Québec French tradi-tional and online media from 2010—when Québec's prison overpopu-lation problem began to filter into the media—to 2022. Although both English and French media stories were collected, analyses showed that English stories were duplicates of the French ones and did not provide new data. These journalistic accounts are of interest, since they represent vivid indicators of social attitudes toward imprisoned women pre and post transfer to Leclerc. They provide a view into recent history and as such are useful witnesses of the prison conditions and enduring path of women's prisoning in Québec. The media data is supplemented by historical and contemporary government reports, task forces, and inquiries on women's prisoning. These documents are taken as domi-nant narratives on women's prisoning whose outcomes are reinterpreted here to widen and hopefully refine our understanding of orthodox Canadian correctional history. Since compelling critical scholarly works already exist about women's prisoning process in Canada, some of these studies are at times introduced into the conversation as secondary

---

2.   While the PTP researchers conducted their interviews across Canada in 2016–2017, so did the researchers of a similar research project, the University of Alberta Prison Project (UAPP) (Jones, Bucerius, and Haggerty, 2019). The UAPP conducted a little over 580 interviews/surveys with prisoners, as well as approximately 130 interviews with correctional officers in four prisons in Western Canada.

sources either to fill in contextual gaps or to provide analytical leads in support of the arguments developed in the book.

The 21 women participants selected their own pseudonym for this study. They were between 21 and 73 years old, with an average age of 42. All used French as a first language. All women served time in provincial prisons in Québec, some for as short a time as five days, and others for as long as 23 months, for an average of 5.7 months.

As per Table 1, the total duration of Jessy's provincial incarceration could not be assessed, since she was detained multiple times in provincial prisons over the study period, a phenomenon often referred to as the "revolving doors" of incarceration characterized by multiple short prison terms (e.g., Padfield and Maruna, 2006). Remembrance of the specificities of each of those jail terms was difficult for her at times. Thirteen of the 21 women interviewed also experienced incarceration in a federal institution designated for women. These federal institutions are located in the cities of Abbotsford, Edmonton, Kitchener, Joliette and Truro. The Okimaw Ohci Healing Lodge, the federal institution designated for Indigenous women, is located on Nekaneet First Nation land near Maple Creek, Saskatchewan.

TABLE 1. Incarceration Profile of Interviewed Women

Pseudonym	Age	Incarceration sites	Total time in prison (provincial [prov] + federal [fed])
Panel A: Women imprisoned at Maison Tanguay			
Cloé	40 to 49	Tanguay; regional prison C;[3] federal prisons A and B	4 to 6 months prov; 10 years+ fed
Jessy	30 to 39	Tanguay; federal prison A	Revolving doors in prov; 31 to 36 months fed
Kate	40 to 49	Tanguay; regional prison C; federal prison A	13 to 18 months prov; 6 to 12 months fed
Linda Côté	50 to 59	Tanguay	1 to 3 months prov
Malory	30 to 39	Tanguay; regional prison C; federal prison A	1 to 3 months prov; 13 to 18 months fed
Revmarie	30 to 39	Tanguay; regional prison C; federal prison A	19 to 23 months prov; 6 to 12 months fed

---

3.   Regional prisons C, D, and E are provincial prisons located across Québec and are designated for men.

Pseudonym	Age	Incarceration sites	Total time in prison (provincial [prov] + federal [fed])
Panel B: Women imprisoned at both Maison Tanguay and Leclerc Prison			
Arlarian	20 to 29	Tanguay; Leclerc; federal prison A	13 to 18 months prov; 13 to 18 months fed
Maddy	30 to 39	Tanguay; Leclerc; regional prison C; federal prison A	1 to 3 months prov; 6 to 12 months fed
Marilyn Monroe	30 to 39	Tanguay; Leclerc; regional prison C; federal prison A	Less than 1 month prov; xx months fed[4]
Maude	50 to 59	Tanguay; Leclerc; federal prison A	7 to 12 months prov; 6 to 12 months fed
Mimi	20 to 29	Tanguay; Leclerc; federal prison A	xx months prov; xx months fed
Peggy	30 to 39	Tanguay; Leclerc; federal prison A	7 to 12 months prov; 19 to 24 months fed
Panel C: Women imprisoned at Leclerc Prison			
Allison	60 +	Leclerc	4 to 6 months prov
Béa	20 to 29	Leclerc	1 to 3 months prov
Chouette	50 to 59	Leclerc; regional prison D	1 to 3 months prov
Jessica	20 to 29	Leclerc	Less than 1 month prov
Mia	40 to 49	Leclerc	xx months prov
Nuage	50 to 59	Leclerc; regional prison C; regional prison E	4 to 6 months prov
Penny	60 +	Leclerc; federal prison A	Less than 1 month prov; 6 to 12 months fed
Roxy	30 to 39	Leclerc	1 to 3 months prov
Tina Diamond	20 to 29	Leclerc; federal prison A	Less than 1 month prov; 6 to 12 months fed

Cloé is the only woman to have been imprisoned at two different federal institutions designated for women. While Cloé spent over 10 years in these federal institutions for women, Kate, Revmarie, Maddy, Maude, Penny, and Tina Diamond were jailed in federal institutions for a period of less than one year. Women's total stay in federal prisons designated for women averaged 19.8 months. Although Canadian federal prisons manage sentences of 24 months or more,

---

4. "xx" means that, for Marilyn Monroe, Mimi and Mia, the question pertaining to the duration of prison terms was overlooked partially or entirely during the interview. The statistical estimates of prison term averages provided below exclude Marilyn Monroe for federal terms only, Mimi for both provincial and federal terms, and Mia for provincial terms.

prisoners are eligible for parole after serving one third of their sentence, or a minimum of eight months. Federal correctional authorities find that women's average federal prison sentence is less than five years (Correctional Service Canada, 2018). Women reported a higher federal full parole grant rate (50%) than men (35%) between 2012–2013 and 2017–2018[5] (Parole Board Canada, 2018: 28). This data partly explains why their average stay in federal prison was approximately 20 months. Together, the 21 women interviewed served an average of 20.6 months of incarceration in both provincial and federal prisons.

A majority of the 21 women interviewed were incarcerated in more than one prison during the study period, between 2011 and 2016. As Table 1 highlights, at any point during that period, 12 women served time at Maison Tanguay in Montréal, 15 at Leclerc prison in Laval, and 13 in federal prison A. Eight of the 21 women also served time in men's local provincial prisons, for example while awaiting official transfer to a prison designated for women such as Maison Tanguay or Leclerc prison.

To protect the women's identity, master lists of interviewees, signed consent forms, and interview recordings (identifiable by numerical codes only) were kept in locked file cabinets in conformity with my university's research ethics approval. Upon the transcription of irremediably anonymized verbatim paper versions of the women's interviews, the audio format of these interviews was deleted. Signed consent forms and anonymized transcripts were eventually transferred to the secure institutional server developed in the early 2020s at Université Laval, with which I am affiliated. The women were guaranteed that these transcriptions would be accessible only to active members of the research team, and that no administrative staff, correctional staff, or government employees (provincial or federal) would access them. Moreover, each member of the Québec research team signed a confidentiality agreement guaranteeing confidentiality as prescribed by Canadian and Québec law.

---

5.   At the time of writing, the Parole Board's Performance Monitoring Report of 2017–2018 was the last one publicly available on Parole Board Canada's website.

The lived prison experience of these 21 women who survived incarceration will be put to contribution in Chapter 4 where I will discuss women's prisoning at the provincial level in Québec. To set the table for this discussion, and to start connecting path dependence ideas with processes of prisoning human beings, the following chapter delves first into a re-reading of the history of women's prisoning at the federal level in Canada.

CHAPTER 3

The Tenacity of Federal Prisons Designated for Women

F ollowing Elizabeth Comack's, and others' questioning of incarceration as the appropriate social response to conflicts the law may have with particular human beings, I adopt the term "prisoning" to envision incarceration as a process without assuming that prison is the appropriate answer to women's criminalization. I posit that prisoning is an institution, in the sense developed by North (1993: 23), in that prisoning comprises the formal rules of the game, such as laws, regulations, penal policies, a bureaucracy and organizations (such as unions and prisons), as well as informal constraints, such as behavioural norms, discretion, and self-imposed codes of conduct. Aoki (2007:6-8) is a major scholar in neo-institutional economics. He expanded on Douglass North's definition of institutions. Following Aoki's lead, I posit that institutions like prisoning also imply collectively acknowledged conventions and representations (e.g., prisons as a fixture of criminal justice), coupled with agents' expectations and beliefs concerning other actors' options and purposes. Prisoning is a set of formal and informal processes charged by a society with crafting, overseeing, and applying correctional regulations or policies. Prisoning is a set of taken-for-granted behavioural routines that ease decision-making, as well as "cognitive scripts" (Ebbinghaus, 2005:6) that lessen ambiguity in an intricate world.

3.1 COMMON GAOLS, PROTO-PRISONS AND ONTARIO'S KINGSTON PENITENTIARY: WOMEN AS AN "INCONVENIENCE"

The 1867 Canadian Constitution divided responsibility for imprisonment between provincial and federal governments, and from this emerged parallel prison systems for men and women. Women's prisoning in Canada is unique in part because of the "country's origins in a series of disparate French and English colonies and Indigenous lands forcibly welded together in an only partially successful exercise in nation-building" (Fyson, 2017: 175). It is also unique because of Canada's geographical immensity, its small-scale but broadly spread population, and significant culture and language differences. The prisoning of women is also historically a male-centric process (Hayman, 2006).

From the beginning of New France in the 1600s to the 1820s, gender-mixed and multi-function asylums and common gaols were used to keep the condemned before their punishment, to house witnesses and defaulting debtors, to redress persons inept at providing honestly for themselves, and to offer refuge to destitute vagrants. At the time, common gaols were not yet used primarily as a means of punishment, since the actual punishments were capital executions, corporal chastisement (Cooper, 1987; Fyson, 2006) or penal transportation—the relocation of prisoners to distant places, often in colonies. Transportation was practised by some European countries as a means of reducing prison overcrowding, whereby convicted men and women could escape death sentences by being sent to penal colonies in coerced servitude, as was the case in Australia (Boritch, 1997) and in French Guyana (Fournier, 1989).

In New France, a French colony in North America (1534–1763), corporal chastisement, torture, or execution were the predominant modes of punishment. The first person executed in New France in 1604 was a young 16-year-old woman found guilty of stealing (Cooper, 1987). Focusing on the United States, Rubin (2019a) argues that, in the late 18th and early 19th centuries, capital offences, colonial executions, and corporal punishment lost favour to incarceration as the primary form of penal punishment for serious crimes. Although a similar transfiguration happened in Canada, physical deprivations, torture, and brutality remained ubiquitous in this newly adopted form of penal punishment that was the prison (Société Elizabeth Fry du Québec, 2011). In the wake of this search for alternatives to traditional modes of punishment, the pioneering proto-prisons were born. They were state-run institutions detaining convicted individuals often required to perform hard labour. While other modes of punishment coexisted, proto-prisons dominated and were adopted as a prototype that many states emulated. This was especially the case of the 1776 late-colonial Walnut Street jail in Philadelphia that I introduced in Chapter 1. Under the aegis of the Quaker prison reformers and high-ranking officials of the state of Pennsylvania, this jail became the first state "penitentiary house" in the United States, a place to reflect and repent. Starting in 1790, the revamped Walnut Street jail became a widespread taken-for-granted benchmark erected in many states at the turn of the 19th century despite riots, escapes, fires, and disorderliness within its walls.

Eventually, such problems precipitated the demise of proto-prisons based on the Walnut Street design as a next generation of prisons emerged, partly inspired by the English workhouses based on strictly enforced discipline, control, and personal reform (Rubin, 2019b). Workhouses began to emerge in the 1600s in the United Kingdom as hospices dedicated to the social assistance of human groups temporarily or permanently unable to provide for themselves. They housed, in common areas, persons rendered vulnerable because of age, physical impediments, cognitive impairments and teenage pregnancies, for example, who were given accommodation and, for the able-bodied, unpaid employment in return for the handout. In an effort to begin the physical segregation of groups of indigents, namely the "aged and impotent, children, able-bodied males, and able-bodied females" (May, 1987: 122–123), many workhouses built after 1835 adopted a Y-shape or cruciform architecture as material expressions of English philosopher, jurist, and social reformer Jeremy Bentham's (1748–1832) panopticon ideal which, among its main characteristics, provides for the separation of occupants and locates the surveillants' room as central point, thereby ensuring maximum visibility from the centre. Panopticon-inspired workhouses comprised three- or four-storey buildings joined in the centre by central administrative buildings and surrounded by work and exercise yards enclosed within brick perimeter walls. To effectively segregate the different groups of poor, these workhouses comprised separate work and exercise yards for each group (Fowler, 2007) to nurse those in need of medical treatment, to dissuade others from indigence, and to act as physical barriers against illnesses (Driver, 2004).

Contrary to the traditional period breaks whereby Walnut Street inspired designs are thought to have died down before the birth of modern prisons, Rubin (2019a) convincingly demonstrates that Walnut Street inspired proto-prisons and modern prisons overlapped and coexisted in time and space. Confronted with growing prison popula-tions and increasing disorder, several state prisons sought to expand control through tighter prison schedules and harsher segregation. The initial intent was to build larger and better controlled proto-prisons, since these remained the dominant exemplar. However, as construction plans were crafted and revised, a new design model emerged, that of the "modern" prison. In part to do away with the "flagrant evils" (Skidmore, 1948:180) of the Walnut Street inspired prison designs, alternative plans emerged aimed at modifying the Pennsylvania system of solitary confinement that the Walnut Street prison and its derivatives embodied.

Several versions of the modern prison sprouted, but it is the New York State Prison at Auburn that spread most rapidly and became the new archetype in the United States between 1822 and 1860 (Rubin, 2019b). This new prison model was based on prisoners having access, in silence, to daytime communal workstations, while solitary confine-ment was preferred at nighttime. With its innovative factory-style hard labour, solitary meditation, and religious instruction, the Auburn "penitentiary" was intended, similarly to the Walnut Street inspired proto-prisons, to be a place where prisoners would do "penance," become repentant and eventually be reformed.

While the Walnut Street inspired proto-prisons were among the forerunners of an entire school of thought on prison construction and reform, Rubin (2019a) argues that the rapid and wide adoption of the modern Auburn prison system marked what path dependence scholars call a critical juncture in the history of penal reform:

> By 1835, a plurality of states had authorized or built a modern prison, the vast majority following the Auburn System. At this point, the modern prison template (virtually synonymous with the Auburn System version)

had become so widespread and taken for granted, that it created its own gravitational force (p. 545).

According to path dependence scholars, critical junctures are moments of institutional fluctuation that make remarkable changes possible. Although they refer to random or accidental events, critical junctures occur when new conditions either lock in an ongoing path or redirect the institution toward a different path. With hindsight, it is safe to assume that the rise of the Auburn System of imprisonment was a critical juncture in the sense that, according to Rubin (2019a: 546), it continued to shape correctional innovations for decades, as most subsequent new prisons (for men, for women, for youth, for serious offenders, etc.) became but "variations on a theme" as the gradually entrenched Auburn System progressively limited the creativity of carceral decision-makers to think "outside the box" of the Auburn System.

In the wake of this paradigmatic change and of the corollary desire to conform to the new trend, Canada undertook to build prisons, or to restructure existing locally run colonial common gaols into prisons following the increasingly institutionalized Auburn System. Conforming to a new trend is part of what path dependence scholars call a bandwagon effect, one of the positive feedback mechanisms responsible for the lock-in process into a trajectory. A bandwagon effect had already been developing in the United States since the 1820s, and was taking root in Canada. The first prison to become a "penitentiary"—rooted in ideals of penance, repentance, and reform—was the Provincial Penitentiary of the Province of Upper Canada, which opened in 1835 in Kingston as a maximum security institution designed for men.

Kingston Penitentiary's architect was William Coverdale, a master carpenter who became "master builder" at the penitentiary following the dismissal in 1834 of John Mills, who had been brought originally from Auburn, New York. Hired at one fifth less pay than Mills, Coverdale remained as the "master builder" of the penitentiary for 14 years, during which the main building as well as the gatehouse were erected, chiefly with prisoner labour (McKendry, 1991). According to Edmison (1954: 26), not only was "[t]he Penitentiary . . . built upon the plans and lines of the Auburn, N.Y., prison [but] [t]he [former] Deputy Keeper of Auburn, William Powers, was hired, at £350 per annum, as building superintendent." Kingston Penitentiary's intended capacity of 880 beds ranked it among the largest prisons in the Western world, the biggest being Millbank in England with its 1000 beds at the time (Johnson, 2015). Since the prison's design did not have women in mind, when the first sentenced women arrived at Kingston Penitentiary on August 28, 1835, they were detained along with children:

> [T]hree women were sentenced to serve penitentiary terms on the same day, August 28, 1835. All were from the Gore District (the Hamilton, Ontario area). They were inmates #33 – Susan Turner; # 34 – Hannah Downes and # 35 – Hannah Baglen. All were sentenced for the crime of "Grand Larceny". Susan Turner and Hannah Downes were sentenced to serve 1 year, and Hannah Baglen was sentenced to 2 years. . . . The youngest female inmate appears to have been # 9207 – Sarah Jane Pierce, a 9 year old [*sic*] from Brockville, Ontario. She was sentenced on March 4, 1878 for house breaking and larceny and given a 7 year sentence. Among the items that she was found guilty of stealing were a quilt, a ladies [*sic*] hat, a towel, a pitcher, some beef, raisins, biscuits, tea and sugar. Her mother received a sentence of 6 months in the County Gaol for receiving the stolen goods.[1]

To be isolated from the men, both women and children were detained, at turns, in the prison's infirmary (Société Elizabeth Fry du Québec, 2011), the attic (Boritch, 1997), the old dining hall (Neufeld, 1998), the north wing of the building starting in 1839, or in other makeshift arrangements, such as leaving them to sleep in corridors when their numbers grew in the 1850s (Cooper, 1987). Between 1835 and 1913, the women were moved several times within Kingston Penitentiary, with each move being hastened because the existing space was needed by the male population. In such circumstances, the women had little to no access to workshops and recreation, and spent their day making and mending prison clothes and bedding (Boritch, 1997). They seemed forever in the way of the prison's expansion. As noted by Boritch (1997: 172), correctional authorities appeared not to know what to do with the women: "From the beginning, prison officials viewed female inmates as a nuisance to be housed and managed in whatever ways were least disruptive to the dominant male population." The prison staff themselves testified to Kingston Penitentiary's incompetence and disinclination to deal with women prisoners (Neufeld, 1998), considered to be an inconvenience, hence further silencing differences.

---

1.   https://www.penitentiarymuseum.ca/history/interesting-facts/, accessed November 25, 2021.

Moreover, prison officials expressed divergent and often conflicting views on the best way to rehabilitate women, thereby offsetting efforts to change women's prison conditions during the 19th century (Cooper, 1987) and putting women's welfare second to the space required by the men prisoners.

In 1849, the Penitentiary Board of Governors, as well as the Royal Commission of Inquiry to Investigate into the Conduct, Discipline, and Management of the Provincial Penitentiary (Brown Report) recommended that a suitable building be dedicated for women to alleviate their unhealthy living conditions and end their corporal punishment at the hands of Kingston Penitentiary authorities (Canada, 1849). Apart from the 1851 Penitentiary Act, which imposed rules to control corporal chastisement and to move women prisoners with mental health issues to the Upper Canada Insane Asylum (Cooper, 1987), the women remained a hindrance in Kingston Penitentiary, designed for men.

In the meantime, Kingston Penitentiary, which was initially a provincial penitentiary, became a federal penitentiary following Confederation in 1867. However, one had to wait until 1909 before a decision was made to build new quarters to house the women at Kingston Penitentiary. Resorting to men prisoners as construction labour to minimize costs, the 32-cell Northwest Cell Block opened in 1913 on the penitentiary premises (Société Elizabeth Fry du Québec, 2011), that is within the maximum security male designed perimeter, some 65 years after repeated calls for adequate housing for women. Since this separate building was the only federal penitentiary designated for women Canada-wide, many women suffered from geographical dislocation and social isolation, being separated by thousands of kilometres from families and communities. For their part, federally sentenced men could be detained in the growing penitentiary estate across Canada.

One year later, in 1914, the Royal Commission on Penitentiaries (MacDonnell Report) suggested that, since federally sentenced women constituted a low risk to society, the new quarters ought to be demolished, and federally sentenced women sent to their respective province of origin in prisons accessible to their families to promote women's community resettlement upon warrant expiry. According to Cooper (1987: 133), this idea of surrendering federal women prisoners to provincial jurisdictions was regarded by federal corrections officials as "a retrogressive step," mostly because a new facility had recently been delivered for the women on penitentiary grounds. It is interesting to note here that reducing women's severe geographic and social displacement was considered a retrogressive step, which suggests that the argument was monetary and political, since Canada was in the middle of building and reinforcing a centralized system of federal prisoning. Hence, the idea to cede federally sentenced women to provincial jurisdictions was not acted upon and was taken again for many years without success. According to data reported by Cooper (1987), the only time the possibility of returning federally sentenced women to provincial jurisdictions was considered in a genuine manner was when the matrons working at the women's unit at Kingston Penitentiary demanded a raise in pay: "they were informed that the unit would be closed, and the inmates sent to the provinces if the matrons persisted with their requests for increased wages" (p. 136).

Turn-of-the-century employed women asking increased wages amounted to a counter-reaction against the stabilization of the embryonic Auburn-derived male-centred prison path, where male guards outnumbered by far the number of matrons employed to manage "inconvenient" women prisoners. I have argued previously that to potentially disrupt path dependence, exogenous shock or critical mass may be needed. Here, critical mass is something that matrons did not have the luxury of possessing. Moreover, demanding increased wages did not support a power-based gender role reproduction whereby actors come to resort to power to assert their gendered interests in preserving male dominance within the birthing prison system. Thus, matrons' demands did stand out as a "formative historical event" (Beyer, 2010:190), an event that eventually contributed to rule out alternative developments to a power-based gendered role reproduction in prisons. One had to wait until 1973 when interjurisdictional Exchange of Service Agreements finally allowed eligible federally sentenced women to serve their sentence in a provincial prison closer to family and community (Dion, 1999).

3.2 AFTER A HUNDRED YEARS OF SQUATTING, THE 1934 PRISON FOR WOMEN

In 1921, the Report on the State and Management of the Female Prison at Kingston Penitentiary (Nickle Report) stated that women prisoners' salary should be increased, that they spent too much time in cells with cold cement floors and walls in need of new paint, and that they worked with antiquated laundry equipment and were compelled to do the personal laundry of prison staff (Cooper, 1987). It also recommended, once again, that a fully autonomous prison for women be built, but this time outside the premises of Kingston Penitentiary (Hannah-Moffat, 2001). However, Commissioner Nickle did not support the 1914 recommendation to ground women's prisoning process on their geographic proximity to their community of reintegration. Although W. F. Nickle entertained popular views of women prisoners as sexually abnormal, his report was nonetheless a landmark in the history of the treatment of women prisoners, since it resulted in an improvement of women's prison conditions at Kingston Penitentiary, and led to the construction, 13 years later, of the Prison for Women across the road from the Kingston Penitentiary for men (Cooper, 1987). After almost one hundred years of makeshift accommodation and mistreatment, the construction of the Prison for Women was an opportunity for correctional authorities to think outside the box and bifurcate toward a different correctional model from the one based on the institutionalized Auburn System design. However, the Prison for Women turned out to be but another variation on a theme, since it reproduced Kingston Penitentiary's maximum security, male-oriented design and programming. Even its management continued to be a task delegated to Kingston Penitentiary's warden, its doctor and its two chaplains. The administration offices of the new Prison for Women, not fully autonomous, were amalgamated to those of Kingston Penitentiary in 1933 within the luxurious official residence of its warden, built entirely by prisoner labour. The residence was converted for administrative purposes following the penitentiary's 1932 riot. Before this incident, wardens resided with their families within the Kingston Penitentiary security perimeter.[2]

---

2.   https://www.penitentiarymuseum.ca/history/cedarhedge/, accessed November 25, 2021.

Later, the Prison for Women's management was fulfilled jointly by Kingston and Collins Bay[3] penitentiaries for men until 1960, when an independent woman warden was designated finally for the Prison for Women (Cooper, 1987; Hayman, 2006).

It is ironic that, after 99 years of women squatting in Kingston Penitentiary without a separate prison designated for women, the first prisoners to inhabit the Prison for Women would be 100 men transferred from Kingston Penitentiary while renovations were undertaken at the men's penitentiary following rioting (Hannah-Moffat, 2001). The women were made to wait to access their own prison until men no longer needed it.[4]

The design of the new federal Prison for Women was a congregate-style prison surrounded by a five-metre wall topped with barbed wire, in which cells no longer had outside windows and women had no recreation ground and no provision for outdoor exercise or education; a "great big barrack . . . cold and empty" impressed a matron about her move to the new prison (Cooper, 1987: 137). This largely reproduced the increasingly dominant modern male-centred prison model despite growing evidence that women's crimes were occasional and accidental (Elliot and Morris, 1987), that they constituted a low risk of recidivism, and experienced and responded to imprisonment differently than men (Hannah-Moffat and Shaw, 2000a). For a century before the opening of the Prison for Women, federally sentenced women had been imprisoned at Kingston Penitentiary, certainly, but also in men's federal penitentiaries located in various Canadian provinces, thus creating a fragment of decentralization. However, the opening of the Prison for Women meant the repatriation of these women into a single, central penitentiary to increase the cost effectiveness of the prisoning operation.

Self-reinforcing mechanisms may have affected the decision process not to thread off the beaten path. First, financial concerns pushed decision-makers to build the Prison for Women across the road from Kingston Penitentiary, since men prisoners, already employed in the penitentiary as ropemakers, blacksmiths, carpenters, and

---

3.   Collins Bay Penitentiary opened in 1930.
4.   https://www.csc-scc.gc.ca/text/pblct/brochurep4w/4-eng.shtml, accessed June 22, 2021.

stonecutters (Dickens, 1874:362) were used to build this new prison (Société Elizabeth Fry du Québec, 2011). Kingston Penitentiary architect William Coverdale (Edmison, 1954:26), as well as men prisoners, who had been used in the past to building portions of Kingston Penitentiary itself, had acquired skilled knowledge of the Auburn System model. Financial concerns also motivated decision-makers to favour a congregate-style rather than a cottage-style prison, which would have been more in line with a motherly (caring, protective) type of regulation of women prisoners (Hayman, 2006). There was therefore a "learning effect" (Arthur, 1994), which swelled benefits as the familiarity with the Auburn system model itself increased. There were likely also "adaptive expectations" at play, since decision-makers may have adapted their actions to options expected to breed wide-ranging approval.

Hence, the benefits of model reproduction were beginning to augment, further insulating decision-makers from the adoption of a creative carceral design or philosophy different from the modern prison. Arthur (1994) and Pierson (2000) identified financial cost as a major incentive to "stick with" a preferred environment. As such, costs are an increasing return mechanism precluding change. Thus, the Prison for Women further entrenched a self-reinforcing institutional pattern despite growing evidence noted in government inquiries that lamented the demonstrated failure of Auburn inspired imprisonment (Canada, 1849; Neufeld, 1998).

The second self-reinforcing mechanism at play involved the prevailing historical stereotypes as to the nature of "criminal" women. According to Cooper (1987), the penitentiary system of the time entertained contradictory characterizations of women prisoners as either poor unfortunate souls or perfidious seductresses. Similar characterizations concurrently employed in the media perpetuated Manichean notions of dangerous, irredeemable, yet exposed and fragile criminalized or imprisoned women (Faith, 1987; Martel, 1991). Such dichotomy may have generated a mixture of protectionism and public antipathy toward women prisoners. Both cost and stereotypes, as self-reinforcing mechanisms, may have contributed to crafting an interdependent web of positive feedback processes favourable to increasing returns. By ricochet, such increasing returns tended to generate organizational stability within corrections.

Between the opening of the Kingston Penitentiary in 1835 and that of the Prison for Women in 1934, several other federal penitentiaries and provincial prisons were built in Canada upon the modern Auburn System prison model. As far as women's prisoning is concerned, I argue that the decision to build the Prison for Women largely upon the modern prison model marks the continuation of what Schreyögg and Sydow (2011) named the "formation phase" of the organizational process of becoming path dependent, whereby a dominant action pattern began to emerge. According to the authors, the formation phase begins with a critical juncture, a decision or an action that is taken in the "preformation phase" in a period when a wide range of plausible actions or alternatives were still financially and culturally accessible for correctional authorities. Prior to the birth of Kingston Penitentiary, Canada had not yet embedded punishment "within a formal, rational, semi-permanent organization" (Rubin, 2019b: 158) and so did not possess a long heritage of correctional rules and culture that shaped organizational decision-making (Pierson, 2000). Historically, one can locate the main critical juncture in penal reform in the wide adoption of the Auburn System model, since it was being reproduced over a certain timespan, in the United States and in Canada since the first half of the 19th century. A critical juncture is the period during which organizations enter "into the dynamics of a self-reinforcing process" (Schreyögg and Sydow, 2011: 323) through increasing returns processes and positive feedback mechanisms.

In the "formation phase," decision processes begin to reflect the building up of a dominant action pattern, "alternative patterns face problems in getting attention and acceptance, which renders the whole process more and more irreversible. By implication, the range of options narrows, and it becomes progressively difficult to reverse the central pattern of action, i.e., an organizational path is evolving" (Schreyögg and Sydow, 2011: 324). Building the Prison for Women upon the Auburn system model while disregarding the multiple admonitions and recommendations of previous governmental inquiries and reports signals the possible progression of an organizational persistence onto one prevailing path.

Moreover, in the 15 years prior to the construction of the Prison for Women, the prison population averaged 25 women, which did not justify the construction of a 100-bed institution (Cooper, 1987). Thus, in 1938, four years after the Prison for Women's opening, the Royal Commission to Investigate the Penal System of Canada (Archambault Report) recommended its closure because of appalling prison conditions and the modest number of federally sentenced women, as well as their population profile, which justified neither the Prison for Women's construction or its maximum security design or continuance (Canada, 1938) based on "the heavy operating expense" of such a large facility (Canada, 1978a: 4). Along this line, the report recommended the women's transfer to their province of origin for detention closer to family and community of resettlement. Commissioners swept aside with a wave of the hand federal correctional authorities' financial argument to the effect that one centralized penitentiary was less costly. Again, set-up costs, as well as substantial short-term savings (Cooper, 1987), were invoked by federal correctional authorities as a major argument supporting the preservation of one centralized prison for women, although provinces responded positively to the idea given appropriate transfer or federal monies.

With hindsight, it is safe to assume that a move toward decentralization via provincial prisons early in the 20th century could have significantly reduced the overall human and fiscal costs and could have been a more efficient alternative. It is also safe to assume that politically motivated expediency (i.e., high set-up costs and substantial short-term savings) nurtured federal correctional authorities' actions and decisions to remain on the status quo path. By ricochet, this contributed to a build-up effect leading to further self-reinforcement of one institutional pattern.

The 1950s saw a sharp increase in the number of federally sentenced women in Canada due, in part, to drug offenders entering the criminal justice system in droves as well as to the incarceration of Doukhobor protesters. The Doukhobors were Russian dissenters engaged in radical pacifism essentially in the province of British Columbia. Members of a small radicalized sub-group were jailed in the 1950s and 1960s for nude protests, parades, and involvement in several bombings of buildings (Friesen, 1995).

Consequently, even in 1960, after a decade of increasing overcrowding in the Prison for Women, correctional authorities felt it was best to expand the prison by 50 beds rather than force a shift toward the decentralization of federal women's prisoning (Boritch, 1997) with the agreement of the provinces. This decision was taken despite a reduction in journalistic reactionism toward criminalized or imprisoned women. Indeed, between the 1930s and the 1950s the media abandoned its sarcastic or pathetic narrative widely used against criminalized or imprisoned women at the turn of the 20th century. The decision to expand the Prison for Women instead of privileging a decentralization approach (in provincial prisons) was reached despite the media's progressive immunization against contemptuous or sanctimonious descriptions of women's criminalization and the emergence, in the 1950s, of more restrained and neutral journalistic accounts of criminalized or imprisoned women (Martel, 1991).[5] Such a neutral journalistic tone could have, in turn, helped dispel myths used to justify maintaining women in over-secure prisons. Without the corollary self-reinforcing mechanism of reactionary public opinion, correctional authorities' decision to expand rather than decentralize reverts to "cognitive stickiness" (Larason Schneider, 2006:466).

Throughout the 20th century, repeated pleas for the decentralization of women's federal prisoning stemming from government inquiries and committees as well as from private sector reports were ignored by decision-makers. The 1947 Gibson Report on the Canadian penitentiary system underscored the lack of adequate services for federally sentenced women housed at the Prison for Women to no avail (Canada, 1947). Within the next two decades, two smaller governmental committees, the Fauteux and Ouimet committees, supported the principle of the Prison for Women as a central prison (Canada, 1956) and of a centralized prison service throughout Canada (Canada, 1969). The Canadian Corrections Association also produced an official statement of policy in 1968 which once again stressed the isolation of the Prison for Women and once again recommended that the provinces assume responsibility for all women prisoners (Canada, 1978a). Like the Archambault commissioners before them in the 1930s, Fauteux committee members travelled extensively in Canada and abroad and observed "a remarkable uniformity of informed opinion throughout the country" about prisoning (Fauteux 3 cited in Anonymous, 1977: 6).

---

5.   Martel's (1991) work centred on Québec media. It should be noted here that the journalistic restraints of the 1950s were followed by a return of backlash media comments on criminalized and imprisoned women in the 1960s and 1970s as a result of feminism's second wave.

Borrowing from political scientist Paul Pierson (2000: 260), such a "communit[y] of discourse" may be likened to the entrenchment, across Canada, of confirming information into mental maps increasingly shared among political and correctional actors. These maps, in turn, generate network effects that replicate ideological paths. With such uniformity of thought, it becomes more difficult to reverse course. Unlike the Fauteux and Ouimet reports, the 1977 MacGuigan Report by the Sub-Committee on the Penitentiary System in Canada was a major government report that focused on male federal offenders (Canada, 1977a). Commissioners took notice of federally sentenced women as one witness at the Commission decried the Prison for Women as "unfit for bears, much less women" (p. 135). In relation to the obsolescence of the Prison for Women, the sub-committee found "remarkable indifference to a casual neglect of women's needs by both region and [national] headquarters" of the federal Corrections Branch (p. 137).

Simultaneously, a National Advisory Committee on the Female Offender was formed to assess federally sentenced women's situation exclusively (Canada, 1977b). Its report (Clark Report) also recommended the closure of the Prison for Women based on the repeated denunciation of the geographical dislocation and unwarranted classification suffered by the women, and the prison's lack of adequate correctional programming. The Clark Report prompted the creation of a National Planning Committee on the Female Offender responsible for assessing Clark's recommendations either that federally sentenced women be housed in smaller regional facilities or that they be managed by the provinces. The Planning Committee's Needham Report opted for the closure of the Prison for Women and its replacement by two regional facilities under the purview of the federal government (Canada, 1978a). The same year, the Chinnery committee, established to write an action plan for the replacement of the Prison for Women by regional facilities, also rejected the idea of keeping the Prison for Women (Canada, 1978b). By 1981, the Canadian Association of Elizabeth Fry Societies had submitted a statement brief to the solicitor general advocating for the closure of the Prison for Women. The same year, the Canadian Human Rights Commission favourably received a charge of sexual discrimination against the federal government filed by Women for Justice, a group of women outside the field of corrections. Although the Commission declared that the treatment of incarcerated women was inferior to that of men and that, consequently, they suffered discrimination in Canada, prison conditions continued to deteriorate at the Prison for Women (Frigon, 2002).

Programming seemed to suffer particularly. In 1985, the prison had a clinical intervention team dedicated to assisting women in crisis situations or those considered to have behavioural problems, on an ad hoc basis. Near the end of the 1980s, the prison employed one part-time psychiatrist on a three half-day per week basis, one full-time as well as one part-time psychologist, the latter having expertise in the thera-peutic approaches to sexual abuse. The scarcity of therapeutic services at the Prison for Women was offset by providing women access to five beds in the treatment unit of the Kingston Penitentiary for men, as well as to the St. Thomas Psychiatric Hospital located in Brampton, Ontario, a city some 300 kilometres west of Kingston (Canada, 1987). Alcoholics Anonymous delivered regular therapeutic sessions, while the Elizabeth Fry Societies of Ontario provided individual consultations, group discussions, social activities, and basic education (Martel, 1990). Along similar lines, there lingered a dearth of dedicated programs for federally sentenced women, especially in addictions. Educational and profes-sional training consisted of outdated courses except for those courses which women could follow in surrounding men's prisons. There was no community service program or pre-release program at the Prison for Women (Canada, 1990).

The deteriorating conditions fuelled the recurrent calls for closure. These were followed by a report of the Canadian Bar Association Committee on Imprisonment and Release, which, among other proposals, recommended that legislation be introduced to coerce the definitive closure of the Prison for Women (Jackson, 1988). Yet, switching women's prisoning to some other plausible alternative seemed difficult, since the financial, political, and cultural costs of switching remained allegedly high despite contemporary *savoir-faire* showing the modern prison model to be less tailored to, or ineffective, with criminalized women. In 1990, however, the official limestone residence that the Deputy Warden of Kingston Penitentiary inhabited from the 1910s to the 1930s, when it became the official residence of the Warden, was given a new purpose and became a minimum security prison for federally sentenced women. It was located a stone's throw from Kingston Penitentiary and from the maximum security Prison for Women. Upon its reassignment, the building was renamed

Isabel J. McNeill House after the first superintendent of the Prison for Women.[6] Designed to accommodate 10 women, it offered employment training, and sustained interactions with the community via programs and leisure activities.

3.3 THREADING OFF THE BEATEN TRACK? THE 1990 TASK FORCE ON FEDERALLY SENTENCED WOMEN

Pressure from government studies, investigations, and reports from the private sector, the media and feminist, Indigenous, and reformist organizations (Boritch, 1997; Hannah-Moffat, 2001; Frigon, 2002; Hayman, 2006)[7] mounted for years about the inappropriateness of the Prison for Women. Martel (1991) points out that, in the 1980s, the dominant media narrative still conveyed a masculinist conception of women. The representation of the emotional, passive, dependent, irrational, and irresponsible woman that had been ambient at the turn of the 20th century, seemed to persist in the 1980s, at a time when pressure was building leading to the implementation of the Task Force on Federally Sentenced Women. Despite, or thanks to, such media representation of incarcerated women, recurrent proposals to shut down the Prison for Women culminated in 1988 when the Daubney Report (Canada, 1988) recommended that the prison be closed within five years and that a task force be instituted to decide on the best way to facilitate the closure. No longer able to ignore shifts in power relations induced by new interest groups and to diffuse continuous collective and public pressure via a smokescreen of delaying tactics such as inquiries and commissions, in 1989, the federal government implemented the Task Force on Federally Sentenced Women. This Task Force fell, notably, under the impetus of the newly appointed commissioner of corrections, Ole Ingstrup, who, in 1988, brought with him a Scandinavian perspective on corrections resting on humanism and correctional programming rather than on security management

---

6.   http://www.stoneskingston.ca/penitentiary-city/isabell-macneill-house/, accessed March 21, 2022.
7.   For an account of feminist involvement in Canadian prison reform since the 19th century, see H. Boritch (1997: 178-180). For an account of feminist legal and political advocacy associated with the inequities faced by federally sentenced women in the 1980s, see S. Hayman (2006: 22-26).

(Hayman, 2006). Ingstrup's commitment "represented a radical departure from that of his predecessors, who generally dismissed female offenders as insignificant or beyond rehabilitation" (Adelberg and Currie, 1993: 19).

The Task Force on Federally Sentenced Women was unusual in Canadian politics notably because it was based on the combined participation of government officials, the voluntary sector, representatives of Indigenous and minority groups, and women with lived experience of the prison. This singular constellation of actors stimulated the design of a correctional and social innovation. The Task Force's objective was to assess the appropriateness of the male-centred correctional model and its use with women prisoners. Specifically, the Task Force addressed current and historical issues in the women's prisoning process such as geographic remoteness, program limitations, the over-security of facilities, the unacknowledged realities of Indigenous women, and the legacy of male-centred programs and facilities.

Until the implementation of the Task Force on Federally Sentenced Women in 1989, conditions in prisons designated for women were the mirror of class and gender conventions that fashioned the inauguration and evolution of other prisons designated for women in many Anglo-Saxon countries in the 19th century. However, in its 1990 game-changing report, *Creating Choices*, the task force working group recommended yet again that the Prison for Women be closed in part because the prison had been the theatre of a recent series of suicides (Hayman, 2006). Among its more innovative recommendations, it advocated for the implementation of a women-centred correctional philosophy set in a holistic conception of women's experiences and needs. In the hope of heralding a "broader justice and social reform," (Canada, 1990: 77) task force members imagined five principles for correctional change based on: women's empowerment; their treatment with respect and dignity; the provision of holistic programming and meaningful options to make responsible choices; in a prison environment that is positive and mutually supportive. These four principles were to be embedded in the fifth one: a shared, collective responsibility for incarcerated women from all levels of government, corrections, private and voluntary sector services, businesses, and community members.

Task force members recommended that prison design and operations follow these five principles and led to the construction of four decentralized, minimum security, cottage-style facilities across Canada in addition to an Indigenous healing lodge. Undergirded by non-intrusive security, these facilities comprise individual rooms and make the most of "natural light, fresh air, colour, space, privacy, and access to land" (Canada, 1990: 84). They must offer Indigenous programming and services and a mother-child unit, have civilian clothed staff, and adopt new terminology whereby, for example, women prisoners are referred to as "residents" and no longer as "offenders." Observers agree that the implementation of the task force's recommendations by the federal government has been the most important correctional reform for women in Canada's history, as well as a vanguard pioneer on an international level (Hannah-Moffat, 2001; Hayman, 2006).

Yet, shortly after the opening of one of these new women-centred institutions, I sat on its Program Advisory Committee—a committee established at the discretion of the local warden—from 1996 until 1999, when she unilaterally disbanded the committee. During my numerous visits to the new prison, I was able to observe that this facility included one "resident bathroom" and one "staff bathroom" almost side by side in the central administrative building. Despite the innovative correctional vision based notably on the promotion of women's respect and dignity, the design of this new prison still marked distinct spaces for the condemned and for their keepers, much like conventional prison designs.

The new women-centred prisons opened over a nine-year period: The Nova institution in Truro, Nova Scotia, the Okimaw Ohci Indigenous lodge in Maple Creek, Saskatchewan, and the Edmonton institution for Women were the first to open in 1995. They were followed by the Québec prison in Joliette and the Ontario prison in Grand Valley in 1997. The last one to open was the Fraser Valley prison in Abbotsford, British Columbia, which opened in 2004 in a campus-like federal prison no longer needed by authorities to detain federally sentenced men. Prior to its opening, federally sentenced women were incarcerated in a British Columbia provincial prison, the Burnaby Correctional Centre for Women (BCCW) under the Interjurisdictional

Exchange of Service Agreements[8] between the federal Minister of Public Safety and Emergency Preparedness and provincial and territorial jurisdictions. Such agreements allow for reciprocal exchanges of prisoners between jurisdictions, information sharing, etc. The intent behind Exchange of Service Agreements is to "facilitate and enhance offender related objectives,"[9] such as preventing geographical dislocation, guaranteeing access to specialized programs and services, and meeting the needs of persons of various ethnocultural origins. When the provincial Burnaby Correctional Centre for Women closed in March 2004, federal correctional authorities reclaimed federally sentenced women and housed them in a decommissioned minimum security men's prison in Abbotsford.

As illustrated in Figure 1 at the end of this chapter, I argue that Schreyögg and Sydow's (2011) third stage of path dependence development, the "lock-in" stage, took form between the opening of the Prison for Women in 1934 and the *Creating Choices* report in 1990, the latter being considered, with hindsight, a critical juncture. The lock-in period of 1934–1990 amounted to a further constriction of possible alternatives to the growing authority of one pattern. Practices became established, and operational procedures became long-standing, such that women's prisoning as an organizational process lost flexibility to consider alternatives. It must not be assumed that a locked-in mode of prisoning women arose because it served some particularly useful purpose. Functional accounts are not the only plausible ones. According to path dependence scholarship, many events may generate or sustain positive feedback in a variety of ways. Such events may be: 1) the timing and sequencing of political decisions or accidental events; 2) the short-termism of electoral politics; or 3) the swift staff renewal rate in strategic bureaucratic ranks (Pierson, 2000).

According to Schreyögg and Sydow (2011), the lock-in period may be cognitive, normative, or resource-based in nature. In the case of Canadian federally sentenced women, the **path stabilization** period seems to be a blend of these three types of lock-in. It is cognitive in the sense that interpretive frames were initially built that later became

---

8.   Interjurisdictional Exchange of Service Agreements, https://www.csc-scc.gc.ca/
     politiques-et-lois/541-1-gl-eng.shtml, accessed November 19, 2021.
9.   Ibid., note 8, art. 2.

dominant in managerial decisions, creating a "community of discourse" (Pierson, 2000:260) based on widely shared and replicated mental maps about women's prisoning. It is also cognitive in that the short-time horizon of political actors—based on the logic of electoral politics—as well as the rapid turnover in key bureaucratic positions, tend to make self-reinforcing processes in politics intense and learning difficult, thus susceptible to path stabilization. As cognitive components, short-termism political foresight and lack of political will tend to be less conducive to major institutional reforms.

The lock-in is also normative in the sense, firstly, that Canadian correctional decision-makers contributed to the emergence of an international bandwagon effect, whereby the male-oriented modern prison design was adopted widely and became hegemonic, thus increasing the price of dissension. It is normative also in the sense that the preservation of a centralized federal prison for federally sentenced women was part of a larger nation-building political agenda in Canada (Hayman, 2006). Through positive feedback, the newly established prisoning model was frequently repeated and "cast into a pattern which [became] reproduced with an economy of effort and which, *ipso facto*, [began to be] apprehended by its performer *as* that pattern" (Berger and Luckmann, 1967: 53). It became "habitualized action" (p. 53). Whenever habitualized actions become typified and shared by an assortment of actors in the context of a shared history, institutionalization takes place. Habitualized actions become institutions. By ricochet, institutionalization allows for the societal acceptance of newly established prisoning models, thus providing legitimacy to and objectivation of these new prisoning models since they result from human subjectivity but become objects readable or "catchable" for others (Berger and Luckmann, 1967).

Finally, the lock-in is also resource-based in the sense that financial arguments have been invoked extensively by correctional authorities over the course of the 20th century to justify keeping the centralized Prison for Women. These components may become routinized and come to imprint correctional services' organizational structure and behaviour long after the advent of the organization itself (Schreyögg and Sydow, 2011). Following path dependence ideas, one could argue that the erection of the Prison for Women was part of a growing national and international adoption of an increasingly dominant prison design (i.e., a bandwagon effect) and was (presumably) underlain by high start-up financial costs. Its persistence for most of the 20th century, however, sat on already prohibitive maintenance costs (financial, material, and cultural), the consolidation of learning effects, the safeguarding of a fleet of correctional staff increasingly qualified in women's prisoning, and adaptive expectations. Such expectations imply that opting for an alternative prison design, or decarceration, or abolition depends to a considerable degree on correctional decision-makers' certainty that many other correctional entities will follow suit. It is safe to assume that the above components engendered a reduction in political and managerial discretion to do otherwise. As already discussed, correctional decisions made in the 19th century, once institutionalized, tended to configure the decisions about alternatives that could be made later in the 20th century.

As mentioned above, and illustrated in Figure 1, *Creating Choices* may be viewed as a critical juncture in the Canadian penal reform landscape, a historical event that, in retrospect, constituted a fork in the road, an opportunity to stray beyond the locked-in path on which corrections had been since 1835. Following Capoccia and Kelemen (2007:343), it may be argued that the Task Force on Federally Sentenced Women occurred in a temporal moment where "cultural, ideological and organizational influences on political action [may have been] relaxed for a relatively short period of time." On a cultural level, specifically in the 1980s, a subdued and more neutral media stance had overtaken the 1970s' media trend of portraying "pariah femininity" (Kilty and Bogosavljevic, 2019) through sarcastic and sexist journalistic accounts of women in Québec and elsewhere in Canada. It has been argued (Martel, 1991; Faludi, 1991) that such media representations could have been a reactionary stance to the protest movements of the 1960s and 1970s, especially the second wave feminist movement. Thus, ambient cultural influences—including the 1980s feminist political activism toward women and justice—may have stimulated political action toward more seriously addressing perennial problems with the conventional process of prisoning women. Ideologically, turn-of-the-century positivistic criminologists as mythmakers of misogynist assumptions about women's hidden aptitude for malevolence and cunning had been losing hegemonic ground since the ideological turn in the 1960s and 1970s, which offered alternative sociological, feminist, and critical theorization on women's victimization, criminalization, and incarceration (Carlen, 1983). It is reasonable to assume that these new theories percolated into federal correctional services. On an organizational level, since 1988, Correctional Service Canada had been under the guidance of Commissioner Ole Ingstrup, who looked to imprint humanism and rehabilitative programming into corrections for both men and women. In sum, *Creating Choices* was the result of the interactions of collective action by individual, community, and ministerial actors in a given conducive historical moment. At this intersection, collective actors determined which of the available pathways they would pursue.

Following path dependence scholar Bernhard Ebbinghaus (2005:17), I suggest that three scenarios of institutional transformation presented themselves to these collective actors. The first is "path stabilization" (full institutional persistence), whereby deeply rooted institutions tend to marginally adapt to environmental changes without altering the foundational principles of the preferred path. Ebbinghaus equates path stabilization to the maxim "plus ça change, plus c'est pareil" (the more things change, the more they remain the same). Under this first scenario, the stakeholders of *Creating Choices* would have persisted in the line of the Prison for Women in Kingston, for example. The second scenario is that of "**path departure**" (partial institutional persistence), characterized by intermediate change and steady adjustment through limited rejuvenation of institutional arrangements with some rerouting of foundational principles. Here, earlier decisions constrict the set of alternatives but do not define the next adaptive move. In the second scenario, *Creating Choices* stakeholders would have encouraged the construction of one new federal prison designated for women, centralized yet sporting a women-centred correctional philosophy. Path departure sits between the locked-in inertia of path stabilization and the third least likely scenario, "**path cessation**" or path switching (no institutional persistence) (p. 17). This last scenario is that of radical transformation and paradigm change set off by a change in the opportunity structure, a critical juncture. In such "revolutionary change," self-reinforcing processes have terminated, and a new institution is founded in lieu of the institutionalized, hegemonic one (p. 17). In the latter scenario, *Creating Choices* stakeholders would have directed federal authorities to abolish the practice of prisoning women, for example.

Although plans for a new prison designated for women had been abandoned by federal correctional services in 1956, 1965 and 1968,[10] *Creating Choices* did generate the adoption of a new physical style of imprisonment designated for women, and the construction of regional cottage-style women-centred prisons away from the fortress-like design of the Prison for Women, itself borrowed from the dominant Auburn system and its derivatives. The dominant modern prison design was not completely evacuated, though, since an "enhanced unit" meant to be a maximum security unit was built on the premises of each of the new facilities designated for women, complete with one wing containing cells with steel beds, integral lavatories and the control post for the entire prison (Hayman, 2006). Moreover, in anticipation of the closure of the Prison for Women, all Prairie[11] women classified as needing maximum security were transferred to the Edmonton Institution for Women in Alberta. In so doing, the *Creating Choices* philosophy and its subsequent implementation adopted a particular institutional arrangement from two or more alternatives (Mahoney, 2000).

It introduced institutional flexibility that, I argue, disrupted a long phase of corrections' institutional stability set on the Auburn system design as a dominant organizational arrangement. I would argue that, at the time of its conception, *Creating Choices*—as a critical juncture—constituted path departure because significant changes in the environment occurred (as discussed above) and self-reinforcing mechanisms (e.g., new political alliances between correctional authorities and the volunteer sector) provided sufficient resources for gradual adaptation, hence changing the foundation of women's prisoning process.

Creating Choices did not constitute path cessation because, in their promotion of an innovative feminist correctional philosophy, members of the task force did not entertain the radical idea of decarceration, hence remaining well within the frozen institutional landscape of the prison paradigm. However, historical studies of welfarism, for example, were able to demonstrate that states said to be frozen

---

10. https://www.csc-scc.gc.ca/text/pblct/brochurep4w/8-eng.shtml, accessed May 10, 2021.
11. Within Correctional Service Canada, the Prairie administrative region includes Manitoba, Saskatchewan, Alberta, the Northwest Territories, and Northwestern Ontario. https://www.csc-scc.gc.ca/contactez-nous/index-fr.shtml, accessed February 9, 2023.

landscapes have been able to adopt substantial reforms and reintroduce stifled historical substitutes in times of crisis (e.g., Hinrichs, 2000; Palier, 2000; Reynaud, 2000), showing that locked-in paths need not be thought of as eternal.

However, while the Canadian government publicly accepted the report in its entirety in September 1990, the vision carried in *Creating Choices* was altered before it had morphed into a complete physical reality. The full implementation of the vision detailed in *Creating Choices* failed due to several circumstances, one of them being costs. Hayman (2006) argues that design teams were pressured to abide by Treasury demands, as well as by parallel demands from Correctional Service Canada for further savings, with the result that architectural components were either suppressed (e.g., workroom), deferred (e.g., gymnasium), or reduced (e.g., administrative space). Among other things, the National Implementation Committee consisted solely of public servants at first, but eventually allowed Indigenous partners to join the planning process while representatives from the voluntary sector—often more in harmony with prison abolition than prison construction—were removed (Hayman, 2006). As Frigon (2002: 20) aptly noted: "feminists and activists were included only marginally in the implementation process of the *Creating Choices*' vision. Thus, Correctional Service Canada retreated into traditional bureaucratic correctional models."[12]

In a similar vein, federal correctional authorities unilaterally selected the building sites and nominated wardens with little consultation of women's groups or local communities, in direct contradiction with the task force's philosophy (Hannah-Moffat, 2001). For example, the task force recommended that the new facilities be built at sites that best provided established support networks needed to activate the community release strategy (Hayman, 2006). Thus, in accordance with *Creating Choices*, the facilities needed to be built "in or near Halifax, Nova Scotia, Montréal, Québec, central/Southwestern Ontario, Edmonton, and the lower mainland of British Columbia" (Canada, 1990:84). Yet, federal correctional authorities secretly decided to allow communities within a 100-kilometre radius from the targeted cities to

---

12. All quotes from French-speaking authors have been freely translated by the author of this book.

bid as potential sites (Hayman, 2006). As a result, authorities selected three small communities located close to 100 kilometres from the larger targeted urban cities considered to be more accessible to most women and their families. At these sites, networks of women's groups and public transportation were almost nonexistent (Frigon, 2002).

Other exogenous and endogenous pulls also contributed to the failure of *Creating Choices*' full implementation (see Hayman, 2000: 43). From report to planning, *Creating Choices*' ideals were watered down and compromised to the benefit of correctional authorities, which reclaimed almost full penal governance in how the vision would deploy physically and operationally. In his theory of policy generations, Netherlands public administration scholar Michiel de Vries (2000) argues that, during the life of a policy—such as the women-centred correctional philosophy contained in *Creating Choices*—governmental problem-definition and problem-solving are characterized by emphasis on certain political or democratic values and the disregard of others, depending on the time period.

Specifically, in the first generation of a policy, governments may stress short-term goal fulfillment (e.g., the preservation of the sole Prison for Women in Kingston) to the neglect of longer-term issues. Then, to amend errors arising from decisions related to short-term goal fulfillment, governments enter a second phase, that of long-term planning which, according to de Vries (2000) is technocratic and elitist, ignoring social interests and democratic procedures. As a result of democratic neglect, governmental attention will eventually glide toward integration through heightened deliberation and collective cooperation (e.g., the drafting of the *Creating Choices* report). However, as focus on democracy may lead to neglect or a deficit in efficiency, governments tend to revert to short-term goal fulfillment, thereby repeating the sequence (e.g., the watering down of *Creating Choices*' ideals). In this last process, governments tend to seek sources of stability, looking back at policy legacy anchored in the old.

3.4 THE CATALYTIC ROLE OF THE APRIL 22, 1994, INCIDENTS AT THE PRISON FOR WOMEN: A PUSH BACK TOWARD THE HEGEMONIC MODERN PRISON

As did the proto-prisons, reformatories, plantation-style prisons, and the Auburn-style modern prison, among others (Rubin, 2019a), the idealized model of prisoning that was *Creating Choices* obviously diverged, as a guide, from its on-the-ground implementation, as do all ideal types. One patent example is that, between the moment the Canadian government accepted the *Creating Choices* report in 1990 and the actual opening of the five new facilities, the Prison for Women in Kingston remained operative, but the prison's atmosphere deteriorated as incarcerated women and staff alike were growing apprehensive about the opening of the new facilities based on a correctional philosophy completely foreign to them. Following path dependence literature, I would argue that the linear equilibrium that had crystallized since the middle of the 19th century in relation to women's prisoning that had allowed the carceral apparatus to retain its same essential shape was about to burst out of its linear state of homeostasis and be upset by changes likely to exceed the carceral system's adaptation capacity, thus leading to a possible new equilibrium (Howlett, 2009). As a result, the women's transfer to the new facilities closer to families but away from prison buddies, as well as the imminent transfer of staff, generated considerable tension and anxiety at the Prison for Women, since this substantial change was not welcomed by all.

In anticipation of its closure, many experienced staff at the Prison for Women had requested transfers to other federal institutions in and around Kingston. In the spring of 1994, there was an unusually large number of inexperienced staff members at the prison. This is when incidents took place at the Prison for Women which led to the implementation of the Commission of Inquiry into Certain Events at the Prison for Women (Arbour Report) (1996) led by Madam Justice Louise Arbour. These incidents happened four years after the 1990 tabling of the *Creating Choices* report and during the construction of the new facilities. They spanned from April 22 to 26, 1994, and began when six women physically assaulted four women officers in the infirmary at about 6 p.m., the usual time slot for the distribution of medication. The incident was reported to have been a very brief (one to three minutes), but violent and unpredictable group attack on staff. Criminal charges were laid against the six instigating women, five of whom pleaded guilty, but two of whom recused themselves during their testimony before Judge Arbour and exonerated their companions. The six women were taken to the prison's segregation unit without proper eye decontamination after the use of mace (in violation of correctional procedures), and without prior strip searches. At the time, internal Post Orders at the Prison for Women dictated that strip searches be executed on every woman upon transfer to the segregation unit. Following the 1994 incident, the instigating women were not strip searched, nor were they for the following four days, in violation of internal correctional procedures (Canada, 1996).

Although correctional procedures at the time required that incident observation reports be written by staff prior to their leaving the building, officers involved in the 1994 incident wrote these reports a few days after the incident and following both formal and informal consultation between the officers involved (Canada, 1996). The April 22 incident engendered a deep loss of confidence, whereby fear and mistrust sprouted in the prison already characterized by exhaustion and exasperation in relation to the operationalization of the *Creating Choices* correctional philosophy. According to Justice Arbour (Canada, 1996), such distrust explained, in part, the actions of several parties immediately after the incident.

Following the incident, the women involved were transferred to the segregation unit where, between April 22 and 26, unprecedented tension grew, in part because the women had no way to decompress emotionally from the events. Consequently, women were throwing trays of food, juice, water, and urine, and lighting small fires in the segregation cells. Three women already segregated before the April 22 incident either self-inflicted injuries, took a hostage, or attempted suicide. Between April 22 and 26, 1994, none of the segregated women were informed of their right to counsel, and none had access to counsel, in violation of the existing statutory, regulatory and policy arrangements. Justice Arbour described the level of agitation with these words:

> From the beginning of these events, there were periods in which the inmates were acting out and engaging in verbal abuse ranging from demands (for amenities or rights to which they thought they were entitled, and which were being denied), through insults, and threats. Sometimes

the noise level was so high that the entire unit seemed to vibrate (Canada, 1996: 28).

On April 26, 1994, the Warden of the Prison for Women requested the intervention of Kingston Penitentiary's Institutional Emergency Response Team, a group of elite male staff trained in intimidation and cell extraction. According to federal correctional authorities, an Institutional Emergency Response Team only intervenes as a last resort, when all lesser alternatives have been tried. Justice Arbour believed that this was not the case on April 26, 1994 (Canada, 1996). At the time of the incidents, it was routine for Emergency Response Teams to videotape cell removals and strip searches. The all-men emergency response team was called in to remove eight women from their segregation cells and strip search them. Among these eight women, six had been involved in the April 22 incident, and two others had been housed in the segregation unit well before the incident took place.

According to federal correctional Commissioner's Directives and standing orders, no male staff may strip search a woman, except when the delay in locating a female officer would endanger the life or safety of any person or could result in the loss of evidence. Justice Arbour believed that the actual staffing situation at the Prison for Women on April 26, 1994, did not substantiate the need to resort to male staff to strip search the women (Canada, 1996). In Canada, before April 1994, no all-men Emergency Response Teams had ever strip searched a woman prisoner. The eight women were undressed by men and videotaped by men, at times under the gaze of male maintenance staff who happened to be working in the segregation unit at the time of the cell extraction (Canada, 1996). Regarding the use of Emergency Response Teams, Justice Arbour made nine recommendations related directly or indirectly to the fact that men may not strip search women (Canada, 1996: recommendation #6 a) to i)). Justice Arbour made 14 recommendations in total, each with multiple sub-recommendations that amounted to approximately 85 recommendations. Most of these recommendations required that Correctional Service Canada review the totality of its directives, regulations, standing orders, regional instructions, etc., to ensure compliance with the law. In this line of thought, Madam Justice Arbour also recommended "that the position of Deputy Commissioner for Women be created within the Correctional

Service of Canada, at a rank equivalent to that of Regional Deputy Commissioner (Canada, 1996: 132, recommendation #4a).

Following these events and the subsequent egregious conditions in which the women were kept in the segregation unit for several weeks, on January 20, 1995, federal correctional authorities tabled a Report of the Board of Investigation into the April 22 incident and subsequent events in the segregation unit. Within federal correctional services, local, regional, or national boards of investigation are set up 1) to assess and report on circumstances surrounding incidents involving a prisoner in federal penitentiaries or an offender under community surveillance; and 2) to learn about and share best practices to prevent similar incidents in the future. The most serious incidents are the subject of national investigations.[13]

This report of the Board of Investigation made some general criticisms of certain aspects of the administration of the Prison for Women (Correctional Service Canada, 1994). The report significantly exhibited the offending histories of the instigating women. According to the Office of the Correctional Investigator (OCI)—the Canadian ombudsman office for federal prisoners—an incorrect description was provided of the Institutional Emergency Response Team, while little attention was paid to its own response at the Prison for Women. The report did not address many aspects of correctional services' response to the April 22 incident or what happened afterwards. Justice Arbour would add the following comments later in her 1996 report (p. 54):

> The allegations that were being made that female prisoners had been strip searched by males were very serious allegations. The failure of the Correctional Service to take steps to verify these allegations by reviewing the videotape throughout the many months over which these allegations were growing, amounts to either a disregard of its motto of integrity and accountability, or to a misguided wishful thinking that the issue would disappear from further scrutiny. I believe that it was a combination of both. The significance of the failure to release the video in a timely fashion is exacerbated by the grossly inaccurate depiction of what happened which emerged from the final draft of the Board of Investigation Report.

---

13. Commissioner's Directive 041 – Incident Investigations, https://www.csc-scc.gc.ca/acts-and-regulations/041-cd-en.shtml, accessed May 5, 2023.

To characterize correctional authorities' lethargy in verifying the allegations as "misguided wishful thinking" resonates with path dependence scholarship regarding the temporal bracketing (putting aside) of human dramas within organizations and institutions. Specifically, Correctional Service Canada's historicity and the continuity of its organizational life is rife with human incidents obscured from public view possibly for the sake of reputational risk management. One telling example is that of a 19-year-old "relationship-wounded" young woman (Cadieux, 2003: 13 min. 25 sec.) who, in 1981, was sentenced to life in a Canadian federal penitentiary and spent the following approximately 20 years involuntarily or voluntarily isolated 23 or 24 hours a day in segregation cells because of mental health problems, since segregation cells were often considered to be the "safest spot" within prisons (Cadieux, 2003: 30 min. 46 sec.). The tragedy of her human drama in prison (prisons that she called "destruction machine[s]" (Cadieux, 2003: 25 min. 16 sec.) was well known to all hierarchical levels within Correctional Service Canada, since she became the embodiment of every flaw within federal correctional services. She also embodied correctional authorities' shame of the infernal cyclical pattern of prison/psychiatric hospital she had to endure while under federal corrections' responsibility.

As a result, her prison release was carried out with great organizational discretion[14] as a means to manage Correctional Service Canada's reputational risks. According to a former warden of one of the new women-centred federal prisons, once sentenced, human beings "belong to correctional services" (Cadieux, 2003, 59 min., 20 sec.), whose legal responsibility entails the management of sentences much more than the management of human beings. As managers of sentences, correctional services put sentences before humans. In the human drama at hand, failing "to take steps to verify . . . allegations [that women had been strip searched by men] by reviewing the videotape," or to release the compromising videotape amounts to strategic inertia within the organization. It is part of the management of reputational risks.

On February 14, 1995, the Office of the Correctional Investigator tabled a special report to the solicitor general that severely condemned federal correctional authorities' own January 20 report, the Institutional

---

14. Personal conversation with Elizabeth Fry Society staff in 2003.

Emergency Response Team intervention at the Prison for Women, and the conditions and duration of the women's confinement in segregation afterwards. According to the Correctional Investigator, it was almost impossible to determine what really happened on April 22, 1994, because of the poor quality of correctional authorities' own report.

One week later, on February 21, 1995, extensive film footage of the Emergency Response Team intervention was shown on the CBC's highly rated television program, *The Fifth Estate*.[15] The same day, the Solicitor General tabled the Correctional Investigator's Special Report in the House of Commons and announced its intention to launch an independent inquiry to examine the 1994 incidents at the Prison for Women, giving birth to the 1995 Commission of Inquiry into Certain Events at the Prison for Women (Canada, 1996).

Federal correctional authorities' response is difficult to reconcile with the spirit of *Creating Choices*, which was to underpin the entire strategy for dealing with federal women prisoners at the time. Virtually all correctional authorities' actions in response to this incident contradicted the intent behind *Creating Choices*.

Considered by Frigon (2002) and others to be a catalyzing moment, the April 22 incident at the Prison for Women in 1994 launched the Arbour Commission of Inquiry and resulted in its landmark report for corrections in Canada. Justice Arbour's scathing 1996 report about federal correctional authorities' lack of compliance with the law provided both an impetus and an environment for federal correctional authorities to commit to operational principles to undergird women's prisoning. In addition to passing extensive comment on correctional services' "disturbing lack of commitment to the ideals of justice" (p. 108), Justice Arbour's 1996 report offered 14 specific recommendations designed to ensure that future correctional practices would meet the needs of women prisoners. However, these principles were soon tossed aside with the inauguration of the new regional facilities designated for women.

According to Pierson, (2000: 263), political life is characterized by four features: multiple equilibria, contingency, the critical role of

---

15. "The Ultimate Response" (1995), *The Fifth Estate*, Canadian Broadcasting Corporation https://curio.ca/en/video/the-ultimate-response-4162/, accessed May 23, 1996.

timing and sequencing, and inertia. In a set of initial conditions favourable to self-reinforcing mechanisms, several potential outcomes generally cohabit, and allow for the simultaneous creation of multiple equilibria within an organization or institution. In such an organizational backdrop, incremental actions, or random events, if they occur at the right moment (contingency), can generate sizeable and durable outcomes. However, the occurrence of these events is insufficient in and of itself to generate an increasing returns process that could lead to organizational path dependence. A critical feature is also when an event occurs. According to path dependence approaches, earlier segments of a particular sequence matter more than later segments, hence "an event that happens 'too late' may have no effect, although it might have been of great consequence if the timing had been different" (Pierson, 2000: 263). The timing and sequencing of events is thus important in the establishment, or not, of an increasing returns process. Once such a process becomes established, positive feedback, if sustained, may guide the organization toward a single (rather than multiple) equilibrium which, in turn, may become resistant to change. The events at the Prison for Women in Kingston, Ontario, though not small, happened only four years after the *Creating Choices* report was tabled in 1990. They happened during the organizational implementation of its idealized model, a period of organizational flux where a new equilibrium (i.e., *Creating Choices* ideals), alien to federal correctional services, had potential to supersede the dominant modern prison design. Moreover, the 1994 events at the Prison for Women happened when self-reinforcing processes were not yet rooted and thus could not fortify *Creating Choices* ideals as a potential path departure. As a result, the recent bifurcation, at the time, toward path departure away from the locked-in path (i.e., Auburn modern prison and its derivatives) was fragile in terms of implementation, physical infrastructure, and social acceptability.

What is more, two years later, the Arbour Report (Canada, 1996) revealed federal correctional services' lack of compliance with the law, as well as with the principles of *Creating Choices*, as illustrated, for example, by the use of a male emergency response team to strip search women prisoners. Following path dependence scholarship, both the 1994 prison events and the 1996 Arbour Report are significant incidents because their timing was close to the 1990 release of the *Creating Choices* report. I argue that the unique timing and sequencing of these events may have prompted a push away from the *Creating Choices* philosophy and a pull toward reverting to the initial hegemonic modern prison institutionalized path. This is because both revealed little adherence to the principles devised in the *Creating Choices* report. In terms of coordination effects—a self-reinforcing process of path formation—the 1994 incidents and the revelations of the Arbour Report announced a transformation of the purpose of the new network that was developing at the time around *Creating Choices* principles. Therefore, they both may have weakened a possible bourgeoning organizational appeal toward emulation of *Creating Choices*. Had the Prison for Women events and ensuing Arbour Report happened years later, they might have had a lesser influence on the perennity of the potentially new equilibrium emerging out of *Creating Choices*. Figure 1 situates the Arbour Report—derived from the April 1994 incidents—on a path that branches away from the emerging alternative path introduced by *Creating Choices*, a path that leads back toward the hegemonic path. Although the April 1994 incidents, and the resulting Arbour Report, are hypothesized here to have contributed to a certain deviation from the new alternative correctional path, they alone did not trigger a return to the conventional dominant path. They needed a longer sequencing of events. The latter are discussed in the following section on *Creating Choices'* morphed implementation.

Along the same lines, and following path dependence scholarship, I will discuss later how the *Creating Choices* ideals had little positive weight on provincially sentenced women's transfer to Leclerc prison in Montréal, an alarming prison event that took place some 20 years later. The timing of this transfer was too far outside the gravitational pull of *Creating Choices* to be sucked in by its paradigm and its corollary intellectual and political enthusiasm.

The actual opening of the new regional prisons for federally sentenced women between 1995 and 1997 gave the *Creating Choices* vision a physical and material reality. During and around that time, further circumstances morphed original plans and moved the initial "low-risk/low-security needs" vision of *Creating Choices* ever closer back toward the dominant model of the modern prison.

3.5 THE MORPHED IMPLEMENTATION OF THE *CREATING CHOICES* CORRECTIONAL PHILOSOPHY

In 1995, its first year of operation, the Edmonton Institution for Women became the site of a series of incidents that generated much media hype and brought the local mayor to call for the closure of the newly opened facility. Among these incidents were instances of self-injury and attempted suicide (Hayman, 2006), assaults on staff (Boritch, 2001), the "escape"[16] of seven women within a period of 18 days (Tanner, 1996), and the murder of Denise Fayant, an incarcerated woman, at the hands of another incarcerated woman (Hannah-Moffat, 2001). In anticipation of the closure of the Prison for Women in Kingston all federally sentenced women originating from the Prairie administrative region, including those classified as needing a maximum security environment, were transferred to the Edmonton Institution for Women in Alberta, which resulted in a disproportionate number of these women being housed at the new minimum security facility. The media scrutiny that the incidents of self-injury, the assaults on staff, the escapes and the murder of Denise Fayant generated resulted in the almost complete closure of the Edmonton Institution for Women on May 1, 1996. The closure was propelled by intense political pressure from Alberta's Reform Party, which put forth a "law and order" political agenda, as well as by public concerns about the potential dangerousness of federally sentenced women. As a result of the escapes, not only the Edmonton facility but all the new women's federal prisons across Canada—except Okimaw Ohci, the Indigenous Healing Lodge designated for women—witnessed an intensification of their security measures such as the erection of fences, the addition of razor wire, the improvement of alarm systems and the introduction of video camera surveillance as a blanket riposte to all imprisoned women's potential dangerousness. Perimeter fences morphed the new facilities into medium security prisons which became de facto over-secured prisons

---

16. Originally a minimum security facility, the Edmonton Institution for Women was not surrounded by a high perimeter fence, barbed or razor wires, sensors, or other security devices. The women who "escaped" took advantage of the fact that the principal entrance had been left unattended to open the main door of the prison and walk out. Some of them returned to the prison of their own volition a few hours later, while others were picked up by police in the downtown area the following day (discussions between members of the Program Advisory Committee of the Edmonton Institution for Women, 1997).

for women classified as needing a minimum security environment. The minimum security women waited some 20 years after the *Creating Choices* report for the Canadian government to release funds to erect minimum security cottages outside the perimeter fences at four of the five regional prisons (Correctional Investigator Canada, 2014) although these prisons had been planned as minimum security facilities from day one.

Moreover, correctional authorities invested over $500,000 to upgrade one male penitentiary and one regional psychiatric centre to house maximum security women, although *Creating Choices* had envisioned that all federally sentenced women would reside in the new prisons designated for women regardless of their security level (Hayman, 2000).

It quickly became clear to prison sociology scholars that, during the ideation of *Creating Choices* in 1990 and its carefully constructed elaboration stages, task force members had failed to tackle the harsh empirical reality of some women's violence, a reality which, during implementation, exhorted the use of more traditional analyses of violence as a rather hastened solution to such an anomaly to the policy paradigm that *Creating Choices* represented. While some policy problems, such as some women's violence, can be overlooked at least for some time, others demand action to preserve the policy's legitimacy. Correctional authorities' response to the empirical reality of some women's violence guaranteed that the vision embedded in *Creating Choices* was not fully realized.

Over the years, other incongruities with *Creating Choices* emerged, such as the building of maximum security units with segregation cells, the adoption of law enforcement-like uniforms for correctional officers, the increase in the proportion of men correctional staff (Correctional Investigator Canada, 2014), and the neglect of community strategies. These strategies featured new community centres for released women, halfway houses managed by community organizations, Indigenous centres managed by Indigenous groups and communities, etc. (Frigon, 2002). They were carved into the initial report but were not afforded the resources necessary for their development.

Moreover, in 1996, correctional authorities adopted a new male-centred policy and actuarial and risk-based assessment tools for managing women prisoners. Actuarial tools are one of several risk technologies that aim to delineate and accurately measure risk. They are borne out of neo-liberal rationalities that have taken root in increasingly calculated western penalty since the last decade of the 20th century. Prisons, specifically, no longer govern or transform human beings, they manage the risk these human beings are said to pose (e.g., risk of recidivism, risk of escape, risk of violence). Within correctional spheres—including prisons—risk is now a common management ethos, and risk-based assessments have become a currency. Actuarial tools are thus said to provide a more accurate measurement of "true" recidivism risk.

The adoption of such tools by Canadian federal correctional authorities generated a redefinition of women's needs—such as underschooling, victimization, underemployment—no longer considered to be "needs" but risk factors used to predict their recidivism (Hannah-Moffat, 1999). This redefining of women's experiences and realities as "risks" marks a reformulating, perhaps even a reversal, of the task force's women-centred correctional approach.

In a similar vein, federal correctional authorities implemented a new mental health policy for women based on cognitive behavioural therapy, which disguised itself as progressive humane practices (Kendall, 2002; Kendall and Pollack, 2003; Pollack, 2005). According to Pollack (2005: 71), federal correctional authorities have constructed women prisoners as "disorderly and disordered and thus in need of 'taming' by adopting a mental health policy based on cognitive behavioral therapy which tends to over employ psychiatric labels and to devise accordant treatment regimes." Through this mental health policy, women are regulated rather than empowered, thus short-circuiting one of the five crucial principles of *Creating Choices*: women's empowerment.

In addition, in the last decade of the 20th century, as well as in the early 2000s, neo-conservative and neo-liberal political rationalities based on tradition, order, authority, individualism, and market dominance were beginning to consolidate in Canada and, according to political scientist Janine Brodie (1995), were eroding commitments to social welfare and ideals of social citizenship that the Canadian government entertained in the 1980s. By ricochet, these rationalities also were used to demonize criminalized and incarcerated women (Minaker and Snider, 2006; Comack, 2006). Neo-conservative and populist calls to get tough on crime (Audesse and Martel, 2020), became instrumental in encouraging a neo-liberal repositioning by federal correctional authorities when they launched the implementation of the *Creating Choices* correctional philosophy. In and of itself, this correctional philosophy embodied the political mood of the previous decade, when the federal government prioritized gender-specific social and penal policies as a result of its appreciation of women prisoners as a social subgroup suffering the pains of discrimination. Amid such government restructuring, talks of deficit reduction notably translated into short-changing the *Creating Choices* women-centred correctional philosophy to parallel neo-conservative and neo-liberal correctional ideals.

Feminist scholars critiqued this morphing of *Creating Choices* (Hannah-Moffat and Shaw, 2000a) and the use of male-centred actuarial risk tools in women's prisoning process, which revert to individualizing issues and pathologizing women (Hannah-Moffat, 2001; Chan and Rigakos, 2002). Such morphing is akin to "gender path dependence" (Kronsell, 2016: 311), whereby historic gender norms are likely to shape new ones leading to a normalization of male-centredness in formal and informal dimensions of organizations such as correctional services. Feminist institutional theorists within political science (Acker, 1990; Krook and Mackay, 2011) have long recognized the importance of institutions in the production of gender and gender inequalities. In Canada, specifically, the production of gender within correctional organizations historically involved the imprisonment of women for morally connoted crimes (e.g., prostitution, vagrancy), training in domesticity via prison employment such as sewing/mending, cleaning, dishwashing and laundry, and deferring the wardenship of women's prisons to nuns to provide religious and domestic education to women defying the gendered social order. By ricochet, the production of gender inequalities historically involved recurringly reverting to the "too few to count" (Adelberg and Currie, 1987) mantra to justify, for example, housing women in male-centred prison designs, offering them male-designed programs and assessing their needs and risks using actuarial risk predictive tools intended for men. Such decision-making invokes an apparently non-gendered logic of appropriateness of the said prisons, programs, and tools.

As such, correctional services are organizations which, like many others, supply arenas where representations and norms of gender are moulded notably through the compact predominance of male bodies (e.g., male prisoners, male guards) and masculine practices (e.g., correctional programs designed with men in mind) which, over time, confer decision-making power. In turn, these gender norms are replicated, can be reinforced over time, and come to be entrenched in dominant modes of organizational comprehension and action (Pierson, 2004), thus generating "'pattern-bound' effects over time, caused by locking into place certain rules and norms of [organizational] behavior" (Kronsell, 2016: 314). An indication of path dependence would be that history is remembered, that is actuarial tools historically designed for men become a sort of "tradition" within correctional organizations, and thus remain relevant even in the face of potentially pathbreaking women-centred practices such as those fashioned in *Creating Choices*. Thus, it may be argued that this morphing of the correctional philosophy contained in *Creating Choices* and the use of male-centred actuarial risk tools in women's prisoning process promote historical correctional practices which continue to constitute obstacles to "gender mainstreaming."[17]

The Council of Europe, which has been instrumental in the development of this concept since the 1990s, defines gender mainstreaming as "the (re)organization, improvement, development and evaluation of policy processes, so that a gender equality perspective is incorporated in all policies at all levels and at all stages, by the actors normally involved in policymaking."[18] Despite the construction of prisons designated for women, the nomination of a Deputy Commissioner for Women within its executive structure, and the curtailed implementation of a women-centred correctional philosophy, Canadian federal correctional services tend to reproduce common patterns of action and decision-making—like the use of male-centred actuarial risk tools—largely derived from internal expert knowledge and promoting, in this case, gender-neutral logics of appropriateness. By ricochet, such logics become embedded and contribute to path dependence, explaining, as Kronsell (2016) argues, why historic gender notions become tenacious

---

17. "Gender mainstreaming" was first introduced at the Third United Nations World Conference on Women in 1985 in Nairobi, Kenya. Ten years later, in 1995, growing interest about this concept translated into gender mainstreaming becoming a strategic objective in international gender equality policy at the Fourth United Nations World Conference on Women in Beijing, China (Beveridge and Shaw, 2002).

18. Council of Europe, https://www.coe.int/en/web/genderequality/what-is-gender-mainstreaming, accessed March 22, 2022.

and quick to be called upon as recurrent commonsensical ideas of what is normal. Historic consistency is preserved. It is important to recall that feminist institutionalism does not use path dependence in a deterministic manner. Rather, it is used to suggest that opportunities for institutional or organizational innovation and change (such as the women-centred *Creating Choices* correctional philosophy) are constrained by previous choices, and that institutions—or organizations in the case at hand—provide "conditions for action that can make a certain course of action more or less appropriate or promising" (Kulawik, 2009: 265).

In yet another manner, federal correctional authorities' strategic planning in years subsequent to 1990 has also been difficult to reconcile with the spirit of *Creating Choices*, which was meant to bolster gender-responsive correctional policies and practices toward federal women prisoners. Nevertheless, in 2004, the Institut Philippe-Pinel, a high security university psychiatric hospital which opened in 1970 in Montréal and specializes in forensic psychiatry, opened a mental health assessment and treatment unit exclusively for federally sentenced women.[19] The Regional Psychiatric Centre in Saskatoon developed since 1978 as a trailblazing mental health facility with the security provisions to simultaneously act as a federal prison. It provides treatment for "acute and sub-acute mental health needs" (Correctional Service Canada, n.d.). These and other regional accredited psychiatric in-patient hospitals partially embody federal corrections' 2002 Mental Health Strategy for Women Offenders as well as gender-responsive correctional policies and practices.

Nevertheless, in 2008, under a Conservative federal government, federal correctional authorities accepted the 2007 report of a questionable five-member review panel aimed at assessing the processes and procedures of federal corrections "as part of the government's commitment to protecting Canadian families and communities" (Canada, 2007: iii). Although the five panel members had professional experience in agencies such as policing and parole, or in areas such as Indigenous economic challenges and criminal victim advocacy, none of them had academic backgrounds in either criminology, correctional law, offender treatment, or rehabilitation. Moreover, they did not possess expertise in law, policymaking, and imprisonment, which is usually expected of

---

19. https://pinel.qc.ca/historique/, accessed March 21, 2022.

members appointed to sit on such "expert" panels or committees. "Given the breadth, complexity and timeline of its mandate, a panel with a much greater range of expertise was necessary to ensure well-founded recommendations," conclude Michael Jackson, University of British Columbia law professor and human rights advocate, and Graham Stewart, former Executive Director of the John Howard Society of Canada (Jackson and Stewart, 2009: 8).

Published only six months after the panel was convened, the expedited report entitled *A Roadmap to Strengthening Public Safety* (hereafter *Roadmap*) marked the onset of a massive "transformation agenda"[20] within federal corrections undergirded by an apparently "gender-neutral law-and-order discourse" (Struthers Montford, 2015: 285). Observers noted that the 2007 *Roadmap* represented a rupture from the feminist policy of the *Creating Choices* report as panel members imagined a male-centric offender accountability model believed to be applicable to all offenders including women prisoners (Correctional Investigator Canada, 2010; Struthers Montford, 2015). It must be noted, here, that such male-centric approaches to corrections had been hegemonic throughout Canada's correctional history, as shown earlier, and had attracted the ire of observers for decades. Thus, as a proponent of a gender-neutral approach to corrections, *Roadmap* marked a reversal in Canada's international reputation as trailblazer in gender-based policy making (Brodie, 2009), since it drove gender from the centre to the edges of policymaking. Struthers Montford (2015:298) makes a convincing demonstration of the review panel's inclination to consider Correctional Service Canada to be a "business" aimed at becoming "more efficient," and its explicit "condon[ing] of the use of coercion and punishment to have offenders act in productive manners."

Roadmap panel members were also mandated to assess the conclusions of the 40-page Expert Committee Review of the Correctional Service of Canada's Ten-Year Status Report on Women's Corrections (Glube Report). This expert committee had been appointed to "counter the damning findings of the [158-page] Arbour Commission" (Struthers Montford, 2015: 301) and neutralize the 82-page 2003 report of the Canadian Human Rights Commission (CHRC) that found systemic discrimination against imprisoned women in the federal correction

---

20. https://www.csc-scc.gc.ca/about-us/006-0009-eng.shtml, accessed March 3, 2021.

apparatus. The Glube Report featured six recommendations, including for correctional authorities to accord a higher priority to women's community corrections to facilitate successful reintegration; to plan the construction of a second Indigenous healing lodge designated for women for the eastern part of Canada; and to dedicate full-time Indigenous elders to the secure units within federal prisons designated for women especially in the Prairie and Pacific regions.

As for the CHRC report, it was the result of a formal request made to the Commission in 2001 by the Canadian Association of Elizabeth Fry Societies, the Native Women's Association of Canada, the Canadian Bar Association, the Assembly of First Nations, and the National Association of Women and the Law. It regarded the treatment of federally sentenced women in prisons and under community surveillance, with a particular focus on the prisoning of two groups of women: Indigenous women and women with cognitive (e.g., low literacy levels) or mental challenges (Canadian Human Rights Commission, 2003). The objective of the Commission's extensive review was to "identify ways of bringing the correctional system into line with the purpose of the Canadian Human Rights Act"[21] (Canadian Human Rights Commission, 2003: i).

To achieve this goal, the Commission drew 19 recommendations, including the development and implementation of gender-responsive programming and a needs-assessment process that answers the needs of all women; the creation of a security classification tool based on women's documented low risk to public safety; the immediate annulment of the correctional policy[22] requiring a maximum security classification of at least the first two years of imprisonment for all prisoners serving a minimum life sentence for first- or second-degree murder; the mandatory obligation for staff working in prisons designated for women to follow the 10-day Women-Centred Training with an obligatory yearly refresher course; the immediate reassessing of the disproportionate number of Indigenous women classified as maximum security using a gender-responsive reclassification tool; and the inclusion of human rights compliance in the accountability accords for correctional managers (Canadian Human Rights Commission, 2003:

---

21.   Canadian Human Rights Act, Revised Statutes of Canada, 1985, c. H-6.
22.   Policy Bulletin No. 107.

27-69). The above recommendations promoted gender-responsive policies and practices that were in keeping with the 1996 Arbour recommendations.

However, the four-member Glube Expert Committee reported in 2007 that federal correctional authorities had made "remarkable progress . . . in what CSC [had] accomplished over the past ten years in women's correction" (Correctional Service Canada, 2007: 37), and that the recent convergence of reforms "represented a sudden transition in which women's corrections was thrust from the bonds of an antiquated past into the promise of a new future" (Correctional Service Canada, 2007: 6). This committee formulated an enthusiastic opinion of the minimum security Isabel McNeill House which had been housing federally sentenced women since 1990 in Kingston. Committee members believed this facility's "level of interaction, innovation, and support . . . is certainly impressive, as is the commitment to progress on the part of the staff" (p. 32). It also noted "its excellent use of space of [the] small CORCAN shop" (p. 26). Such praise did not deter the federal government from announcing the McNeill House's closure on the same day the Glube Report was released (CBC News, 2007). The 2000 closure of the Prison for Women was no stranger to this decision, since the number of admissions to the Isabel McNeill House had declined steadily since 2000. Only four out of ten beds were occupied at the time of the announcement. The minimum security facility was deemed by government to be "no longer financially viable" (CBC News, 2007). It refused to consent to the monies needed for its refurbishing (Société Elizabeth Fry du Québec, 2011). Upon the 2007 closure, the four federally sentenced women remaining at the Isabel McNeill House were to be "moved to higher-security facilities that have programs geared to minimum-security prisoners" (CBC News, 2007), thus replicating a long-adopted path by Canadian federal correctional authorities based on the periodic incantation of the "too few to count" (Adelberg and Currie, 1987) organizational and financial mantra.

Concomitantly, this expert committee also adhered to the claim that women prisoners' profile was changing toward more histories of violence, more repeat offences, more maximum security classification upon admission, more gang affiliations, substance addictions, and serious mental health conditions, especially among Indigenous women (Correctional Service Canada, 2007: 15-22). Committee members based their claim of a shifting women prison population profile solely on CSC internal documents. The same year, *Roadmap* (Canada, 2007) embraced the Glube Report and contributed, according to Jackson and Stewart (2009), to crystallizing a "misconceived impression" of violent crime trends (p. 22) and of the concurrent "overly simplistic" (p. 27) idea of a changing offender profile via inappropriate utilization or interpretation of crime and correctional statistics. This is important, since the argumentative schema behind the gender-neutral law-and-order *Roadmap* report was based largely on such crime trends and offender profiles.

In sum, by embracing the idea of a changing women prisoner profile and espousing a gender-neutral, law-and-order philosophy, the *Roadmap* Review Panel brought women's prisoning closer to the original path and further away from the alternative path that *Creating Choices* promised to be.

Twenty years after the opening of the first women-centred federal prison, the Correctional Investigator took a snapshot of women's conditions of confinement (Correctional Investigator Canada, 2014). Among other things, he highlighted that women's incarceration rate grew by over 25% in the 2010s; the rate of double bunking (adding a second prisoner in single occupancy cells) rose from 0.4% in 1999 to 10% in 2014; incidents involving the use of force against women had increased by 94% since 1999; and the self-injury rate had increased by 313 % since 1999. He also observed that women were serving a longer proportion of their sentences before being released on parole. Over the years, the regional women-centred facilities operated more and more like traditional modern-design prisons. It is no longer an act of hubris or delusion to consider the persistence of women's prisoning as entrenched in orthodoxy. As a previously viable option, *Creating Choices* became diluted with enduring discourses and practices of the dominant path, notably in the aftermath of a series of random but decisive events and policy decisions. As Hayman (2000: 45) reflected, "new ventures require careful and courageous nurturing if they are ever to be tested fully—and without this testing there is no way of determining where the real flaws, as opposed to the perceived flaws, lie."

Following path dependence literature, in many political (Pierson, 2000) and organizational processes (Schreyögg and Sydow, 2011), prolonged periods of positive feedback and cumulative financial and cultural commitments to a dominant path—such as the Auburn-style modern prison model—make metamorphosis increasingly difficult although not impossible. They influence not only the shape in which a new branching occurs, but also, I would add, its orbital proximity or farness to the stabilized dominant path. The close timing of the decisive events discussed above made it easier for correctional organizations to revert to a more familiar, established, institutionalized, tried and true prisoning model. As the new woman-centred, holistic correctional philosophy had not yet gotten enough orbital distance from the more dominant path at the time these events took place, mechanisms that self-reinforced the dominant path and ensured its persistence for a long time deployed their attraction pull-back toward the locked-in path.

In general, self-reinforcing mechanisms—such as learning and bandwagon effects—play a role as shepherds of organizational dynamics (Schreyögg and Sydow, 2011) because they amount to investments in time, money, skills, and expectations. One such mechanism is the increasing commitment of organizational decision-makers toward isomorphism or coordination. Institutional isomorphism was coined in 1983 by Paul DiMaggio and Walter Powell. It refers to the organizational practice for institutions to copy others, not for efficiency motives, but based on a view that they are legitimate and fitting. Analogously to learning and bandwagon effects, isomorphism also amounts to investments in time, money, skills, and expectations. In turn, these investments yield continuing benefits. The process of institutionalization leads to dominant correctional norms and arrangements becoming internalized as cognitive schemata. These, in turn, ensure that such norms and arrangements become socialized as seldom questioned, taken-for-granted practices. Hence, organizational dynamics have a potent inclination to persist once institutionalized (Pierson, 2000).

A telling illustration of such institutionalization is the multi-billion-dollar international prison industrial complex that maintains the economic health of regions by creating jobs, encouraging real estate purchase, yielding municipal taxes, and bolstering the consumption of local goods and services. It also cultivates a persistent private technological industry. In a conference in March 2021 on another correctional topic, Canada's federal Correctional investigator, Ivan Zinger, argued that, as a vast bureaucratic body, correctional services have persistent difficulty diverting monies from infrastructural budgets toward the betterment of community resources for released prisoners. Such diversion would mean not only operating prisons on amputated budgets but potentially giving up a portion of their personnel as more prisoners find their way into multifarious and improved community resources (Zinger, 2021). Amputating budgets and downsizing personnel are both contradictory to self-reinforcing mechanisms, which, in a large bureaucratic process like prisoning, would tend toward the long-term reproduction of institutional patterns such as securing budgets and protecting jobs. Following the correctional investigator, I suggest that threading on an alternative path to prisoning may be considered as too costly on multiple levels, since it would divert the prison industry from the increasing returns engendered by the continued adoption of set patterns. As Pierson (2000:252) argued, "preceding steps in a particular direction [tend to] induce further movement in the same direction."

Following such a "movement in the same direction" is not unique to Canadian federal corrections. Since no correctional service works in a silo, but rather gives to and borrows from other such services nationally and internationally, it may so happen that provincial correctional jurisdictions could be inclined to follow a similar "movement in the same direction" as that of the Canadian federal correctional authorities. Next chapter explores this idea within Québec.

Figure 1 below is a synthetic historical illustration that summarizes the argumentative framework that is developed in this book. It condenses in one single figure the path dependence tendencies of prisoning processes. The pink boxes highlight the federal prisoning of women sentenced to incarceration for two years or more, while the blue boxes represent Québec's prisoning of women sentenced to incarceration for a few days to two years less one day. Figure 1 also identifies two events—the advent of the Modern Auburn-style prison around 1821 and the *Creating Choices* report of 1990—as critical junctures that have set or could have set correctional policies and practices onto a new untrodden path. A third noteworthy event is the new prison designated for women that Québec correctional authorities plan to build in the future, and which could become a critical juncture and drag the prisoning of women on an alternative path. These three events are highlighted by bold black outlines. As critical junctures are located at the collision junction of two "airflow" paths blowing "winds" in different directions, past historical forces that have been significant "winds" in the advent of critical junctures are identified horizontally and connected by small arrows that indicate the flow of dominant history.

Vertically, a bold black line connects most of the boxes and illustrates the persistence of the dominant prisoning path. Pink and blue boxes are amalgamated on this single bold black line because both federal and Québec correctional authorities developed a similar path dependence toward the Modern Auburn-inspired prison.

Departure from the dominant path is illustrated by a bold black line that originates at the *Creating Choices* critical juncture and deviates to the left away from the dominant prisoning path. However, the deviated bold black line soon branches back toward the historically dominant path, as a series of events, reports, and decisions have moved innovative correctional policies and practices regarding the prisoning of women into the gravitational pull of the hegemonic path.

Since this book does not aim to document the full and complete rotation of women's federal prisoning away from *Creating Choices* and back toward the dominant path, the bold black line branching back toward the main path stops before touching the vertical line representing the locked-in path. Further studies documenting the most recent operationalization of women's prisoning at the federal level are needed to support (or not) a full restoration of correctional services' dependence to the modern Auburn-inspired prisoning model.

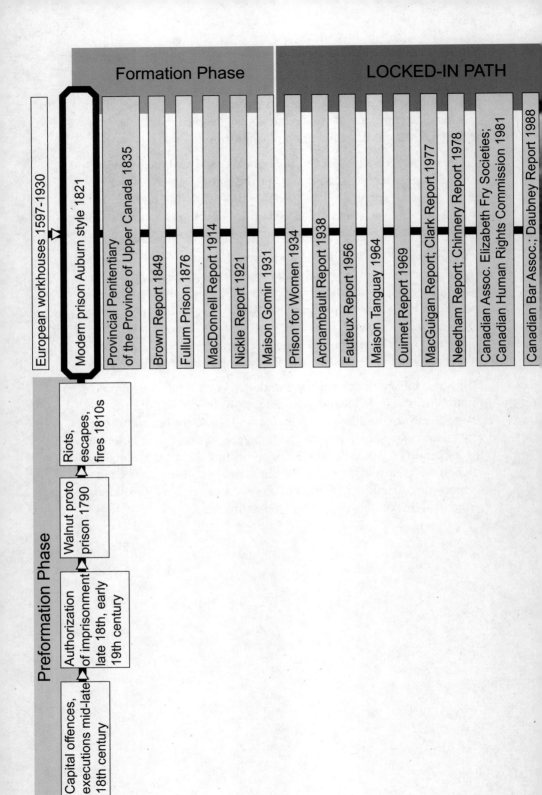

Preformation Phase

Formation Phase

LOCKED-IN PATH

Capital offences, executions mid-late 18th century

Authorization of imprisonment late 18th, early 19th century

Walnut proto prison 1790

Riots, escapes, fires 1810s

European workhouses 1597–1930

Modern prison Auburn style 1821

Provincial Penitentiary of the Province of Upper Canada 1835

Brown Report 1849

Fullum Prison 1876

MacDonnell Report 1914

Nickle Report 1921

Maison Gomin 1931

Prison for Women 1934

Archambault Report 1938

Fauteux Report 1956

Maison Tanguay 1964

Ouimet Report 1969

MacGuigan Report; Clark Report 1977

Needham Report; Chinnery Report 1978

Canadian Assoc. Elizabeth Fry Societies; Canadian Human Rights Commission 1981

Canadian Bar Assoc.; Daubney Report 1988

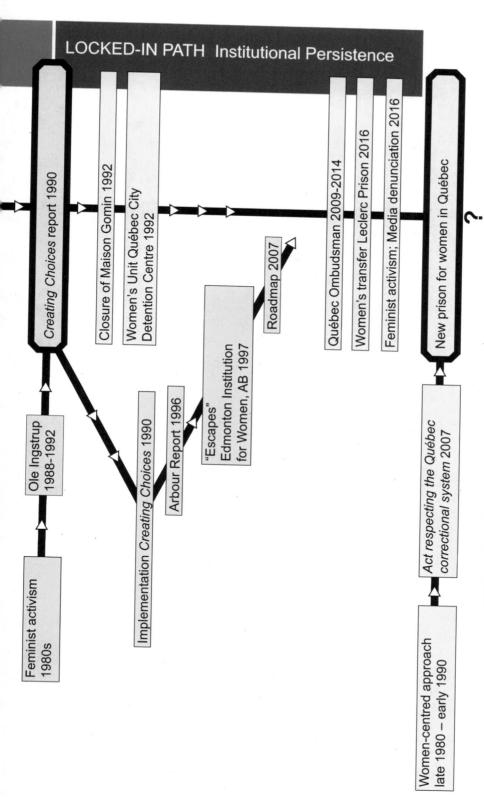

LOCKED-IN PATH Institutional Persistence

Feminist activism 1980s

Ole Ingstrup 1988–1992

Creating Choices report 1990

Closure of Maison Gomin 1992

Women's Unit Québec City Detention Centre 1992

Québec Ombudsman 2009-2014

Women's transfer Leclerc Prison 2016

Feminist activism; Media denunciation 2016

New prison for women in Québec

Implementation Creating Choices 1990

Arbour Report 1996

"Escapes" Edmonton Institution for Women, AB 1997

Roadmap 2007

Act respecting the Québec correctional system 2007

Women-centred approach late 1980 – early 1990

FIGURE 1. Women's Prisoning in Canada: The Incipience of a Path Dependence

CHAPTER 4

The Tenacity of Prisons Designated for Women in Québec

I ncarceration as the primary mode of punishment is considered to have "revolutionized" criminal justice and to be a game changer in the history of penal reform (Rubin, 2019b: 158). Chapter 3 highlighted the male-centrism of the locked-in path followed historically by prisoning practices toward women at the federal level in Canada. Provincial correctional practices have been no less guilty of similar oversights. In Canada, most women prisoners are housed in provincial and territorial prisons, most of which are officially designated as "co-ed" facilities although they may not have been planned or designed to house men as well as women originally (Boritch, 2001). The introduction of women in these prisons has often been an after-thought, especially in areas where, according to correctional authorities, the small number of women did not justify building separate prisons for them. As a result, only a small minority of provincial and territorial prisons house only women, sometimes in prison buildings no longer needed by the male prison population.

4.1 WOMEN IN MIXED PRISON-ASYLUMS BEFORE THE 19TH CENTURY

Documents on the history of Québec situate the onset of incarceration for criminal, vagrant, and furious women in the 17th century, when they were housed in common, overcrowded, and gender-mixed prison-asylums (asylum in the sense of refuge or shelter) (Fyson, 2006). In heavily Catholic Québec specifically, between 1686 and 1871, "women of unfortunate souls" (Berzins and Collette-Carrière, 1979: 88) considered to be morally "fallen" (Laplante, 1991: 18; Fecteau, Tremblay and Trépanier, 1993: 37) were housed in dedicated hospices managed by communities of nuns (Boyer, 1966; Landreville and Julien, 1976). During the 1820s, vociferous debates led to the definition of the chief parameters of a novel criminal justice system based on imprisonment as punishment as well as on prisoner reform (Fecteau, 1989). Consequently, architectural experiments flourished in order to devise an appropriate architectural model for the birthing "imprisonment for punishment" facilities (Caron-Labrecque, 2017).

In the wake of this watershed moment in penal history, and following persistent exiguity and construction defects with its 1811 Champ-de-Mars prison located in the city of Montréal, the government of Lower Canada (the southern portion of modern-day Québec) built a new prison, also located in Montréal. The Patriotes-au-Pied-du-Courant provincial prison opened in 1836, although it would only be completed in 1840 (Noppen, 1976).

Between 1826 and 1830, numerous debates took place within the Lower Canada government relating to criminal justice reforms. They aimed at constructing a provincial penitentiary serving all Lower Canada as a long-term option to endemic overcrowding in countless district prisons. These debates delayed the actual construction of the new Pied-du-Courant prison, as two government emissaries were sent to Philadelphia in 1834 to build on the United States' advancements in penitentiary architecture discussed in Chapter 3. The following year, the emissaries submitted their report to the Lower Canada government, recommending that the Pied-du-Courant prison be built along the lines of the Pennsylvania prison system, thus discarding the Auburn prison system (Noppen, 1976). While the Québec government became busy with the political entanglement that ensued from a governmental committee's dismissal of this recommendation, Upper Canada (the predecessor of the actual territory of Ontario) was building its first provincial penitentiary inspired by the Auburn prison system in Kingston.

The Pied-du-Courant prison was architecturally inspired by the modern prison model (Noppen, 1976) as a middle ground between a still necessary district common gaol and a larger penitentiary fit for the systematic treatment of crime (Fecteau, Tremblay and Trépanier, 1993). The prison was located at the corner of Craig and de Lorimier streets in an area where the St. Lawrence River channel narrows between St. Helen's Island and the northern shore, creating the "courant Sainte-Marie" (Noppen, 1976). Pied-du-Courant literally means "at the foot of the stream." The final location of the prison stems from British prison reformer John Howard's vanguard recommendations toward prison condition improvement (hygiene, prisoner classification, and gender separation) found in his seminal work *The State of the Prisons in England and Wales*, first published in 1777.[1] Following Howard's hygiene recommendations, the land finally selected for construction of the Pied-du-Courant prison is in proximity to a river to take advantage of accessible water and to properly dispose of wastewater through drainage (Noppen, 1976).

The uniformly cut grey-brown stone (typical of the Montréal region) used to build the entire structure bolsters the daunting, colossal, and stern character of the building. Designed for individual cell detention at night and spacious common living areas during the day, its architecture embraces the latest innovations in incarceration, specifically the Auburn prison model aimed at solitary confinement at night and access to factory-like settings during the day albeit in total silence (Rubin, 2019a). The prison's neoclassical architectural conception (Caron-Labrecque, 2017) was audacious at the time and motivated by a forerunner vision aspiring to improve prison conditions. By choosing, in the 1830s, to build a prison inspired by the modern prison template, the Lower Canada government featured among the "early adopters" of the model (Rubin,

---

1. This work had three editions during Howard's lifetime (1777, 1780 and 1784). A fourth edition was published in 1792, two years after Howard's passing. https://wellcomecollection.org/works/hup4h66f, accessed February 14, 2022. Each new edition comprised updated statistics of his most recent findings. https://johnhoward.ca/history/biography-john-howard/, accessed February 10, 2022.

2019a: 544). Within 10 years of their first emergence in the early 1820s, modern prisons following the Auburn system multiplied swiftly across the United States, while the Pennsylvania prison model (total solitary confinement) struggled with a less extensive adoption. At the time, the modern prison, whether in its Auburn or Pennsylvania formats, was becoming a master model for incarceration guiding prison policy and practices around punishment and rehabilitation issues. The Pied-du-Courant prison jumped on the bandwagon and actively participated in the formation stage of path dependence discussed in Chapter 3. Based on the important role the Pied-du-Courant prison played in the renewal of prison architecture in Lower Canada and Québec, the government of Québec classified the building as a historical monument in 1978 (Caron-Labrecque, 2017).

Between 1836 and 1876, women were imprisoned in the Pied-du-Courant prison, where they were mixed in with sentenced and remanded men prisoners, vagabonds, and debtors, although they were housed in a rear wing of the prison and guarded by a matron, following prison reformer John Howard's recommendation for gender separation (Noppen, 1976). The predominance of men prisoners in Québec common gaols is a recent phenomenon. In 1865, women accounted for 40% of all admissions to Pied-du-Courant prison. However, between 1865 and 1913, their overall proportion steadily decreased and reached 10% by 1913, a percentage that remained constant throughout the 20th century. Most of these women were imprisoned for minor crimes such as vagrancy and prostitution (Fecteau, Tremblay and Trépanier, 1993). Prison conditions were difficult, especially for women, who were not allowed outdoors into prison yards because the architectural design of the Pied-du-Courant prison was such that women could see men prisoners, be seen by them and even speak to them from the prison yards (Fecteau, Tremblay and Trépanier, 1993).

Thirty years later, in 1867, in reaction to mounting criticism about chronic overpopulation, gruelling prison conditions and gender mixing (Berzins and Collette-Carrière, 1979; Fecteau, Tremblay and Trépanier, 1993), prison inspectors advocated for the construction of a separate and isolated building for women prisoners, a kind of house of corrections or penitentiary guided by the establishment of a "perfect discipline,"[2] combining work, schooling, and religious practice.

4.2 THE FIRST DEDICATED WOMEN'S PRISON (1876): HINTS OF HEGEMONIC MALE-CENTRED PRISONS

In 1876, the Québec government finally opened the Asile Sainte-Darie for Catholic women on Fullum Street in Montréal. Although women prisoners of Protestant faith were originally to be integrated into Asile Sainte-Darie, they remained at the Pied-du-Courant prison for men and were ultimately housed in a fully separate unit (Fecteau, Tremblay and Trépanier, 1993).

Asile Sainte-Darie was a three-storey high cross-shaped building that looked like a convent and adopted a religious regimen, since authorities of the time counted on religious education and the power of example to reform women prisoners (Fecteau, Tremblay and Trépanier, 1993). This prison would remain operational until two other provincial prisons for women were built in Québec's two largest urban centres; Québec City's Refuge Notre-Dame-de-la-Merci in 1931 and Montréal's Maison Tanguay in 1964.

Borrowing from the Pennsylvania penitentiary system of the 19th century,[3] the first of these two prisons designated for women was the Refuge Notre-Dame-de-la-Merci, a "modest" castle-like architecture adopted "to create a decor that ennobles a facade behind which a harsh reality is lived" (Noppen, Jobidon and Trépanier, 1990: 116). Characterized by individual cells along a central corridor, the prison was located on agricultural land in the village of Sainte-Foy near Québec City. It opened in 1931, and was managed by the Good Shepherd Sisters, who inhabited the west wing of the building.[4] The Refuge was the first prison for women in the Québec City area. In 1968, Refuge Notre-Dame-de-la-Merci was renamed in memory of the 17th-century owner of the land on which the prison was built,

---

2. *Rapport des inspecteurs de prisons et asiles de la province de Québec*, 1867-1868, cited in Fecteau, Tremblay and Trépanier, 1993.
3. https://www.ville.quebec.qc.ca/citoyens/patrimoine/archives/pages_histoire/maison_gomin.aspx, accessed February 15, 2022.
4. Ibid.

surgeon Anet Gomin.[5] In keeping with the gendered social expectations of the time, and contrary to men's prisons, this prison designated for women was not renamed Gomin prison, but Maison Gomin, a "home" intent on recreating the family sphere and where provincially sentenced women had access to sewing, knitting, moulding, and weaving. In Maison Gomin, the "girls," as the women prisoners were then called, were addressed by their first name, a paternalistic practice which infantilized women and relinquished the respect of labels like "Mrs." or "Miss" (Berzins and Collette-Carrière, 1979). Thus, similarly to their federal counterparts discussed in Chapter 3, Québec provincial prisons designated for women also hint at hegemonic gender pedagogy. In 1972, Québec's Justice Ministry took over the management of the prison and custody of its prisoners from the Good Shepherd Sisters. However, one sister continued to hold the directorship of the prison until 1981, and another sister acted as a peace officer until the prison's closure in 1992.[6]

Maison Gomin remained ill-equipped in terms of psychosocial intervention practices. By 1985, the prison employed only four correctional officers specially trained in individual counselling and assistance, as well as one psychologist who, according to Adelberg and Laprairie (1985), infrequently visited Maison Gomin, and whose chief occupation appears to be the provision of psychological assessments. During the 1980s, the prison also offered the women prisoners remunerated employment, as well as recreational and educational activities (Martel, 1990).

This prison designated for women was in use until 1992, when the Québec government shut it down largely as a result of its small capacity and architectural design deficiencies, which may have been detrimental to the safety of the premises. It then transferred the women to the Québec (provincial) Detention Centre designated for men, in a newly added, fully independent division complete with pink walls on the units.[7] This

---

5.   Ibid.
6.   http://www.soeursdubonpasteur.ca/fr/oeuvres/w5/, accessed February 15, 2022. https://www.ville.quebec.qc.ca/citoyens/patrimoine/archives/pages_histoire/maison_gomin.aspx, accessed February 15, 2022.
7.   Information confirmed by a support worker employed by a prominent community organization and responsible for program delivery at the Women's Unit of the Québec Detention Centre (email dated February 26, 2002). This experienced worker confirmed that the walls of the common areas, such as the visiting room and the

decision to move women prisoners from a women-only prison to a men's prison took place two years after the publication of the *Creating Choices* report in 1990, the critical juncture highlighted in Chapter 3 which was highly critical of the Canadian historical trend to incarcerate women in men's prisons: a paradox if ever there was one.

Québec's second prison designated for women, which replaced the Fullum Street Asile Sainte-Darie, opened in Montréal in 1964 on governmental land, where the Prison de Montréal (also known as Bordeaux prison for men) had stood since 1912. The opening of the Bordeaux prison in 1912 spelled the end of the Pied-du-Courant prison, which closed that same year (Caron-Labrecque, 2017). Women imprisoned at Asile Sainte-Darie on Fullum Street were transferred to this new prison, "Maison Tanguay,"[8] and one by one they crossed its iron door bristling with spikes (Guénette, 1983).

In an archival nine-page article published in 1983 in *La vie en Rose*, a feminist current affairs magazine (Guénette, 1983: 26), journalist Françoise Guénette described Maison Tanguay as

a high school, a mass of concrete with a poorly fenced perimeter, 200 feet from a quiet street in Ahuntsic [a neighborhood in the City of Montréal], and in the otherwise impressive shadow of Bordeaux, the men's prison, the big brother.

At the time of Guénette's visit to Tanguay, the prison comprised a canteen, a disco room, a chapel, a hairdressing salon, rooms for schooling, an infirmary, a super maximum security unit, and segregation cells. In the prison, units comprised a common room used alternatively as a TV room, a kitchen, or a cards room. The common rooms were separated from the corridor and the matrons' security posts by large glass walls—"like a nursery in a hospital" (Guénette, 1983: 29). At the opposite end of the unit, there was another glass door leading to the shower and laundry room area and then to the 13 to 17 individual cells arranged face to face. These cells were concrete cubes of 182 cm by 243 cm with iron doors equipped with peepholes. Then, as now, most women imprisoned in Maison Tanguay in the 1980s had been

---

classroom, were of a neutral beige/white colour, but that those within the living units were "pink/beige."

8.   In Québec's 2018-2028 Infrastructure Plan, in which the province plans to expand and revamp the prison, it is still called "Maison Tanguay" (Québec, 2018a: 72).

convicted of non-violent crimes such as shoplifting, fraud, and fine defaults (Guénette, 1983).

In the early 1980s, women imprisoned at Maison Tanguay were, at the time of arrest, "unskilled workers, unemployed, welfare recipients, dancers, prostitutes" (Guénette, 1983: 27). For many decades, employment possibilities would continue to push what Pat Carlen (1983) referred to as gender pedagogy, whereby training for domesticity and motherhood have been dominant attributes of carceral regimes in prisons designated for women, notably in Anglo-Saxon countries. Housework and an ethos of care and dependency remained deep-seated in correctional practices and programming for over a century. In this line of thought, Maison Tanguay essentially offered jobs such as cleaning, laundry, dishwashing, and sewing (Berzins and Collette-Carrière, 1979).

A few years after Maison Tanguay's inauguration in 1964, and following the detention of a few young teenage girls in Tanguay's infirmary amid the "crazies," the prison opened a "juvenile" wing complete with "outdoor activities, TV, cards" (Pelletier, 1983: 24). Below, 13-year-old Danielle D. describes the situation of several of the adult women with whom she was imprisoned in the infirmary at Maison Tanguay in the early 1980s, before the opening of the juvenile unit:

> I saw some extremely lost . . . women. One in particular who was hooked on a drug trip, spent her days talking to the ashes in her ashtray. I also saw women who had done nothing but leave their husbands. There were women who were locked up in a cell all day long who should not have been in the cell; others who were not allowed to read books and to whom I would give some reading material from time to time; there were some who did not even have sheets, who slept on the mattress; another who was tied to her bed by her ankles. Supposedly to prevent suicide attempts. (Pelletier, 1983: 24)

In the early 1980s, the Québec Human Rights Commission established that no complete therapeutic programming existed yet at Maison Tanguay (Commission des droits de la personne du Québec, 1985). In 1990, the first international conference of the Research Group on the Study and Production of Order was held at the University of Ottawa, the same year the Task Force on Federally Sentenced Women submitted its ground-breaking *Creating Choices* report. The conference focused essentially on the state of psychosocial service delivery within the criminal justice system. In a review document that provided an update of psychosocial practices in Canada and Québec produced for the conference, Martel (1990: 33-34) concluded that:

> there is almost no therapeutic treatment for women. Whether through institutional services or programs or even through other public agencies or external residential programs, psychosocial service delivery for criminalized women is characterized by its near absence and lack of integrated policy. . . . Nevertheless, it appears from the documents reviewed that residential programs in Québec—separate from those offered in prisons [such as programs offered in halfway houses]—do . . . base their service delivery on certain objectives that are much more specific than those used by prison staff. The focus of the vast majority of these [residential] programs centers on the development of self-control and self-determination in the context of encouraging integrative activities.

Indeed, in 1985, the Tanguay prison employed one recreation specialist, three social workers, one permanent psychologist and one psychiatrist working two half-days per week and affiliated with Institut Philippe-Pinel, a high security university psychiatric hospital which opened in 1970 in Montréal, and specializes in forensic psychiatry. During that period, the prison dedicated about a dozen cells in its infirmary for women with psychological issues. Treatment in these permanently occupied cells appears to have lacked integration, since the part-time psychiatrist and the full-time psychologist seemed to intervene mainly in cases of crisis. Their consultations aimed to prepare assessments required by the courts and prescribe medication to ease mental disorders. The general practitioner was left to attend to lighter psychological issues such as anxiety, insomnia, and minor depression, which were treated mostly with medication, as were agitated or recalcitrant women, according to the Québec Human Rights Commission (Commission des droits de la personne du Québec, 1985). During that same decade, Institut Philippe-Pinel opened a 21-bed women's unit in 1985. At that time, the unit accepted only women exhibiting the most severe psychiatric issues with associated dangerousness, as well as women assessed to be "not criminally responsible on account of mental disorder" (Criminal Code, 1985, Part XX.1, s. 672.1(1)) (Commission des droits de la personne du Québec, 1985; Société Elizabeth Fry du Québec, 2011). Criteria for transfer from Maison Tanguay to the women's unit at Institut Philippe-Pinel were dangerousness, hallucinations, and delirium. Requirements of concomitance between these three criteria rendered the use of the women's unit either improbable or reserved to extreme psychological conditions (Commission des droits de la personne du Québec, 1985). In other words, mental health care was not available to all women incarcerated at Maison Tanguay in the early 1980s, but rather was restricted to a small fraction. In sum, even after decades of mounting multifarious problems with the modern prison template, and rather than seeking alternatives to this prevailing template, Québec correctional authorities in the 1980s retained many features of the modern prison rather than divert women prisoners who seemed a poor fit for prison, like those diagnosed with or exhibiting mental health issues. In relation to mental health, Maison Tanguay retained its constitutive power as a variation of the modern prison.

Moreover, Maison Tanguay offered no therapeutic treatment for substance abuse, instead favouring the management of such situations via disciplinary measures such as reclusion. Although referring women to the Portage Centre, an outpatient facility specializing in multi-drug addiction, was an option at Maison Tanguay, the Québec Human Rights Commission's 1985 investigation of Maison Tanguay concluded that very few women could undergo treatment at the Portage Centre because of the repressive and punitive ethos advocated by Maison Tanguay's administration with respect to alcohol and drug use (Martel, 1990).

Several studies conducted in the late 1980s continued to confirm that women detained at Maison Tanguay still had little access to alcohol and drug abuse treatment in specialized outpatient facilities and lacked access to comprehensive therapy as well as institutional programs aimed at community reintegration or prevention. Moreover, most provincial prisons for women did not deliver services for sexual abuse survivors (e.g., Brunet, 1989; Canada, 1990).

As discussed in Chapter 3, starting in 1973, Exchange of Service Agreements were reached between the Canadian federal government and provincial governments to counter the geographical dislocation engendered by the fact that all women from across Canada serving a federal term of imprisonment were housed in Canada's sole federal Prison for Women located in Kingston. Exchange of Service Agreements allowed for federally sentenced women to serve their prison term closer to home, in a provincial prison of their province of origin. The agreement with Québec was signed in 1979 (Société Elizabeth Fry du Québec, 2011). Thus, starting in 1979, Maison Tanguay also began to house women serving a federal term of incarceration. This accommodation agreement would be pursued until federal authorities opened five geographically dispersed federal prisons designated for women throughout the country between 1995 and 1997 as a direct result of the *Creating Choices* report of 1990 (Hannah-Moffat and Shaw, 2000a). One of these new federal prisons was in Joliette, Québec. Upon losing the federally sentenced women who transferred from Maison Tanguay to the new Joliette federal prison in 1997, Maison Tanguay saw its carceral population fade substantially, which led to a reduction in budget allocations. In turn, decreased monies led to progressive building deterioration and a reduction in the quantity and quality of programs and services to women (Giroux and Frigon, 2011). Women prisoners once again became "too few to count" (Adelberg and Currie, 1987) in terms of budget and personnel allocations.

Simultaneously, while the building degraded and programs and services were on life support, policy changes abrogated some forms of early release, multiplied or intensified release conditions, and increased rates of intermittent/weekend sentences. Women's incarceration rates swelled, and Maison Tanguay began to experience overcrowding. Grievances emerged about the presence of mildew, rats, sewer backflow in drinking water pipes, delays in changing medical prescriptions, suppression of paid employment in prison, diluted and rationed cleaning products, lack of food in appropriate quantities, etc. (Manifeste des détenues, 2015).

The crime rate of women imprisoned in Québec's provincial prisons was five times lower than that of men, and their sentence length averaged half of the men's, with around 70% of the women serving a sentence of less than 30 days (Giroux and Frigon, 2011). Research on provincially incarcerated women is limited in Québec. Extant studies tend to be health related (e.g., Gormley et al., 2020) and use mixed samples of both women and men (e.g., Lasnier et al., 2011). Fewer studies address sociopenal issues such as multiple reincarcerations (Roy, Laberge and Cousineau, 1992), prison conditions in remand (McLean, 1995), self-mutilation (Frigon, 2001), Indigenous prison identities and trajectories (Martel and Brassard, 2008; Brassard and

Martel, 2009), or post release employment (Strimelle and Frigon, 2011). It is notoriously difficult to access prisoners detained in prisons for research purposes in Canada and elsewhere, since prisons are infamously opaque organizations that tend to cultivate a culture of secrecy (Bandyopadhyay, 2007; Pace Law Review, 2010; Piché, 2012; Reiter, 2014; Drake, 2018; Whittaker, 2021). Such prison opacity is similar within provincial correctional services. Many Canadian scholars have attempted, in the past, to obtain authorizations to enter provincial prisons across the country for research purposes. To my knowledge, mostly researchers who were contracted by provincial correctional services to investigate phenomena of interest to them have had access to provincial prisons and prisoners. Yet, women prisoners experience often gruelling prison conditions, more so than women incarcerated in Canadian federal prisons.

4.3 THE MAISON TANGUAY OF MONTRÉAL (1964): PRISON CONDITIONS

A small portion of the prison conditions analyzed in the following two sections of this chapter stem from institutional reports such as those of the Québec Ombudsman (2014; 2016; 2018; 2020) as well as from media reports. However, a large portion of the analyses stem from the semi-directed interviews conducted in French with 21 women who have lived experience of incarceration in provincial prisons in Québec (note that several of these women have also been incarcerated in federal prisons designated for women). As examined earlier in Chapter 2, at the time of interview, all women had experienced incarceration in Québec's provincial prisons, some of them in several different prisons. A little over half of these women served time at Maison Tanguay in Montréal, while 15 experienced incarceration at the Leclerc prison in Laval, and 13 in federal prison A. One third of the 21 women also served time in regional provincial prisons designated for men, for example while awaiting official transfer to a prison designated for women such as Maison Tanguay or the Leclerc prison.

Prison conditions at Maison Tanguay are challenging. The Québec Ombudsman noted in 2014 that Tanguay is "in a bad state of dilapidation and overcrowding" (p. 67) and is plagued with conditions such as "bad hygiene, unsuitable facilities, . . . and shortcomings in the assessment of women's needs" (p. 68). One of the most enduring problems is Tanguay's almost perpetual state of overcrowding. To reduce such overcrowding, in 2013 Tanguay management put an end to the established practice of using the prison (designated for women) as a landing spot for men prisoners from a nearby prison in need of therapeutic programming (Québec Ombudsman, 2014). It appears that hard-earned prisons designated for women may have been used by male prisoners when necessary.

The women interviewed who had been housed at Maison Tanguay between 2011 and the time of its closure in 2016 recount living often in overcrowded single- or double-occupancy cells. Carceral architecture usually privileges individual cells with one bed, one toilet, and one small sink. During periods of prison overcrowding, the process by which a single-occupancy cell is swollen with an extra prisoner is referred to colloquially as double bunking. Many women with lived experience of Maison Tanguay endured unsanitary conditions in their double bunked cells such as "*disgusting*," poorly lit cells where they would sleep on a mattress on the floor close to mildew and mice: "*you had thin, thin, thin, thin sheets there* [and] *thin, thin, thin, thin mattresses. You always had lower back pains when you woke up*" observed Jessy,[9] a woman who was "*in and out*" of Maison Tanguay for years. In that regard, Malory, who was incarcerated at Maison Tanguay for one to three months[10] on remand before integrating a federal institution designated for women, would claim that she had "*always been part of someone's floor*" in Tanguay. Maddy experienced one to three months of provincial incarceration at a regional prison designated for men, Maison Tanguay, and Leclerc prison combined. This was followed by six to twelve months of federal imprisonment. She details her experience as the extra prisoner in a single-occupancy cell while at Maison Tanguay:

---

9. To protect the women's anonymity, pseudonyms are used in this portion of the manuscript. To ensure that the women's unicity still transpired through the anonymization process of the data, they each chose their own pseudonym.

10. Also, to protect the women's anonymity, their total incarceration time is indicated using six-month time range estimates at the federal level. The federal ranges used are: 6-12 months; 13-18 months; 19-24 months: 25-30 months; 31-36 months; one additional time range used is the 10 years+. Since prison sentences are much shorter at the provincial level, different types of time ranges are used: less than one month; 1-3 months; 4-6 months; 7-12 months; 13-18 months; 19-23 months. Ranges make it possible to remain unspecific enough not to risk identifying the women participants while still providing an adequate sense of how long each woman experienced prison life.

Tanguay, it's hell, hell, hell, hell! I had never seen that in my life. I didn't sleep because when [the prison was] *overcrowded, I slept on the floor in a single cell, in the back, on a comfortable mattress, but on the floor. You could see mould at the bottom, the beautiful little mice were passing by, at which point, I stopped sleeping at night. I slept during the day* [on my roommate's bed] *while* [she] *worked, because I didn't want to sleep on the floor. It's very small, it's very confined. I never locked myself in my cell. Even if it was mayhem in the common room, I couldn't go* [to my cell for downtime].

Among other women, Marilyn Monroe had a similar experience. During her less than one-month detention period at Maison Tanguay, she slept on the cell floor with her head near the toilet bowl. Disgusted about her cellmate's nightly toilet routine, and worried about being trampled, Marilyn rolled over almost completely under her cellmate's bed at night:

You can't sleep well. You hide your face with the blanket to be sure to be in your cocoon a little bit. The woman who accessed the cell before you, well, she does what she wants. [My cellmate] *was with her five girlfriends on the bed talking all day long, then smoking, then taking illicit drugs. It wasn't fun because I hate the smell, I don't even smoke cigarettes. Ah! It was messed up; it was like a jungle.*

A single cell is a cell designed for one prisoner but in which two or more prisoners could be housed during periods of overcrowding. Some prisons also have double-occupancy cells comprising one small sink, one toilet, and two bunk beds. When a third prisoner is added to a double-occupancy cell already housing two prisoners, it is called triple bunking. Kate spent less than a month at Maison Tanguay. She details the triple bunking process at Tanguay:

It already happened that [a sector] *was full, full, full. When you are already* [housed] *in a double cell, it is a bed on top of the other. Then they put a third* [woman] *in and must add a mattress on the floor. That is for one night only. Just for bedtime. She would arrive in time for night lockup, she would go to bed, and then in the morning, when* [staff] *unlock cell doors, she would go to another sector, because it is full. . . .* [Triple bunking] *usually doesn't happen often, but if you're in a single room, it happens very often that there are overpops* [overpopulation], *very, very, very often. In* [regional prison designated for men] *when there are over-pops* [among women prisoners], *they transfer* [them] *immediately to Tanguay.*

Many also reported that women knitted blankets for themselves and other women to keep warm, since the prison only provided one bedsheet and a single polar fleece blanket (*"the old kind of lumpy covers that ambulances used to have,"* Kate described), often with cigarette holes in it, a situation that Revmarie confirmed. In her 2022 published testimony, Louise Henry added that these institutional blankets were not only *"very thin"* (p. 82), but they were also not of standard dimensions to fit the beds in the cells. The women especially experienced the cold when sleeping on the floor. Kate, who spent 13 to 18 months in a regional prison designated for men and Maison Tanguay, explains:

> *Oh my God! In Tanguay, sometimes, it was freezing. You know when you're stuck, you're double* [bunked] *in the room, but there's only one bed, the other is lying on the floor, it's cold, you know. Sometimes, you arrive,* [the prison is overcrowded], *it was a mattress on the ground, you know. It's cool. . . . sometimes it's freezing. You must have good blankets. . . .* [Correctional staff] *turn on the heat late. Let's say it's cold in October, November, but they wait* [until] *the building is at zero. They are big buildings; it must be expensive* [to heat]. *But sometimes they* [turn the heat on] *late. Sometimes it can be mid-November, late November but they* [turn on the heat]. *There are evenings when it's cold. Sometimes it starts to freeze, in the evening.*

For many, the cold essentially appeared to be experienced while sleeping on the floor of a double- or triple-bunked cell, but other women, such as Jessy, who never drew the winning ticket of *"being part of someone's floor"* as Malory explained earlier, also experienced the cold in general during her numerous prison terms at Maison Tanguay: *"it's not warm, there at Tanguay, it was not warm."* Revmarie is the sole woman interviewed who, contrary to all others, holds a different opinion of the ambient temperature at the prison:

> *Tanguay, it's crazy, but it was hot. We were dying, we had to open our windows. Even in winter. In the summer there is no heating, but when the heating started* [in the fall], *we had to open our windows. But at least we weren't cold.*

As Revmarie remarks, the cold was far from being the only extreme temperature to intensify the unsanitary conditions in prison. Summers might be *"very hot, very hot"* in most if not all prisons where Kate was incarcerated. To endure the heat, she and other women reverted to buying *"little fans, the little, little ones, but that's it. It's seriously hot in the summer."*

In addition to experiencing cramped cells, mould, and mice, Maddy adds that, whenever she was assigned to a particular cell in a prison, she "*scrubbed the thing from top to bottom*" as much as she could. Having been incarcerated in several different federal and provincial prisons designated for women, she is adamant that "*the worst* [in-cell toilets] *were pretty much in Tanguay.*" To her, Maison Tanguay is also the prison "*where there's the least amount of light. There are no windows except for the coloured squares at the end* [of the aisles], *so there's not much light, but there were windows in the common rooms.*" Kate is of the same opinion: "*In Tanguay, the light is not strong, it's like nuns' lampshades, all flat.*" She as well as Jessy experienced the disturbing sight of mice in her cell and assesses that Tanguay is worse in terms of squalor than regional prisons designated for men where women may be imprisoned temporarily:

> [Tanguay] *is an unsanitary place, it's mice, it's not clean, it's old there. It's cement walls, you know, brick tiles, all dirty, yellow, full of sludge dirt. I don't know how many years it's been unpainted, it's old. . . . I used to wash my floor on all fours. My cell was clean, but there are cells there, my God, smeared, scratched, it's hard, there.*

All the women with lived experience of incarceration at Maison Tanguay remarked on the general filthiness of the prison as well as the ubiquity of bugs, mice, and mildew. For her part, Cloé laments that, as a result of the unsanitary condition of the shower area, she developed two skin fungi while incarcerated at Maison Tanguay.

Women reported that other women were falling sick because of deficient ventilation and the presence of mildew. Moreover, Marilyn Monroe, who was incarcerated at Maison Tanguay for less than a month, confirms that the cells and their toilets were soiled, that it was up to the women to do the cleaning: "*you didn't arrive with a nice room all done.*" Counting on incarcerated women to clean their own cell, and often the surrounding spaces such as common rooms, is very much akin to Carlen's (1983) gender pedagogy. In prison, the latter tends to remain an organizational attachment, a comfortable value to which correctional authorities may be inclined to hold on. Cox (2004: 207) referred to such tendency as the "path-dependency of an idea," whereby a policy paradigm such as gender pedagogy engenders persuasive effects on organizational staff's thoughts and expectations to the point where they may remain reluctant to revise their view even when strong evidence—such as the *Creating Choices* report—refutes the paradigm.

Not only were spaces such as cells and common areas in questionable sanitary condition, so were meals. Maddy explains that, when her entire unit was under lockdown at Maison Tanguay, correctional staff exceptionally would bring prisoners' meals up to their respective cells instead of leaving collective food trays in the wings' common rooms where women would fetch their own meal. During one such lockdown procedure, Maddy felt violated in her humanity as one female guard once commented: "*Here is your feed* [animal feed], *girls.*"

For her part, Maude experienced repulsion at the food served at Maison Tanguay:

> [The prison] *was full of vermin, rats, mice. We had a locker, and if we had the misfortune of leaving things there, the rats ate them. They gnawed at everything,* [including objects]. *At night, you could hear them. I'm talking about it, and I am nauseous. Even if you're clean in your room, they would come in on all the floors, so that was the hardest part. At Tanguay, it was very hard for me. I didn't eat any more, I had become a vegetarian, and even then, I hardly ate at all. I bought things from the canteen and ate that. Food was really disgusting.*

While Gresham Sykes had long identified eating unpalatable food as a punitive feature of imprisonment in his 1958 seminal work *The Society of Captives*, the consumption of food in institutional settings such as prisons became an increasing research interest starting in the early 2000s (e.g., Godderis, 2006a and b; Earle and Phillips, 2012). Scholars were especially interested in prison food as a conduit for expressions of power and resistance to oppressive environments as alluded to by Maude, who resisted bad prison food by adopting a vegetarian diet.

In this renewed enthusiasm for prison food analyses, women's experiences of prison food also attracted scholarly attention. Apart from Milligan, Waller, and Andrews (2002), who focused essentially on aspects of eating psychopathology in prison, several studies documented food consumption experiences as part of the disciplinary machinery of the prison (Smith, 2002), as resistance via food consumption and practices (Smoyer, 2015), or as patchworks of unique structures, meanings, and food systems (Smoyer and Blankenship, 2014). Others centred on social networks related to food (Smoyer, 2014a), identity building .

(Smoyer, 2014b), or prison food to convey social, political, and institutional disdain for prisoners (Struthers Montford, 2022). Smoyer and Lopes (2017), for their part, examined women's lived experiences of deprivation of adequate food, even hunger, in prison. Analyzing women's narratives of positive and negative prison food experiences, Smoyer and Lopes argue that negative experiences are not only concrete occurrences of material deprivation, as Maude's repulsion described above, but also are akin to symbolic punishment.

For imprisoned women, the inability to make food choices, combined with the lack of control they have over the timing of meals, may be experienced as a loss of freedom as well as a loss of prerogative over food-related activities such as meal scheduling, food shopping, and meal preparation, often traditionally considered as women's domestic work, a conventional gender practice. Since women may have been more engaged in these undertakings prior to incarceration, the loss of control over such food-related activities while in prison exacerbates women's sense of loss of self-sufficiency, being, and personhood.

Maddy, who related above an incident where a correctional officer brought food to cell-confined women, surreptitiously referring to them as animals ("*Here is your feed* [animal feed], *girls*"), was particularly pained by the way food was served and considered the officer's demeanour harsh and unnecessary punishment. The power of such negative, uncaring food-related interaction resides notably in the alteration of women's self-image. Feeling compelled to change her nutritional intake, Maude became a vegetarian by necessity, not by choice, and fed herself essentially from items she bought from commissary, as several other women also reported during our interviews. At great distance from socially accepted behaviour related to food, Maude and others' feeding habits in prison brought them far outside community norms, hence heightening their sense of degradation.

Smoyer and Lopes (2017) note that their research participants consistently referred to prison food as "nasty" (p. 245), and eating periods as precipitated, automated, and animal-like while under the intimidating and oppressing watchful eye of correctional staff. They found food-related activities to be degrading in prison, a sentiment akin to a constraining of human kindness that left them feeling uncared for, deprived of the usual control afforded to adults in the community, humiliated, and in despair (p. 250). In this vein, Rebecca Godderis (2006b) argued that prisoners' loss of control over the process of food consumption is a significant dimension of metamorphosing human beings into "inmates," notably by generating a sense of rupture between the corporeal body that ingests food and self-identity.

Such mortifying experiences may have been heightened when the quality of the meal plan appeared to worsen during the last few months prior to the February 2016 transfer of the women detained at Maison Tanguay to the Leclerc prison. In this regard, Maddy reported that several months before the closure of Maison Tanguay, the prison no longer had a cook and the women were given frozen meals: *"small white dishes with a powdered potato section, then another section next to it with* [something] *that you don't really know what it is, those were our meals."* Mimi concurred.

> *Because we were moving, we had trouble getting soap, shampoo, laundry soap. Even the meals, sometimes, were really restricted because* [staff] *didn't have groceries as such. There were meals where we didn't have anything to drink.*

While it must be functionally legitimate for correctional authorities to reduce food stocks in anticipation of Maison Tanguay's impending permanent closure and the women's transfer to Leclerc prison to minimize food waste or the cost of moving remaining stocks from one prison to another, the fact remains that such a decision engendered human consequences such as hunger and dehumanization for women at Maison Tanguay, albeit temporary ones.

Abandonment derived from negative relationships to food, as well as negative food-related interactions with correctional staff, were not the sole form of neglect. Women reported enduring an assortment of prison conditions at Maison Tanguay which they experienced as indifference at best and oversight at worst. Although Maison Tanguay's policy stipulated that two one-hour yard periods were allowed per day for fresh air, several women explained being frequently *"forgotten"* in the yard for much longer periods of time, sometimes in the winter.

On another note, Revmarie observed that two telephones were located in the common areas of each living unit and could be used for a maximum of 20 minutes at a time per prisoner. Others noticed that they were often defective, severing women's already difficult connection to the community via their access to family members, lawyers, and community resources. Knowing that each wing at Maison Tanguay housed approximately 20 women, having access to two potentially defective telephones per wing seemed highly insufficient to Peggy, imprisoned at Maison Tanguay for seven to twelve months. In relation to telephone access, correctional staff at times have used their discretionary powers to allow demonstrations of their own humanity toward prisoners.

This was the case of Linda Côté. During her one to three months' imprisonment at Maison Tanguay, she was allowed by floor staff to use their unit telephone to maintain an uninterrupted long-standing weekly telephone pattern with her mother. Jessy explained that there was indeed a telephone next to the guards' post, probably on each unit that correctional staff used to dial a number and transfer the line to women for brief and important calls such as emergencies or legal matters. This is most likely the telephone of which Linda Côté speaks. Since Linda's frail and ageing mother was unaware of her daughter's incarceration, Linda preferred not to use the prisoners' in-wing telephones to contact the local seniors' home where her mother resided because Tanguay's telephone system permitted only collect phone calls, a practice that could have tipped off Linda's mother about her daughter's imprisonment. In exchange for obeying all instructions, correctional staff allowed this bending of the rules for Linda. Such forms of leniency on the part of correctional staff indicate that moments of empathy, not only apathy, occur. Imprisoned women recognize these moments of empathy, since they stand out in their minds as humanness. They remain conscious, however, that such moments may be an atypical commodity in prison. Such empathetic incidents also illustrate correctional staff's use of their discretionary powers to perform their professional responsibilities while allowing their own humanity to surface (Smoyer and Lopes, 2017), creating a feeling of shared humanity between staff and women prisoners during and following positive prisoner-staff interactions.

Other indicators of the inconspicuousness women often felt are materialized in the non-functionality of the mandatory in-cell panic buttons which send alarm signals to the correctional staff's post. Several women remarked that these buttons often appeared to be faulty: *Three quarters of the panic buttons in the cells no longer worked,"* says

Malory. Other women, like Jessy, added that "*it took a long time before* [correctional staff] *responded* [to the panic buttons]. . . . *It takes time. They don't respond immediately within five minutes or ten minutes. They don't necessarily respond. . . . They come by when they come by; every hour or half hour.*"

Revmarie reported similar delays in correctional intervention following the activation of a panic button. Along the same line, a few women noticed that mandatory defibrillators were absent either on the units at Maison Tanguay or in other common areas. In this instance, being forgotten may translate into not being resuscitated in the case of arrhythmia or sudden heart failure.

In a more metaphorical manner, being forgotten also transpired for Maddy from the correctional practice of imposing "*compulsory two-hour naps every day*" while she was incarcerated at Maison Tanguay, which made her feel neglected as well as infantilized as if "*in a children's daycare centre.*" Prison practices are heavily scripted in relation to time and to space. Every prisoner has her "proper place" at any time of the day (Martel, 2006: 595). Yet, exercising control over time and space is key to self-actualization because, as I have argued elsewhere:

> [situating] oneself in time and space allows one to preserve a continuous biographical narrative in which discrete moments in time—as well as one's positioning within recognizable locales—connect prior experiences to subsequent ones in an organized, (relatively) undisrupted identity trajectory (Martel, 2006: 594).

As such, temporal and spatial experiences are anchoring features of modern individuals' ability to sustain identity safeguarding. Daily "compulsory two-hour naps" do not permit women in Maison Tanguay to hold a "real" dialogue with time and space because of the prescribed nature of these naps, but also because they may conceal disregard toward incarcerated women and prompt the disempowerment of women such as Maddy who felt like they were in nursery school. "Compulsory two-hour naps" that engender feelings of being treated as preschoolers are not times or spaces adapted to adult human beings, or to their self-actualization. Being thwarted from holding a genuine dialogue with times and spaces adapted to adulthood may interrupt imprisoned women's biographical narratives, thus discontinuing the fine tuning of the self and compromising identity preservation (Martel, 2006).

I noted earlier that, in 2014, the Québec Ombudsman documented Tanguay's state of collapse, its overcrowding, and its unsuitable facilities, as well as its deficiencies in the appraisal of women's needs. It also noted Tanguay's failings in medication distribution. In this regard, Jennifer Kilty reported in 2012 that such shortcomings were also endemic at the federal level. Specifically, she reported situations where federally sentenced women had been either denied medication they were used to taking prior to their imprisonment or were compelled to replace this medication with new ones. She reported also instances of overmedication, which left women feeling like "walking zombies" (Kilty, 2012: 169). Imprisoned at Maison Tanguay for seven to twelve months, Maude experienced similar shortcomings in the distribution of medication, notably the deficient management of medication and the resulting overmedication and contraband among women prisoners.

> It's terrible the pills they gave you at Tanguay, it's unimaginable. The girls just had to holler a little, and then they would come down [from the infirmary] with all kinds of pills. It was frightening, appalling. And the girls would talk about it, and there was no hiding from it. Just say [to the infirmary staff]: "Look . . . the other girl gave me 50 bucks worth of canteen items for such and such a pill," and the staff would give it to you. [One] girl came back [from the infirmary] and she had her prescription, she had her pills. [When] I arrived [at Maison Tanguay] I was not a delinquent, but if I wanted to be a delinquent, I had everything I needed to become a delinquent. At Tanguay, [the staff] were the ones who gave us our pills. You stuck it to the roof of your mouth, you took a bottle [of water], and the way [the women] placed their tongue, they were able to hide their pills. Hey, just knowing that the girl had the pill in her mouth, and then you're going to [swallow it]? Lots of tricks of the trade in terms of the pills; how to swallow them, how to spit them out in your glass, how to hurry to get the pills out of there. That was common. At Tanguay, it was awful the pills that were [in circulation] there.

In a comparative thrust, Jessy, who returned to Maison Tanguay for numerous short periods of time over several years and also served 31 to 36 months in federal prisons designated for women, concludes the following about access to health care services at Maison Tanguay:

> At [federal prison designated for women], . . . they took [me] into consideration, they took the time to check my medication and my mental health. I went through psychological evaluations and all. They did all their tests and all. At Tanguay, they did none of that. I asked for help, [but] there's no real help, there's nothing there.

Not only access to health care services, but also access to basic hygiene conditions seemed problematic, especially in the maximum security unit at Maison Tanguay. Indeed, the Québec Ombudsman (2014: 63) reported that problems persisted in that unit of Maison Tanguay.

> Since 2009, the Québec Ombudsman has been denouncing the fact that women confined to their cells as a result of a restrictive classification do not have access to a sink to allow them to have basic hygiene conditions. Such conditions of detention are all the more unacceptable as these women can remain in their cells for up to 17 hours a day. In November 2010, the institution's management asked for the necessary budget to add sinks. As of March 31, 2014, the Québec Ombudsman had not noted any concrete results.

Along the same lines, and although studies and governmental reports have documented for decades that most imprisoned women are not dangerous to the community and have low reoffending rates (e.g., McDonnell Report, 1914; Archambault Report, 1938; Canada, 1990), policy at Maison Tanguay required the use of restraining devices notably during prison transfers. Women are then being hand and ankle cuffed with restraining chains; what Malory referred to as "*being charcoaled.*" Nuage will describe, later in the chapter, that while at Leclerc prison she was handcuffed while attending a medical appointment at a community hospital.

Such correctional procedure on the use of restraints is a top-down governmental policy and, as such, applies to all provincial prisons in Québec, since they are multi-level prisons; that is, they comprise both maximum and medium security sectors, and at times also minimum security units. Maison Tanguay being a multi-level prison—with a maximum-security unit—implements the policies that apply to this type of prison. Nonetheless, the restraining procedure is in contradiction with scientific data about women's modest level of dangerousness (e.g., Bertrand, 1979; Carlen, 1983; Hannah-Moffat and Shaw, 2000b).

Malory and Nuage's experiences with restraints are illustrative of the cognitive stickiness of ideas and practices about dangerousness, a sort of attachment to what Pat O'Malley (1999: 175) called "nostalgic" policies such as the protection of the public, which remains a key ideology of neoconservatism, a long-standing paradigm. I discussed earlier how core values and long-standing norms command expectations of what should happen in an institution. Applying this path dependence-related idea to the field of corrections, we could argue that the continuing dependence on "protecting the public" as a core value crystallizes cognitive maps within the realm of corrections. In turn, protecting the public sustains gender-neutral correctional policies and correctional practices of dangerousness—such as the use of restraints—making these practices liable to perpetuate only the most unsuitable prison conditions and service provision to women prisoners. As criminologist Allison Liebling once argued (2004):

> Prisons are special communities . . . which exist at once outside and inside the social community. Their form is shaped by social and political ideas held about crime, punishment, social order, and human nature. Many of the practices within them are also shaped by these ideas (p. 462). . . . Ideas and beliefs shape practice, that is, they shape the deep structures of penological action (p. 463). . . . Prisons have "value cultures" (p. 464).

When Arlarian was pregnant during one of her several periods of incarceration at Maison Tanguay, she reported being treated like any other "*inmate.*" She was not offered extra food, even near the very end of her pregnancy, she did not "*have any more to eat.*" She even lost weight during her pregnancy, becoming "*anemic.*" About halfway through her pregnancy, she fell "*Pow! Flac! On* [her] *belly*" because of water on the prison floor, but no staff brought her to the infirmary. However, one staff member came over and asked if she was okay: "*Oh yes. I think so. I hope so,*" she replied. Following Arlarian's answer, no preventive measure was initiated by this staff member to help her further. Fellow prisoners saw the accident as well, but no one appeared to react.

Arlarian explains that women were not forewarned that medical appointments in the community were imminent: "[One correctional staff] *calls you up at the control booth and tells you to get dressed and be ready. Once you are dressed, then they tell you that you have a medical appointment.*" The pregnancy follow-ups, specifically, were completed at the community hospital in the following conditions: "[correctional staff] *put the handcuffs on, they put the hat on, and then you go to your* [medical] *appointment. They treat you like a prisoner, not like a normal person.*" Arlarian added that, during medical examinations, such as ultrasounds, she remained "*chained up*" although hands and feet were not chained together at that point. After the birth of her child, she remained in the hospital for a few days, after which she was taken back to Maison Tanguay while her grandmother took care of the newborn in the community. Arlarian accessed no medical follow-ups, services, or support after the birth, either by prison staff or by hospital staff. She concluded, like many other women, that health services were absent at Maison Tanguay.

Access to health care services is one of prisoners' rights as per the United Nations' 1955 Standard Minimum Rules for the Treatment of Prisoners, revised in 2015 as the Nelson Mandela Rules (United Nations, 2015: rules 4.2 and 24 to 35). It is also featured in the United Nations' Rules for the Treatment of Women Prisoners and Non-Custodial Measures for Women Offenders (Bangkok Rules), which offer health-related supplemental rights to the 1955 Standard Minimum Rules for the Treatment of Prisoners, specifically gender-specific health care measures (United Nations, 2010: rules 6 to 18). However, while some prisoners may be quite attuned to rights litigation, most are not conversant in prisoner rights.

To remedy such rights illiteracy, in 2009-2010, the Canadian Association of Elizabeth Fry Societies initiated a special project entitled "Human Rights in Action," which was dedicated to safeguarding the protection of all prisoners' human rights, especially those of women and gender-diverse persons. Part of the project consisted in the creation of a comprehensive information manual entitled *Human Rights in Action: Handbook for Women Serving Federal Sentences*, "designed to assist prisoners, peer advocates, and regional advocates in ensuring that those whose rights are interfered with have support to address the discriminatory treatment, in addition to identifying and addressing areas that require systemic advocacy."[11] Created in collaboration with formerly federally incarcerated women and prison law students at Dalhousie University and the University of Ottawa, with the help of

---

11. https://www.caefs.ca/human-rights-in-action, accessed on January 15, 2022. The concept of "systemic advocacy" is defined in the 2021 version of the information guide as follows: "In this handbook, we also identify and address areas that need 'systemic advocacy'—advocacy that is not just for individual issues, but issues related to larger structures of power" (p. 5). https://www.caefs.ca/_files/ugd/d2d30e_555aa2bf08064c39a63fa736340d44d8.pdf?lang=fr, accessed on January 15, 2022.

regional advocates with the Canadian Association of Elizabeth Fry Societies, the manual also provided practical information related to early release and parole preparation.

With the assistance of the Canadian Association of Elizabeth Fry Societies, each provincially bound Elizabeth Fry Society concocted its own information manual adapted to provincial correctional laws and practices. As part of this process, in 2010, the Société Elizabeth Fry du Québec devised a 77-page *Guide d'information pour les femmes sous sentence provinciale*, complete with detailed information on the admission/assessment process, classification, programs, remunerated work, access to health care services, right to counsel, segregation, transfer procedures, disciplinary system, cell/body/visitor searches, temporary absence criteria, internal complaint system, Québec Ombudsman, etc. All of the 12 women with lived experience of prison conditions at Maison Tanguay between 2011 and 2016 who were interviewed confirmed that they did not receive a copy of the information guide or any other prisoners' rights manual upon admission to Maison Tanguay. When contacted for this book, staff of the Société Elizabeth Fry du Québec could not confirm when or why the resource had stopped supplying the guide to women in Québec provincial prisons.[12]

Yearly since 2009, the Québec Ombudsman reiterated recommendations to recondition Maison Tanguay and regretted in 2014 that no concrete action had been taken on its recommendations (Québec Ombudsman, 2014). Concurrently, Québec's correctional directorate implemented a Correctional Services Branch – Women and Specialized Activities with the mandate to "analyze the needs of the female clientele, particularly in terms of security at the Maison Tanguay detention facility" (Québec Ombudsman 2014: 64). One year later, in a "context of budgetary austerity," no work had begun, and the closure of Maison Tanguay was publicly announced by the Québec government "due to its deterioration and its incapacity to meet the growing operational needs of the prison population" (Québec, 2015: 1). Upon closure, Maison Tanguay housed approximately 80% of the female provincial prison population in Québec (Québec, 2015).

---

12. Email conversation with staff at the Société Elizabeth Fry du Québec, March 2, 2022.

4.4 THE CLOSURE OF MAISON TANGUAY AND THE WOMEN'S TRANSFER TO THE LECLERC PRISON (2016): THE RELENTLESSNESS OF THE PRISON

4.4.1 The "Déjà vu" Living Conditions at the Leclerc Prison

To end women's exposure to such precarious prison conditions, Québec's Ministry of Public Safety transferred them to the Leclerc prison, a former federal medium security prison designated for men and decommissioned in 2012 by federal correctional authorities given its state of disrepair. Federal authorities then leased the building to the Québec government in 2014 to alleviate overcrowding in men's provincial prisons in Québec. By the fall of 2014, a little over 240 men prisoners were transferred to Leclerc, many of them for violent crimes (Messier, 2016).

In her recent biography, Sister Marguerite, who has been volunteering at Maison Tanguay and later at the Leclerc prison since 1977, explains that the staff of Maison Tanguay (approximately 120 workers) were upset by the "unrealistic" plan to move the women to Leclerc prison in 2016.

> It was as if death had passed within the walls of the prison so much the atmosphere was changed. Tanguay staff had not been consulted. This move could not be completed in just five months, as the authorities had planned. It was obvious! And there was no emergency to explain such a hasty decision! (Rivard and Lavigne, 2022: 85-86)

During the actual transfer of the women to the Leclerc prison, teams from Maison Tanguay were sent to Leclerc to provide training in the incarceration of women (e.g., working with remanded prisoners, pregnant prisoners, etc.). According to Sister Marguerite, the reception of the Tanguay teams was "disrespectful to say the least" (Rivard and Lavigne, 2022: 87), since the women's transfer had been imposed on Leclerc staff, who appeared to show little interest in working with women prisoners. For trade union reasons, only approximately 25% of the Tanguay staff were allowed to transfer to Leclerc, which left a notable void in knowledge and women-centred expertise.

In February 2016 the prison became mixed with the arrival of nearly 250[13] women from Maison Tanguay, a vast majority of whom had been sentenced to less than three months. From that point, women suffered imposed mixed gender confinement. While only 84 men eventually remained at the Leclerc prison, they regularly encountered women, especially in certain hallways or common rooms, on their way to access the visiting room or the infirmary or when women trained in the gym, each encounter being conducive to sexual or degrading statements or harassment (Messier, 2016). Knowing that imprisoned women often have lived experiences of physical or sexual violence, such gender-mixed encounters violate women's fundamental right to human dignity. It is interesting to note that, in a September 2015 press release (Québec, 2015), the Québec Ministry of Public Safety appeared adamant that the upcoming 2016 transfer of the Tanguay women to the Leclerc prison signaled an upgrading of incarcerated women's well-being from the deleterious prison conditions at Maison Tanguay.

> This transfer will allow employees and incarcerated individuals to evolve in an adequate, adapted, and safe environment. The change of vocation of the Leclerc detention facility in Laval [to become a mixed prison] will allow us to take advantage of a location that is equipped to offer services to the female prison population, while ensuring that the quality of these services and programs is maintained.

As a result of government authorities' fantasy of an unproblematic transfer, the Québec Ombudsman had to intervene because of the inadequate planning of the women's transfer, which caused non-access to personal effects and to hygiene products, strip searches in spaces that lacked privacy, housing of women with incompatible profiles, difficulty in accessing sanitary facilities for women with intermittent sentences, and non-delivery of personal effects upon release (Québec Ombudsman, 2016). In its 2016-2017 annual report, "the Québec Ombudsman [was] critical of this lack of planning by the [Ministry], which was long aware of the dilapidated condition of Maison Tanguay. Forced to act, the

---

13. In 2015-2016, the average capacity of Maison Tanguay was 220 beds, with an overpopulation rate of 111%. In 2014-2015, the occupancy rate was 101%; in 2013-2014, 98%; in 2012-2013, 105%; in 2011-2012, 90%; and in 2010-2011, 102%. Ministère de la Sécurité publique du Québec (2016), Études des crédits budgétaires – 2010-2011 à 2015-2016, https://www.securitepublique.gouv.qc.ca/fileadmin/Documents/ministere/diffusion/documents_transmis_acces/2016/119707.pdf, accessed February 6, 2023.

[Ministry] opted for a solution that did more harm than good" (Québec Ombudsman, 2017: 80). Another indication of the hastiness with which the closure of Maison Tanguay occurred was revealed in 2020 by *Le Journal de Montréal* journalist Erika Aubin, who exposed that administrative documents containing confidential information (such as social insurance number, date of birth, personal address, phone number, email address) on over 400 correctional employees had been left unattended for almost four years in abandoned Maison Tanguay (Aubin, 2020). Photos attached to the newspaper article show documents and personal photos left in a cell, along with dictionaries, a lamp, papers, an electronic calculator, and other supplies left in an administrative office as if an evacuation had taken place.

Post-transfer conditions at Leclerc were utterly challenging and, indeed, tell of an ill-prepared transfer of the women. Many women, such as Maddy, Chouette, Mimi, Béa, and Revmarie noted the lack of cleanliness of their respective cramped cell space upon their arrival at Leclerc, similar to Maude's experience below:

> Leclerc [was] a total shock because we expected to be [housed in] the new [renovated] part [of the prison]. I [eventually] had a cell alone, it was all smeared by the guys [previous occupants]. There were drawings of penises, all kinds of vulgar writing stuff, and dirty, broken razor blades all over the cell. The guys, I imagine, were lighting up, they take razor blades and put them in the sockets to light up cigarettes. On the window-sill, there were lots of orange and banana peels. Bedsheets were worn out, and dirty. The guys made drawings on them, but they give them back to you. I washed them with bleach, they changed color a little bit. I didn't even lie on them, I laid on top of another blanket that was more or less clean, that I had washed, then rewashed, before lying down on it. It was really disgusting. I thanked God that [I left for another prison after] just [xx] days at Leclerc because I think I would have left my skin there.

Bed linens, although clean, were often full of cigarette holes, noted Béa, a young woman incarcerated at the Leclerc prison during the spring season. Béa and Maddy's descriptions of the lack of appropriateness of the sanitary facilities such as the toilet, the sink, the shower, summarize well the living conditions at the Leclerc prison depicted by all the women interviewed:

> At Leclerc, the first time I went there, there was no shower curtain for privacy. . . . And they often had male officers and not women officers. So, they used to see everything. When I arrived, that lasted three days.

Then, they installed curtains. I don't know how long that lasted before I arrived, though. . . . At one point, we were putting up bedsheets—we wanted to shower without being seen. Then, an officer forced us to take the sheets down. The following day, we had shower curtains. This situation did not encourage us to wash up. Some girls just washed in their cell with facecloths. – Maddy

Mushrooms in the sink. I was on the . . . floor. The sink [had] no elbow, so we could no longer use the sink. The girls would sometimes put food in the [sink], and then you'd end up with an industrial quantity of flies. . . . The shower also full of flies. We had little white worms once in the shower pipes . . . so there were grubs coming out of the little hole where the water is running. . . . "Pour some Javex [chlorine bleach] on it," [the correctional staff said]. We put Javex in, [the bugs] came out even more. Then at some point, I guess someone came by, because it stopped. – Béa

As Chouette noted, overcrowding problems at Leclerc also affected the cleanliness of the shower area:

There were some who went to relieve themselves in the showers, because there were no toilets for the "overpopulation." If we had six overpops come to our floor who didn't have their own toilet [since they don't have their own cell], they had to ask girls who had their own cell to use their toilet, but I guess some of them can't ask, and went in the showers because [in the shower areas] we had urinals instead of toilets. You go and wash up and the shower is full of shit! Before bringing the women [at Leclerc] they could have removed the urinals, [and] installed at least one toilet there, a toilet to sit on.

Mimi, who experienced the 2016 transfer from Maison Tanguay to the Leclerc prison, experienced conditions that further expose the unpreparedness of the transfer:

When we transferred to the Leclerc, we had to fight to get a bar of soap. We walked around with sheets around our waists to wash our clothes. We went for weeks and weeks without getting our own clothes [from Maison Tanguay], for the little the girls had. You could go at least a week without washing your hair. There were no curtains in the bathrooms, the guards could see us. It was supposed to be all renovated before we got there, nothing was done. They made us move, because it was unsanitary in Tanguay, but it was as bad in Leclerc. It was hell! I became ill at Leclerc while I was fine at Tanguay. Nausea, headaches, dizziness probably because of the mildew, there was mildew everywhere in the air vents. While there were rats, mice in Tanguay, I didn't see any in Leclerc. But it wasn't any better, there was mould on the bars, in the windows, on metal, which is almost impossible, so the building had to be quite contaminated for that to happen. We wrote petitions and tried to do everything we could, but [correctional staff] *used to tell us to clean it ourselves, but we barely had any soap, and a little bit of bleach. We were really restricted on cleaning products. Every time we needed a new mop, we had to really annoy* [correctional staff] *for almost a week.*

Chouette, who was moved several times from cell to cell, witnessed first-hand—along with several other women—that the Leclerc cellblocks were still unkept in the months that followed the transfer, and that women still had to rely on their own initiative to clean their living space:

[At Leclerc], *before I had my own cell, I was transferred twice to a* [double bunked] *cell, then to another* [double bunked] *cell. I cleaned from top to bottom because the walls were filthy, there were monster faces, spiders. . . . I scrubbed, I scrubbed. I cannot live in there, I cannot sleep in there, I'm going to have nightmares, I would go crazy looking at it. You move about* [in the cell], *and there are big red eyes! The girls thought I was a little crazy about it, but I'm going to clean it up, then I'm going to sleep in peace.*

Women admitted to Leclerc totalled more than the number of beds in the sectors summarily renovated to house them. In Québec's provincial prisons, sentenced prisoners often share cells, or may be housed in dormitories, gymnasiums, visiting rooms designed for visitors and lawyers, classrooms, or other "non-traditional accommodation spaces" (Québec Ombudsman, 2018: 15). At times, they may sleep in bull pens[14] or in hallways. During the day, they often wander through the prison carrying their bundle. Kate and Chouette experienced such wandering:

At Leclerc, there were always two of us in the cells. . . . When I arrived, there were too many of us, so they took us to where the cuckoos live, the women who wanted to fight or who were too violent. . . . They took us out [of the cells] *to go to unit A or B. We were in B to sleep, that lasted at least a week. . . . They would transfer us with all our belongings, all our luggage, and then we would go* [to Unit B] *at night. We would pack up* [our things], *go back* [to Unit A during the day]. *After three days,*

---

14. "Bull pen" is a colloquial prison term referring to large, enclosed holding areas where prisoners are detained temporarily while waiting, for example, to undergo the prison admission process or to be brought to court or to other community venues for purposes of education, employment, or health services.

I said, "Shit, look, they'll give me blankets, I'm tired of dragging this around." I was having a hard time. – Chouette

"Still in these non-traditional spaces, we see that people are often crowded together in the same room, that the quality of the air leaves much to be desired, that the air quality is poor, heating is inadequate, and crowding is such that it is difficult to circulate, especially when there are mattresses on the floor" (Québec Ombudsman, 2018: 16). Since such spaces not designed as cells do not contain toilets or sinks, prisoners must await correctional officers' next round to access basic sanitary facilities located elsewhere in the prison. This practice is in contradiction to Québec's Charter of Human Rights and Freedoms, which commands the human and respectful treatment of prisoners, as well as to the United Nations' Mandela Rules, which include reasonable access to sanitary facilities and toiletries essential to the health and cleanliness of prisoners (United Nations, 2015: 11, rule 15).

In Québec's more remote areas, women serving intermittent sentences are not transferred to the Leclerc prison in the city of Laval because of the distance to be covered and the limited duration of their stay. Instead, they are housed in regional prisons designated for men under difficult prison conditions. For example, women tend to be admitted after all the men have been, they may be refused access to goods, are housed in small non-traditional accommodation spaces without windows or running water, since the men prisoners requisition the larger spaces such as dormitories and gymnasiums (Québec Ombudsman, 2018). This situation is akin to accommodation arrangements that women prisoners suffered in the 19th century.

The current paradigm imposed on provincial correctional services in Québec derives from the New Public Management (NPD) philosophy. Applying mindsets and practices derived from the business realm, this managerial ethos is based on efficiency imperatives centred on streamlining bureaucracies, standardized measures of organizational performance and financial cost control (Turnbull, Martel, Parkes, and Moore, 2018). Under such imperatives, it makes rational organizational sense not to undergo long and costly transfers to incarcerate a few women on weekend sentences. Historically in Canada, women prisoners have always been "too few to count," that is, too few to justify the financial means to build detention centres in sufficient number to provide the women with nearby accommodation, as well as gender-sensitive correctional programming and services (Adelberg and Currie, 1987).

Since men were imprisoned at Leclerc prior to the women's transfer, it would have been reasonable to expect satisfactory meal plans. Chouette tells a different story and decries the absence of fruits and vegetables:

> I had my Pepsi, my chocolate, my chips. Look, I'll eat this. I saw the goulash we [were fed], I wasn't able to, you know. I don't lack meat, but we only have oranges, bananas, and apples on weekends. The [one to three] months I've been here, I've had salad twice. Then soup, I've had it once, because there's no soup. It's all goulash, goulash! Then cakes, cakes, no icing, so it's not edible. I often exchanged with the girls on weekends: chocolate bars, chips, or Pepsi for oranges, bananas, or multigrain cookies, it was always the same damn cookie. I provided myself with apples, oranges, and bananas, so that I could eat a little solid. When there were carrots in the goulash, I waited until everyone was served, then I went to get all the little carrots. Because chocolate, I couldn't digest it any more, I would throw it up from eating nothing but chocolate. So, I began to eat toast, toast, toast.

As mentioned before, a particular dimension of the experience of imprisonment that engenders recurring suffering affecting prisoners' sense of self is one's relationship to the food made available in the prison. Another such dimension is that of being consigned to oblivion, of being unremembered. Incidents that induce such a state may take multifarious forms. Our interviews are replete with occurrences where incarcerated women momentarily evaporate from correctional staff's individual memories or from the collective memory of the carceral system. Fading into nothingness then becomes a taxing and afflicting aspect of identity negotiation in prison.

Access to in-house phones did not seem problematic for most of the women interviewed, apart from moments where women would linger on the phone past their allocated 30-minute period and cause the wrath of other prisoners. However, mandated daily yard time appeared as challenging as it had been at Maison Tanguay prior to the 2016 transfer to the Leclerc prison. Béa, a woman imprisoned at the Leclerc prison for one to three months, illuminates her experience of the mandated 60-minute daily yard times as moments of effacement, of reduction to insignificance:

We had yard time every day for one hour. Sometimes [correctional staff] *would skip it. Sometimes we didn't have one. They weren't telling us that we would not be going outside. They didn't give us a reason why, because it's not the decision of the officers in the wing, it's the decision of the officers in the administration, so we just didn't hear about it.* [When we did have yard time], *everyone who wanted to go* [could go]. *There could be about 40 of us because sometimes they would send two sectors at the same time.* [In the yard], *you walk in circles in a chicken coop. You walk around, you get some sun. I went* [in the yard] *maybe four times* [during my one to three-month detention]. *I found it a little bit demoralizing, because it's really a small courtyard and it's all fenced in with barbed wire. I felt like I was in a chicken cage, I didn't think it helped me. You must be in by 10 o'clock p.m.,* [but sometimes] *they would allow yard time at 9 o'clock p.m. You know, when it's 28 degrees all day, you want to go out in the sun, but then they* [would only] *allow yard at 9 o'clock p.m.!*

Others, such as Allison, who spent four to six months at the Leclerc prison soon after the 2016 transfer, reported that the scheduling of yard times tended to fluctuate at the Leclerc prison.

Sometimes [yard access] *was at six o'clock, sometimes it was at nine o'clock, from nine to ten o'clock* [in the evening]. *When we'd get back into* [the building] *it was already time for bedtime lockup.* [Correctional staff] *gave us an hour. If you went outside and it started to rain, they wouldn't let you in. They would leave us in the rain. We would bang on the window: "It's raining, let us in!" "No, you wanted to go outside, you have an hour, stay there." If a girl needed to use the bathroom or anything else, you were out for an hour, she had to go* [to the bathroom] *before.* [In the yard], *we had nothing, it was nothing but asphalt, so we walked in the yard. Then, in July* [the prison authorities] *decided to add two picnic tables for us. So, there was a gang of us walking, and a gang of us sitting at the picnic table talking.*

This is confirmed by Revmarie:

At Leclerc, it was quite cold there. They let us outside, and you never knew when you were going to be let back inside, so it wasn't interesting to go outside [during yard time]. [Yard time lasted] *an hour always* [in every prison], *except at Leclerc,* [where] *we never knew when we were going to be let back inside* [the building].

It is probable that management, at times, may have to reschedule yard times because of staff shortages or incidents in need of attention. However, women experienced such lack of predictability in their otherwise regimented daily prison routine as moments of inconspicuousness, remaining nameless and faceless in some liminal space, waiting, and not knowing when they would be remembered by staff.

In a previous study, I argued (Martel, 2006: 596-597) that the observation in prison of a highly routinized daily structuring of time governed by the clock provides an unwavering and sturdy footing on which prisoners structure their own time. It allows them to situate themselves in a precise moment in time. Prison time routines, thus, become institutionally recognizable temporal patterns, as revealed in the typical daily prison routine shown in Table 2 below.

Yet, prison time is an alienating time because the prison's time schedule restricts human activities. The structuring of prison schedules breaks up time into microparcels of planned, regulated, and broken up time inhabited by multifarious duties, each contributing to generating long periods of waiting alternating with short periods of haste. Nonetheless, it remains that the women who collaborated in this study retain some decisional control over their use of institutional time. They can choose, for example, to retrieve their mail (or not), partake in recreational activities, use the telephones, meet legal advisers, or waive parole. During incarceration, women prisoners are removed from socially recognizable temporal patterns—specifically those in use in the community. As a result, they come to ascribe meaning to the timing of prison activities.

TABLE 2. Typical Weekday Schedule in Canada's prisons[15]

Time	Institutional activities
6:00 a.m.	Wake up
6:45 a.m.	In-cell morning institutional count
7:00 a.m.	Breakfast
8:00 a.m.	Remunerated or non-remunerated work, school, workshops, specialized programming or back to cell
11:45 a.m.	In-cell midday count
12:00 p.m.	Lunch on the units
1:00 p.m.	Remunerated or non-remunerated work, school, workshops, specialized programming or back to cell
4:30 p.m.	In-cell afternoon count
4:45 p.m.	Dinner on the units
6:00 p.m.	Recreation, sports, self-help groups, church, etc.
10:30 p.m.	In-cell evening count[16]
11:00 p.m.	Lockup, lights out

Women confined at the Leclerc prison are, at times, notified in extremis of a change of plan (e.g., cell move, transfer, visit), or may be taken early to court or to medical visits, even if it means waiting around longer, as was the case with Nuage (above), who was informed by correctional staff of her community hospital appointment without warning, was strip searched and left in the bull pen for one hour while staff had lunch before taking her to the hospital. In the excerpt above, Allison recalls how yard access appeared to escape such routinized, deliberate, and predictable compartmentalization of prison time. Yard periods could be granted at fluctuating times or could be altogether cancelled. Such delays or cancellations tend to weaken the spatio-temporal benchmarks that prisoners use, since the prison encourages them to develop fixed ideas about appropriate times for activities. "However rigid, dominating and time-consuming it may be, the carceral

15. Table produced by combining information provided by Correctional Service Canada at https://www.csc-scc.gc.ca/correctional-process/002001-1000-eng.shtml, the John Howard Society of Ontario at https://johnhoward.on.ca/wp-content/uploads/2014/09/counter-point-3-a-day-in-the-life-of-a-prisoner-in-ontario.pdf, and Québec (2014).
16. Evening lockup at Tanguay appears to have been at 9:45 p.m., while the Leclerc lockup is at 10:15 p.m., and federal prisons designated for women's is at 10:30 p.m., according to Arlarian, who served 13 to 18 months at Maison Tanguay, less than one month at the Leclerc prison, and 13 to 18 months at a federal prison designated for women.

schedule becomes vital to prisoners, as it gradually becomes familiar and provides much needed reference points to those estranged from their habitual environment in the community" (Martel, 2006: 597). Consequently, allowing yard time at irregular moments may exacerbate not only frustration but also an anxiety of being forgotten, of being meaningless human beings. The predictable compartmentalization of prison time—via foreseeable daily periods of access to the prison yard, for example—provides reference points used by prisoners to locate themselves and adapt confidently to manifold identity exigencies they may encounter during incarceration.

Along similar lines, Allison recalls a particular situation when she could no longer reach the floor where her cell was located and had to migrate temporarily to another prison floor, one which was wheelchair accessible. She explains these circumstances which precipitated her situation of indeterminacy leading to her being neglected by prison staff:

> *I had . . . surgery. . . . Since that time, I've had problems with my knee, makes the circulation difficult. I couldn't go up to the fourth floor any more, so* [correctional staff] *sent me with the "cuckoos" . . . because they are* [housed] *on the first floor where there is a wheelchair ramp. I was in a wheelchair. . . . Those who get psychological treatment, they call them cuckoos in prison. The guards were okay, I didn't have any problems with them. They just sent me with the cuckoos. At first, I didn't like it, but I realized that they were not much crazier than those I was with on the fourth floor. I remained* [in the mental health unit] *for a good* [xx] *weeks. I was wearing a nightgown for the entire* [xx] *weeks. I asked for my clothes* [which were still in her cell on the fourth floor], *but they wouldn't bring them to me. I said, "my nightgown is starting not to smell too good." After two or three days, you know, you're hot. I had the same little underpants too. I washed them at night before going to bed so I could have clean underwear the next day. There was a girl who lent me an extra nightgown. I had two nightgowns so I could change, but I still washed my underpants every night by hand in my sink, with the little soap that you wash your body with. Then, when we went outside for yard time, one girl lent me clothes. She dressed in yo* [hip hop] *fashion: "Mrs. Allison, you're going to dress like a yo, I'll lend you some* [clothes]!" *She wore her clothes a bit large, and she was approximately my size, anyway. So, I dressed up in* [hip hop] *clothing to go to mass.*

Penny, who spent less than a month at the Leclerc prison before being transferred to a federal prison designated for women, experienced a situation like the one Allison described above. During her entire stay, she was compelled to wear the same clothes she was wearing upon admission to Leclerc. During her entire incarceration period, Penny established an evening routine where she would wash the clothes on her back first with soap and eventually with shampoo when the institutional soap with which she was provided ran out.

> I would put on the nightgown that [correctional staff] gave me, which is slit on the side, then I would wash all my clothes and I would take my shower, while the clothes were being washed. Then, when the clothes were dry, I would put the panties back on at least, and the rest [of my clothes] the next morning.

Similarly to Allison but for very different reasons, Penny was in a situation of indeterminacy—being in transit at the Leclerc prison for a short period of time while awaiting a transfer to a federal prison, her final destination. Such a physical stance in a liminal, transitional space in between two prisons also caused her to be overlooked and tossed aside as if the temporary status of her situation were unworthy of consideration.

For her part, Arlarian spent 13 to 18 months at Maison Tanguay, less than a month at the Leclerc prison, and 13 to 18 months at a federal prison designated for women. She recounts that, while at Leclerc, she experienced a challenging moment when a serious health condition deteriorated because she was not provided with the necessary medication for several days, a medication that comprised "*20 pills per day.*"

> I put my panic button down because I felt sick, because I hadn't had my pill for [xx] days. So, one of the guards comes, and he says: "Why did you put your fucking panic button down?" I said, "Well, I haven't got my pills, I need to take my sugar." And I waited three hours to get my sugar. Then when [the guard] came to assess my sugar [level], I was at 90%. . . . Usually it's six, seven, maybe eight, maybe nine, ten percent max. I said, "You see that? You see?" Three hours later, the nurse came. I never want to go back there. I never want to go back there.

It is likely that during the six-hour period when Arlarian's critical health condition may have appeared trivial to correctional staff and to nursing personnel, she experienced neglect and mistreatment to the point where she "*never wanted to go back there.*"

In 2022, Louise Henry, a Québec woman formerly incarcerated in the middle of the 2010s, published a powerful testimony of her personal experience as a prisoner as well as her observations of the treatment of other women while at the Leclerc prison (Henry, 2022). She describes an assortment of challenging situations and violations of human rights that are largely analogous to the ones depicted in this book. In terms of access to medication, specifically, Henry describes how, because of the medication distribution procedure, a correctional staff member once inadvertently interchanged the medication to be given to two different women who had the same family name.

> The pills are passed through a window, and you have to reach through a grid to get your dose. The medication is in a dispill [pill dispenser] that is clearly marked with your name, the officer opens it and gives you your pills in the palm of your hand without you being able to see the name on the dispill. You have to swallow your pills in front of him and show him the inside of your mouth to make sure that everything has been swallowed. This is a safety issue against drug trafficking. . . . It's a good thing the first [woman] realized that the size and color of her pills were not as usual before swallowing them! . . . Taking the wrong pills is a serious matter. Why not just show the dispill to the inmate so that she can check for herself that they are hers? Or name her by her full name? (Henry, 2022: 50-51).

In such a hasty transfer, it was unlikely that health care services be organized, as confirmed by Nuage, a woman who, as part of a single prison sentence, spent less than a month in a regional prison designated for men awaiting her transfer to another prison, then was transferred back and forth between one prison designated for women and the Leclerc prison for a total of six prison transfers over a few months. Prior to her incarceration, Nuage had a primary care physician who was monitoring the progress of a serious health problem. Following an ultrasound procedure, she was informed that she needed a biopsy. At this point, she became incarcerated. Below, in a long excerpt, she explains experiencing not only humiliation rituals during a visit to a local hospital about her condition, but also the effects of Leclerc's lack of systematization in health care service delivery.

> *It was in* [month] *that I entered detention. I met the* [prison's] *nurse* [at a regional prison designated for men], *I told her about* [my condition] *and she said, "You're going to see a doctor." I didn't have the time; I was transferred to Leclerc* [a few] *days later. Once at Leclerc, I was in overpopulation so I didn't get to meet with a doctor. So, I met the nurse*

five days later. She asked me about my medication because I have [serious medical condition #1]. *I told her about the* [serious medical condition #2], *and she said that I was going to see a doctor. Two days later, I was called, I met a doctor. The doctor examined me and said, "Indeed, we'll send for your* [medical] *file in* [city of origin]. *Wait and we'll get back to you about this." One month, a month and a half, two months later nothing, I even had time to be transferred to* [prison designated for men] *and be transferred back to Leclerc. Then, at a certain point, two guards came to get me: "Madame Nuage, get ready, we're taking you somewhere." "Where?" I replied. "We'll tell you later. We'll tell you when we get to the locker room." Once at the locker room: "We are taking you to the hospital, handcuffed, searched." So, they strip searched me and put me in the bull pen[17] while they had lunch. I was there for an hour. I missed my afternoon of work. I said, "Finally, I'm going to get a diagnosis, is it [really serious] or not." Then when we got to the hospital, they put me in a wheelchair and carried me around handcuffed, shackled, chained.... The chains go cling! cling! on the metal frame of the wheelchair. At the hospital, you don't come in through a small door, you come in where the ambulances do, where people are waiting in the emergency room. So, they carried me around, had my* [hospital] *card made. You wait there, everyone sees you. The two guards came back, and we then went to the* [X] *sector. There are lots of children in the* [X] *sector, right? So . . . I attract children . . . I've always attracted them. There are two little boys, one three years old, one about five years old, who come to see me: "Good morning, ma'am." "Well, good morning," I replied. Then they see the handcuffs. They wanted to ask me questions about the handcuffs, but their mother came to get them. It made me sad. That's how it was at the hospital, I couldn't wait for it to be over. So, the guards took me in, the doctor put on his gloves, the doctor was ready to do my biopsy. He said, "Okay, you're going to give me Madame Nuage's file." What file? Oh, there is no file. Where is the file? The doctor said, "I cannot do anything. It will have to wait until you make another appointment." So, the guards pushed my wheelchair through the hospital again, the entire hospital. "Cling, cling!" The van; arriving here at Leclerc; strip search again;[18] bull pen waiting to go back up to my sector . . . all for nothing. That was it. After that, I never heard from the hospital again.*

---

17. Ibid., note 14.
18. Via data obtained through the Québec *Act respecting access to documents held by public bodies and the protection of personal information* (Chap. A-2.1), https://www.legisQuebec.gouv.qc.ca/en/document/cs/A-2.1, accessed 21 October 2022), scholar, lawyer, and activist, the late Lucie Lemonde, showed that searches executed at the Leclerc prison between 2016 and 2019 did not result in the identification

In such an ill-planned transfer to Leclerc, it was also unlikely that women-centred health services would be available and of adequate quality. Below, Roxy and Mia relate their prison experience in relation to mental health situations:

I'm in the hole, I freeze, I have shit on the walls, I have blood [on the walls]. . . . *And* [correctional staff] *only gave me cheese sandwiches, cheese sandwiches, cheese sandwiches. . . . I was in administrative segregation for suicidal thoughts. They took all my clothes away, and gave me this kind of nightgown in heavy, rigid fabric that didn't cover much, with something to put on my cot in the same fabric. . . . I froze, it was really, really, really cold. I froze for 24 hours. Then, at one point, this was a miracle, I discovered there was hot water. So, I warmed up with hot water, I put it everywhere I could. . . . After that, when* [correctional staff] *ask you: "Do you have suicidal thoughts?" for sure you're gonna say no, even if it's yes. . . . Gee, I'm okay for sure, sure, sure. I wanna get out of here. I freeze, this is hell. But I still wanted to do it* [suicide]. *I said, "Now I'm going to a place where I'll be able to do it. And I'll shut my mouth."* – Roxy

And Mia added:

When [a] *woman attempted suicide in her cell, close to mine, the girl next to her said, "Let's all hit our panic button." Then, we all hit the button. The guard who came by when they carried the woman on the stretcher said, "Hey! That was cool, it looked like a Christmas tree in our office earlier with all those lights." He thought it was funny, and you have this woman who is pissing blood.*

As a place of captivity, the prison is legally and morally (Liebling, 2004) responsible for protecting the public, reducing reoffending, and preventing escapes, diseases, and deaths. It is also responsible for all the activities prisoners need to survive, so the prison must feed, clothe, and offer rudimentary necessities to the prisoner. It also must provide heated quarters in the winter and access to minimum medical care. The prison conditions prevailing in pre-transfer Tanguay as well as those in post-transfer Leclerc violate one of the legislated responsibilities of the Québec correctional directorate, specifically to ensure the custody and control of incarcerated persons that is "reasonable, safe and humane" while respecting their fundamental rights.[19] They are also a conviction

---

of prohibited items. Therefore "these searches cannot be justified on the basis of security concerns" (Henry, 2022: 10).

19. *Loi sur le système correctionnel du Québec*, LRQ, c. S-40.1, sect. 1.

of the Correctional Services Branch – Women and Specialized Activities. Since 2014, this branch has been unable to guide authorities toward an alternative path to instil more humanity into Maison Tanguay in terms of its prison conditions. Security issues are often ingrained in prison narratives which, by ricochet, maintain status quo. It is safe to assume that the Women's Branch encountered self-reinforcing mechanisms within the Ministry against selective improvements, since Maison Tanguay's expansion and revamping have been part of Québec's 2018-2028 infrastructure planning since its closure in 2016 (Québec, 2018a).

The research team members of the Prison Transparency Project, from which this book originates, have long research careers on the carceral system and on lived experiences of the prison. In the past decades, we have each documented such conditions in prisons desig-nated for men or for women in Canada. The findings related here are nothing new in Québec and Canada. What they show is a tenacity of prison conditions. It is troubling that we were able to document difficult prison conditions and human rights violations in Canadian prisons and penitentiaries in the 21st century. I argue that these violations are witnesses of an institutionalized, stabilized (and possibly locked-in) path on which we should no longer be. Although the indifference and brutality of women's prisoning has been documented since the second half of the 19th century in Canada, it remains difficult, at political or organizational levels, to guarantee the dignified treatment of imprisoned women in the 21st century.

The pre- and post-transfer prison conditions discussed here are revealing of the myopic, short-term maximizing behavior of Québec correctional services. Québec's historical rhetoric and formal policies tend to be more welfarist and humanist than those of many other Canadian provinces (McEwen, 2006). It is possible that such political alignment may have contributed to deflect attention away from Québec prisons' often inhumane conditions and practices. The findings are also revealing of the durability of conditions in prisons designated for women and of the fact that women remain victims of after-thought planning (of lack thereof) and "temporary" arrangements in Canadian correctional practice. They tend to be kept still in over-secure men's prisons in wings or buildings that men no longer need, and in environ-ments often insensitive to sexospecific issues and ill-adapted to women's specific needs.

Eight months after the completion of the women's transfer to Leclerc, in October 2016, the Minister of Public Safety announced the construction of a new prison designated for women in the Montréal area to replace the decrepit Maison Tanguay. Meanwhile, the women are to remain at Leclerc prison while the 84 men still housed in the prison at the time are relocated, since the cohabitation of men and women prisoners was only a temporary solution to deal with prison overcrowding (Fortier, 2016). In 2021, nothing had transpired about the construction of this new prison. I inquired about the new prison at Québec's correctional directorate. Information received confirmed laconically that as of 2021—that is five years after its governmental announcement—"the project is still active, and that the greater Montréal area is targeted" for this construction.[20]

4.4.2 Media and Advocates' Indictment of Prison Conditions at the Leclerc Prison

Meanwhile, the deterioration of already horrendous living conditions at the Leclerc prison persists and made the pages of *La Presse*, a prominent Québec media, which in 2018 brought to light the "violence behind bars" at Leclerc, where women are "treated like garbage" by certain correctional staff, notably via designations such as "fat bitch," "dirty cunt," "fucking junkie" (Groguhé, 2018). Bullying is also documented by this journalist, notably tactics of "charging violently at a person pretending to hit him or her or pushing him or her into the cell when she is in no danger" or threats of maximum security reclassification should the woman refuse to withdraw a complaint against a correctional staff member (Groguhé, 2018).

Three years later, in 2021, *Le Devoir*, another prominent Québec media, reported the presence of institutionalized contempt, which appears to translate into correctional staff frequently shouting insults like "Shut your fucking mouth," "Hey, Smith, get over here," "stupid bitch," "fuck off," "[You're] already enough of a fat cunt" (Nadeau, 2021a). Along the same line, the Québec Ombudsman (2020: 88) reported that a pregnant woman was refused a special mattress on the basis that policy allows them only to prisoners weighing 136 kilograms or more.

---

20. Email from Québec's correctional directorate received June 8, 2021.

Chouette, who was imprisoned at the Leclerc prison during the months that followed the transfer in February 2016, confirms the existence of this policy, since she used two mattresses in her cell without proper authorization because of health problems unrelated to weight. During a cell search, correctional staff informed her of the existence of the 136-kilogram policy and that it applied not only to special mattresses but also to extra mattresses. Although Chouette did not meet authorization criteria, correctional staff did not confiscate her second mattress and let her keep it. Here too, correctional staff have used their discretionary powers to allow demonstrations of their own humanity toward prisoners.

As a journalist, Jean-François Nadeau reported approximately ten times in 2016 on the Leclerc transfer and subsequent prison conditions (Nadeau, 2016a to h). In 2018, 2019, 2021 and 2022, he continued to report once or twice a year on the endurance of bad prison conditions despite periodical political promises to correct the situation at the Leclerc prison. In 2018, he and other journalists noted the periodic proliferation of bedbugs as well as mice in staircases, toilets and under mattresses, the persistence of brownish water,[21] a heating system so poor that women have to sleep wearing their winter coats (Feith, 2018), soiled living spaces, access problems for visitors, ambient sewage odours and increasingly intrusive and humiliating strip searches performed in front of other women prisoners, "abusive guards" (Feith, 2018), and limited access to medical services and especially to mental health services (Nadeau, 2018; Feith, 2018). June 2018 marked the birth of the Coalition for the Action and Surveillance of Women's Incarceration in Québec, a body that emerged from Québec's Civil Liberties Union. One of its first advocacy engagements comprised a request to compel the Québec Minister of Public Safety to render public a report of its working committee on women's prison conditions at Leclerc, itself the result of public pressures (Dauphin-Johnson, 2018).

In 2019, Jean-François Nadeau, as well as other Québec journalists, reported on an application for an injunction filed on January 31 at

---

21. Lawyers representing women incarcerated at the Leclerc prison, as well as community organizations that deliver programs in the prison, confirm the prison conditions reported by women prisoners, notably that the brownish water was deemed unsafe for consumption and that women prisoners are "asked to let it run for ten minutes until it becomes clear" (Feith, 2018).

the Saint-Jérôme Courthouse by prison lawyer Mélanie Martel on behalf of two women incarcerated at the Leclerc prison, one of whom was 71 years old and had mobility impairments (Radio-Canada, 2019). Injunctions are exceptional judicial measures aimed at allowing citizens to assert their rights by "directing a person or, in the case of a corporation, partnership or association or other unincorporated association, its officers or representatives, not to do or to cease doing a particular thing or act" (Québec Civil Procedure Code).[22] In Québec, the Superior Court is the only tribunal empowered to hear injunctions (s. 33).

The March 31, 2019, request for an injunction targeted the deterioration of women's prison conditions and aimed, specifically, at compelling the Leclerc prison to improve the conditions for the two plaintiffs. The latter invoked problems such as the lack of heating, difficult access to health care, questionable drinking water, lack of cleanliness, verbal abuse by correctional staff, access to showers and strip searches conducted outside acceptable standards (Nadeau, 2019; Radio-Canada, 2019; Hébert, 2019).

The injunction was supported by Québec's Civil Liberties Union, the Women's Federation, and the Women's Centre of the City of Laval (Groguhé, 2019). It followed a May 10, 2016, request to the Ministry of Public Safety to authorize an independent observation mission into the Leclerc prison. This request was formulated by the Québec Women's Federation and the Civil Liberties Union, two reliable and independent community organizations aimed at collective rights advocacy. Seventeen days later, the Ministry's cabinet director refused the request, invoking security reasons and specifying that improvements had been made in the prison (Alter-Justice, 2016).

Yet these improvements did not address the more systemic problems encountered at Leclerc, such as the gender-mixed vocation of the prison, the shortage of correctional personnel or the traditional correctional architecture and approach of a high security prison originally designated for men, which are all deemed inadequate for women (Alter-Justice, 2016). I argue that such systemic hindrances are in line with a dominant locked-in correctional path.

---

22. *Québec Civil Procedure Code*, c. C-25.01, s. 509-515, https://www.legisQuebec.gouv. qc.ca/fr/document/lc/C-25.01?langCont=fr#ga:l_vi-gb:l_i-h1, accessed March 10, 2022.

The injunction also followed a letter sent on December 10, 2018, to Québec's new Minister of Public Safety, Geneviève Guilbault, by the Civil Liberties Union to discuss women prisoners' apprehensions. The advocacy group asked "for an immediate intervention to get women out of this place that is totally unsuitable on a human, architectural and penological front" (Feith, 2018). This letter remained unanswered (Hébert, 2019), which signals a need for improved government transparency. Lastly, the injunction followed two other requests. The first was sent to the Québec Ombudsman, requesting that it open an emergency file to get the women out of the Leclerc prison. The second request was sent to the United Nations' Committee against Torture (TVA Nouvelles, 2018), urging it to intervene considering the scale of the problems, the seriousness of women's rights violations and the inaction of the Québec authorities. Indeed, the Ministry of Public Safety 1) denied the existence of the said problems, "apart from the possible presence of mice for which exterminators had been hired"; 2) left unrequited a request made by the Leclerc mobilization committee of the Women's Centre of the City of Laval; 3) and remained silent vis-à-vis the extensive media coverage of the situation (Groguhé, 2019).

On January 31, 2019, Québec Superior Court Justice Paul Mayer refused to grant the injunction, arguing that the courts are not the appropriate forum to resolve such issues, an opinion echoed by Québec correctional authorities, who reckon that a complaint to the Ministry of Public Safety would be a more direct conduit for such grievances (Radio-Canada, 2019). However, Justice Mayer recognized that the situation at the Leclerc prison was "extremely important and urgent" (Hébert, 2019) and, as such, could not be fully resolved at the preliminary stage of an interlocutory injunction, since such injunctions, when obtained, are effective only for a limited period. He proposed instead to use an accelerated court procedure which consists in going directly to the permanent injunction (Hébert, 2019), which, in principle, would enshrine the rights of the two women incarcerated at Leclerc definitively.

That same year, in a press release, Alexandre Leduc, member of the National Assembly for Hochelaga-Maisonneuve and person responsible for Public Safety for the Québec Solidaire political party, stated that "the Québec Civil Liberties Union, which has been working on the file for a long time, speaks of a quasi-humanitarian crisis. Here, in 2019, in the Laval area!" (Aile parlementaire de Québec Solidaire, 2019). Further expressing his astonishment, Leduc added that, "in 2019, it is something that is quite surreal" (La Presse canadienne, 2019).

The year 2020 marked the advent of the COVID-19 pandemic which killed over seven million human beings across the planet, with the United States, Brazil, and India being the countries mourning the most (Mathieu et al., 2022). In Canada, the COVID pandemic caused over 50,000 deaths, and created havoc in institutions such as community hospitals, long-term care hospitals, and seniors' residences. Prisons were not spared, since they are essentially made to prevent people from escaping, not to prevent viruses from entering the premises. As of January 30, 2023, the Canadian federal correctional authorities reported 7,648 positive cases and 6 deaths since the outbreak of the pandemic in 2020, with 95 positive cases at the federal prison designated for women located in Joliette, Québec.[23] As of March 11, 2020, Québec provincial prisons reported 2,395 cases and 2 deaths since 2020, with 16 women testing positive at the Women's Unit of the Québec Detention Centre and 139 women testing positive at the Leclerc prison.[24] Data updated in mid-January 2022 confirmed that, since the outset of the pandemic, 7 employees of the Women's Unit of the Québec Detention Centre and 79 employees of the Leclerc prison had contracted COVID-19.[25]

Thus, in 2020, media reports of prison conditions at the Leclerc prison became few and far between, and centred essentially on reminders of the persistence of "deplorable" prison conditions since 2016 (Rédaction Laval, 2020a), or on symptomatic women being kept 24 hours a day in individual segregation cells for 14 consecutive days (Drainville, 2020). Media also reported on requests by the Québec Civil Liberties Union to release ageing or ill prisoners, those serving intermittent (weekend) sentences or serving less than three-month

---

23. https://www.canada.ca/en/correctional-service/campaigns/covid-19/inmate-testing. html, accessed January 31, 2023.
24. https://www.quebec.ca/en/health/health-issues/a-z/2019-coronavirus/situation-coronavirus-in-quebec/situation-covid-19-correctional-facility, accessed March 11, 2022.
25. Ibid.

sentences, and pregnant women to counter the proliferation of COVID-19 in Québec prisons including the Leclerc prison (Rédaction Laval, 2020b). One radio show discussed women's fear of COVID-19, notably those employed at the Leclerc prison laundry used as one of Montréal's regional laundries serving facilities such as community hospitals and long-term care hospitals (where most COVID-related deaths were recorded at the time). In the prison laundry, women prisoners were responsible for cleaning human dejections of potentially COVID-infected persons via bedsheets, washcloths, protective gowns for hospital personnel, etc. (Drainville, 2020).

In 2021, media stories reiterated the recurrence of strip searches during which women were forced to take tampons out in front of guards and, at times, to open the lips of their vagina wider each time they were submitted to a strip search (Nadeau, 2021a). Journalist Jean-François Nadeau added that strip searches are experienced as particularly humiliating for transgender women at the prison. In addition to the above-mentioned infringements of human dignity, women still live in deficient sanitary conditions at Leclerc, as evidenced by white worms in the showers, vermin, black flies, lack of heat in the winter, and a shortage of basic hygiene products such as sanitary pads (Nadeau, 2021a). Brown drinking water was still a problem in 2021, a problem to which incarcerated women tried to bring attention in a 2020 collective letter denouncing incidents of nausea, diarrhea, and skin rashes among them, "cloudy" drinking water that "even the staff does not drink . . . they have bottles" (CDEACF, 2020: 1).

Finally, Nadeau mentioned recurrent lockdowns, and added that, partly because of such upsetting conditions, an increase in self-mutilations and attempted suicides was noted at the Leclerc prison. Five suicides had been recorded at that prison since the women's transfer in 2016 (Nadeau, 2021b). As mentioned already, 71% of women incarcerated in Québec's provincial prisons are serving short sentences of approximately 28 days, and they are most frequently found guilty of failure to comply with a probation order, failure to comply with a recognizance or possession of drugs for the purpose of trafficking (Québec, 2020b). Women prisoners at the Leclerc prison tend to be found guilty of what the late Université du Québec à Montréal Law professor, Lucie Lemonde, referred to as "survival crimes," that is poverty-induced crimes such as minor thefts or drug-possession charges (Feith, 2018).

In March 2022, six years after the women's initial transfer to the dilapidated Leclerc prison, Figarol and Descôteaux condemned in *Le Devoir* the still dilapidated physical state of the prison: "Asbestos, mould, vermin, water infiltration, defective heating, stale air, clogged toilets, dirty showers, brown water, cold air coming in through the gaps in the windows, lack of mosquito nets and the presence of bedbugs." They also condemned the disrespectful comportments and attitudes of the surveillance staff such as:

> excessive and humiliating strip searches, multiple remarks and sexist behaviours, contemptuous language, physical threats, medication difficult to obtain, insufficient clothing and hygiene products, exaggerated recourse to confinement, laborious access to adequate medical care, deprivation of outings in the courtyard, repeated cancellations of [in person] visits and [remote] visits, in particular those planned for Christmas and Mother's Day, due to lack of personnel.

Let us recall that women's imprisonment at the Leclerc prison was to be a temporary solution. Six years later, we must admit that the provisional is becoming permanent and that deleterious prison conditions remain the daily lot of women prisoners even though multiple-source voices have exposed in chorus such situations for over one hundred years in Canada.

The *Creating Choices* feminist correctional philosophy, as a critical juncture, took correctional authorities on an alternative path in terms of women's prisoning. I argue that the planned construction of a new provincial prison designated for women in Québec carries the potential of becoming another critical juncture that could take correctional authorities on a historical trajectory of change that diverts from the path-dependent organizational logic. Although in this instance decarceration or abolition do not appear to be options on the table, it remains that designing a new prison carries a potential for imagining a women-centred correctional philosophy. However, as critical junctures are not foreseeable (Mahoney, 2000; Pierson, 2000), it remains to be seen whether the new prison, as a planned (not accidental) occurrence, will be analyzed as a game-changer, a triggering event holding the potential to reverse the initial self-reinforcing institutional arrangements of prisoning women in men-derived prison designs and programming.

As Figure 1 suggests, federal and provincial corrections do not operate in a silo. Interconnections exist. For example, the Task Force on Federally Sentenced Women was instituted on a shared participation of the voluntary sector, notably the participation of the Canadian Association of Elizabeth Fry Societies (CAEFS) and the Native Women's Association of Canada (NWAC). This shared participation in such a significant policy endeavour sent two signals. Firstly, it indicated to the provinces that women's prisoning was resolutely on the national correctional agenda. Secondly, it intimated that the work of the task force could have an impact on women's prisoning processes in the provinces, especially on provincial governments' acknowledgment of local branches of CAEFS and NWAC (Hayman, 2006).

Meticulous rather than haphazard governmental planning of the Tanguay women's transfer to the Leclerc prison would have necessitated the active involvement of the voluntary sector, especially that of organizations like the Société Elizabeth Fry du Québec, which possesses a solid reputation of over four decades in advocacy and service delivery to women in conflict with the law to facilitate their return to the community. Yet, over 25 years after the Task Force on Federally Sentenced Women signalled to provincial governments the recognition of provincial branches of the Canadian Association of Elizabeth Fry Societies (CAEFS) and the Native Women's Association of Canada (NWAC), potentially impacting on women's prisoning processes in the provinces, the Société Elizabeth Fry du Québec was sidelined during the planning phase of the women's transfer to Leclerc prison. It then had little option but to join a chorus of voices including prison volunteers, the Association des religieuses pour les droits des femmes, the Association des services de réhabilitation sociale du Québec, the Association des avocats et avocates de Montréal, the Association des avocats et avocates en droit carcéral du Québec, Femmes autochtones du Québec, Alter-Justice, Stella, Continuité Famille auprès des détenus, the Coalition for Action and Monitoring on Women's Incarceration in Québec, the Civil Liberties Union, the Women's Federation of Québec (Messier, 2016), and the media in multiple public outcries about the transfer of Tanguay women to the Leclerc facility. It appears that Québec prison services had not seized the federal task force's signals. According to political scientist

Paul Pierson (2000: 260), "actors who operate in a social context of high complexity and opacity [such as Canadian and Québec correctional services] are heavily biased in the way they filter information into existing 'mental maps.' Confirming information tends to be incorporated, and disconfirming information is filtered out."

If acted upon as best as Québec correctional services could with the information available at the time, the women's transfer to Leclerc could be considered an unavoidable mistake. With hindsight, one could reasonably describe the outcome as efficient. However, a plethora of government reports exist which, throughout the 20th century, criticized the federal correctional system for its failure to consider alternative options to women's prisoning at Kingston's Prison for Women. Some of these reports also criticized the *Creating Choices* vision. In this light, one cannot intelligibly argue that Québec correctional services acted upon the women's transfer to Leclerc as best it could, especially with the information available at the time, information that had been mounting for over a century. One could oppose the argument that federal and provincial corrections are jurisdictionally impermeable to one another and work in a silo, rarely influencing one another. Thus, what happens in Québec's prisoning of women is independent from women's prisoning at the federal level, and vice versa. This could not be further from reality.

Although it is beyond the scope of this book to document the porous boundaries between federal and provincial corrections, let me bring to attention a few existing situations and practices that tend to support such porosity. The first are the signals that the federal government sent to the provinces by establishing the Task Force on Federally Sentenced Women, which delivered the *Creating Choices* report in 1990. As discussed above, it signalled to the provinces that women's prisoning was on the national correctional agenda. More relevant to my argument, it also signalled that the work of the federal task force could guide women's prisoning processes at the provincial level. Specifically, the work of the task force could guide provincial governments in their recognition of local branches of the two main voluntary sector organizations invited to sit on the task force, the Canadian Association of Elizabeth Fry Societies, and the Native Women's Association of Canada (Hayman, 2006).

The second situation, confirmed by one jurist employed as commissioner at the Québec Parole Board, is that the federal law on parole provides provincial board commissioners with criteria to assess the quantity and quality of conditions of release.[26] Hence, federal laws provide a relevant backdrop on which to anchor provincial parole decisions. Thirdly, there exists a national correctional network in the form of a consultation table of all Deputy Ministers of Corrections in Canada (federal and provincial) that meets once a year to share best practices.

Moreover, in a discussion I had on May 20, 2021, with a researcher employed at the Québec correctional directorate, I was informed that whenever employees of Québec's correctional directorate require information, studies, or know-how, they "search Correctional Service Canada's internet portal." In a similar vein, high-ranking officials and in-house researchers of corrections departments are regularly seen at scholarly or practitioner conferences, where they encounter emerging theories, practices, and innovation. The above-mentioned practices are illuminating examples of the permeability of correctional organizations in Canada despite the jurisdictional cut between federal and provincial services.

The women's precipitated transfer to Leclerc was thus an avoidable mistake, the outcome of which was largely inefficient and, most of all, constitutes a considerable drama—and a shame on how Québec treats women prisoners. Within path dependence approaches, learning effects, as one of the documented self-reinforcing mechanisms to path formation, hold that "the more often an operation is performed, the more efficiency will be achieved when operating subsequent iterations . . . and the more attractive the chosen solution becomes, due to accumulated skills and decreasing costs the less attractive it is to switch to new learning sites" (Schreyögg and Sydow, 2011: 325). It is safe to assume that Québec's correctional system, therefore, lost its original elasticity of the preformation phase, and remains enclosed in path stabilization that reproduces punitive, inefficient, and inhumane prisoning solutions in the form of systemic violence against women prisoners.

As a further example of the path dependence of women's prisoning in Québec, it is interesting to look at Québec Public Safety's 2019-2023

---

26. Meeting between Québec Parole Board commissioners and criminology faculty at Université Laval about possible collaborations (May 2021).

Strategic Plan (Québec, 2021), in which it spoke little of imprisoned women apart from objective #2.2 (p. 19) which targets support measures in prison.

> Over the next few years, women and Aboriginals will be given special attention. An evaluation of the participants' learning will be carried out annually for two support measures, one for women and the other specific to Aboriginal people. These evaluations will make it possible to improve the support offered according to the particular needs of these clienteles.

The 2019-2023 Strategic Plan makes no mention of what the "particular needs" of women may be, especially following several years of women being incarcerated at the Leclerc prison under dire conditions. Although women victimized by crime occupy a considerable portion of the narrative on women within the government's 2019-2023 Strategic Plan (with five out of seven mentions), women prisoners are not featured, nor do they appear in the Ministry's performance indicators of objective #2.2[27] or in any other strategic objectives (Québec, 2021: 21). By advancing that one of Public Safety's objectives consists in the improvement of support measures for Indigenous peoples and women in prison, the Québec government is sending the message that it plans to follow the dominant path of women's prisoning.

Similarly, the 2019-2023 Strategic Plan appears to follow a similar path to the one adopted previously in Québec's 2017-2021 Strategic Plan (Québec, 2018b), in which women's prisoning was all but ignored in terms of strategic planning. One notable exception to such invisibility is that of objective #2.1 which was geared, at the time, to improving services to women and persons diagnosed with mental health problems by assessing "current program offerings and reviewing the ways in which they intervene with these clienteles" (p. 17).

Historically, penal punishment has served as a form of revenge or retribution, to redress or compensate for wrongdoing, to deter individuals from committing other acts of transgression or dissuade communities from ever engaging in criminalized activities, to transform human beings, or to ensure public order. In terms of praxis, penal

---

27. The performance indicators for objective #2.2 are: increase in the proportion of assessments completed within the established timeframes; increase in the number of accompaniment programs aimed at specific clienteles; increase in the number of incarcerated individuals who have completed the Parcours program; decrease in the number of transfers between detention facilities (Québec, 2021: 20).

punishment has taken several forms, including corporal punishment, deprivation of freedom, and more recently, psychological cure. It is safe to say that, regardless of the punitive aims that have become fashionable at various periods of time in human history, penal punishment has spawned and continues to generate heated debates. Punitive ideals are tenacious through time. Within a path dependence perspective, we could argue that punitive ideals fall victims to "cognitive stickiness" discussed earlier in the book (Larason Schneider, 2006: 466), that is, modes of reasoning, or lines of thought that tend to stick and from which it is painstaking to extricate oneself (van Vugt and Broers, 2016). Cognitive stickiness holds the power to drive decisions in the same direction through many, even disperse, institutional locales.

Borrowing from American cultural theorist Lauren Berlant, I would argue that, similarly to "a person, a thing, an institution, a text, a norm, a bunch of cells, smells, a good idea," penal punishment comprises a "cluster of promises" (Berlant, 2010: 93). Proximity to this cluster of promises means closeness to the constellation of things that the object promises. In other words, humans and human groups become attached to objects, values, institutions, ideals for their potentialities. Hence, in an affective manner, they become endurably and optimistically attached. This optimism is depicted by Berlant as "cruel optimism," that is, "a relation of attachment to compromised conditions of possibility whose realization is discovered either to be *im*possible, sheer fantasy, or *too* possible, and toxic" (p. 94, italics in text). This optimism is characterized as cruel in the sense that human beings or groupings that have penal punitive ideals within their affective habitus (e.g., punitivity as a moral value) might not withstand well the loss of such ideals even if these ideals' manifestations may threaten their own welfare. This is because, according to Berlant (2010: 94), the endurance of such punitive ideals may provide "something of a continuity of the subject's sense of what it means to keep on living and to look forward to being in the world."

The concept of cruel optimism makes it possible to grapple with what appears to be a bit mysterious, on the surface, about the sustainment of affective attachments to problematic objects. A similar argument may be offered about punitive ideals which, on the one hand, garner individual and collective re-investments and which, on the other, are projected onto as societies look forward into the future. Punitive ideals, then, may stem from unstated fears of loss of what such ideals may offer, in terms of both empowering and incapacitating power. Hence, the path-dependent continuity of punitive approaches through history may well find one of its sources in the cultural and emotional habitus of social groups.

CHAPTER 5

Imagining a Scenario Without Prisons

I started this book by asking the following question, which stemmed from the data amassed as part of the Prison Transparency Project: How is it possible that, in the 21st century, after more than a hundred years of periodic denunciation of the dire living conditions in prisons designated for women in Canada, Québec women still endure similar appalling prison conditions in the Leclerc prison? Criticisms of prisons and proposals for reform of the penal system are not recent phenomena. Scholarship in criminology, social work, law and society, architecture, human geography, and philosophy to name a few, has long documented the prison's persistence, but few scholars have made it their central point of focus. Path dependence arguments provide helpful insights for apprehending the multifaceted blend of stability and spurts of transformation that surround many sociopolitical processes such as the prisoning of women. Drawing from the path dependence approach, I attempted to identify how imprisoned women's transfer from one deteriorated prison designated for women to another deteriorated prison designated for men—with the prison conditions exposed earlier—could have happened in the early 21st century despite Canada's century-long history of reports, inquiries, and task forces all condemning prison conditions for women. What have we learned about women's imprisonment in this case study? Path dependence scholarship helped identify that contemporary prisoning behaviour or processes may be constrained by an acceptance of past organizational actions or decisions as the norm.

This book hopes to shed some light on the contribution of path dependence approaches in comprehending the persistence of inhumane conditions in the process of prisoning women in Québec. While this book does not attempt to empirically test path dependence arguments through conventional hypothetico-deductive reasoning, I borrowed ideas and concepts from other disciplines such as economics, political science, and criminal justice that may open discussion among students of the prison on how to better elucidate the persistence of prisons despite past failures. As a social praxis device, my study also provides analytical tools that may be useful in the promotion of decarceration or abolition policies. In addition, these same analytical tools shed supplementary light on correctional practices and institutions that regrettably remain entrenched in patriarchal thought. The conceptual schema of path dependence extends the well-documented "institutional turn" within feminist theories, especially in political science (Krook and Mckay, 2011: 2), whereby scholarship and advocacy have championed the advancement and institutionalization of gender equality as social and political goals. However, early feminist institutionalism may not have taken sufficient notice of mezzo-level institutions and organizations as generating gender inequalities as well as multifarious obstacles to gender mainstreaming (i.e., making allowance for gender in policy and institutional growth), as Krook and Mckay (2011: 2) explain below.

> Early feminist work on gender and institutions, however, generally overlooked the role of institutional processes and practices in reinforcing and reproducing gender inequality (Witz and Savage 1992). More specifically, the causes of gender inequality were understood to exist at the macro-level, rooted in a stratifying system or structure known as "patriarchy." Institutions and organizations, therefore, were not the direct cause of inequality in, and of themselves.

Path dependence approaches instruct that organizations, such as correctional authorities in the case at hand, tend to have "patternized" weights. Such weights over time are instigated by locking into place particular gender-related rules and conventions that may prevent institutional or organizational redesign, based on gender mainstreaming, for example. Path dependence, thus, provides additional tools and frameworks to better comprehend in what circumstances historic gender notions and power inequalities become resilient in political, institutional, and often organizational life.

In sum, the rich conceptual schema proposed by path dependence scholarship offers a complementary assortment of theoretical constructs to the extant arsenal of theoretical and experiential frameworks. Many of these, including path dependence concepts, could be invited in scholarly, political, or advocacy conversations that challenge a penal or prisoning framework. By attending to micro-level diffusion processes as well as macro-level institutional arrangements that may mould decision-making, path dependence perspectives offer a view that is more transparent into the often-impenetrable drive to imprison. Bringing to light opaque institutional or organizational processes contributes to a serious rethinking of penal practices by providing argumentative tools and identifying objects for political action and community advocacy.

There are limits to path dependence ideas. One is the danger that such ideas may convey an overly static perception of the social world (Pierson, 2000) and offer a quasi-deterministic view of the dominant path, whereby all further actions are guaranteed to replicate the path (Schreyögg and Sydow, 2011). However, path dependence analyses need not imply that a particular option or alternative is everlastingly locked in following the same self-reinforcing trajectory. Even though continuities are a marked characteristic of the social world, change does happen but, according to Pierson (2000), it is change constrained by often obstinate organizational or institutional policies and practices. In this train of thought, the intentions and efforts of penal reformers may be seen as repeatedly thwarted by more structural factors—such as economic or bureaucratic forces—often considered to be the prime movers of history (McMahon, 1992). However, several path dependence perspectives in economics (e.g., Martin and Sunley, 2006), history (e.g., Mahoney, 2000), political science (e.g., Collier and Collier, 1991; Thelen, 1999; Pierson, 2000), organizational studies (e.g., Garud, Kumaraswany and Karnoe, 2010) or criminal justice reform (Larason Schneider, 2006; Thorpe, 2015; Beckett et. al., 2018; Rubin, 2019b) do not deny the importance of human agency in the making of a path-dependent process.

For example, organizational approaches to path dependence offer a more nuanced conception of lock-ins than offered within economics, since organizations' processes are social in character and, consequently, are more complex and equivocal in nature. For example, Schreyögg and Sydow (2011) allow for some variation in the third and final "lock-in" phase of path formation process. To these authors, in the extreme form of lock-in—especially as related to technological solutions—"the dominant pattern gains deterministic character; all further decisions or actions are bound to replicate the path" (p. 325). However, because organizational contexts, such as the delivery of correctional services, are social and ambiguous, a less deterministic form of lock-in is in order. Similarly to other path dependence scholars, such as Thelen (1999), Pierson (2000) and Thrane, Blaabjerg and Møller (2010) to name a few, Schreyögg and Sydow (2011) argue that the lock-in process of path dependence in organizational contexts allows a "corridor" (p. 325) for possible variations. This cultivates prospects for developing progressive penal politics. Another example of human agency intervening in the making of path-dependent processes is the perspective developed by political scientist Robert Cox (2004:207). Using an ideational perspective, Cox formulated the path dependence of ideas as the "tendency to hold on to comfortable values in a changing world," that is, the shared and strong engagement toward staple values and ideas of a policy model (such as the Auburn system model). Cox argued that such attachment tends to undergird policy leaders' decisions about the appropriateness of diverse policy options, since some options will be considered more suitable than others depending on how bonded they appear to highly shared core values and ideas. Imprisonment is one such shared value and idea. For the moment, the persistent faith in the prison's ability to achieve results regardless of past and contemporary disappointments seems solidly ingrained in the legitimacy of the enduring myth of the reformative aim of prisons, a myth that decision-makers and embedded actors tend to promote (Rubin, 2019b).

Not only do path dependence approaches have certain theoretical limitations, but this book in and of itself also has notable limits. For example, the book does not analyze, or try to explain, some preoccupying trends within criminal justice. Such is the case of the targeting of racialized groups within criminal justice as well as the growing rates of women's incarceration, notably in the Global North (i.e., Chéné and Chouinard, 2018; Chéné, 2020; Québec, 2020a; Correctional Investigator Canada, 2019; Marques and Monchalin, 2020; Jeffries and Newbold, 2016; McIvor, 2010). These phenomena are disquieting, and merit sustained and funded scholarly efforts to shed light on troubling trends which, in essence, originate from organizations other than the prison, such as the police, the judiciary, and the legislative process.

The growing incarceration rates of women derive from early encounters with the criminal justice system, for example via sentencing practices, policies, and decisions made within the courts. However, one of prison's objectives is to manage the prison sentences given by judges in criminal courts, and the courts are not the target of this book. Another important source of the growing incarceration rates of women is found at the far end of the criminal justice system, for example via early and conditional prison release (i.e., parole, statutory release, suspensions, revocations). Indeed, increases or reductions in the number of parole grant rates as well as conservative or liberal supervisory policies and practices may affect women's incarceration rates. Here again, parole boards are not the target of this book. To avoid diluting the problem, this book addresses the persistence of the prison itself, not its ins (courts) and outs (early release programs). However, I recognize that early release decisions are in part tributary to correctional authorities' analyses and reports of women prisoners' progress (or lack thereof) through participation in programs, as well as of their general comportment in the prison.

A similar argument may be made about the targeting of racialized groups. The documented over-representation of certain racialized groups in prison stems from court practices, as well as from the Parole Board of Canada's conditional release practices and decisions that may spawn larger denial rates of early release toward members of racialized groups. However, this book develops an organizational analysis of prison's practices, policies, and decisions as they pertain specifically to the persistence of prisons through time and space. Thus, at the end of this book, path dependence approaches could also shed stimulating theoretical light on the growing incarceration rates of women in Canada and elsewhere. For example, the path dependence concept of "critical juncture" could be useful in bringing into light the advent of a possible turning point or triggering event that may have participated in creating a bifurcation in the historical path trajectory of imprisoning few women toward imprisoning larger numbers of women. Similarly, since the targeting of women from racialized groups is not the focus of this book, the relevance or usefulness of path dependence perspectives to inform the historical trajectories of such a deleterious phenomenon remains an open question to be investigated in future research.

There is no conclusion to this book as to whether Québec's correctional directorate remains on the same path and might or might not choose to convert "emergent ideas into action [or] emergent actions into ideas" (Garud, Kumaraswany and Karnoe, 2010: 762). The future new prison designated for women in Québec could be an opportunity to thread on or bifurcate toward a different path despite the long-established self-reinforcing processes that have become secured in the stabilized (locked-in) path. One thing is certain, though, women's prisoning in the Leclerc prison is a dismal interlude, since Québec's Minister of Public Safety confirmed to me in August 2021 that ministerial discussions about the construction of a new prison "were at the planning stage," but that it "would take a while" before an actual building is standing.

At the time of writing, the Leclerc women have been enduring inhumane prison conditions since 2016, conditions that have been observed by a constellation of actors—such as prison volunteers and community organizations—and documented in the media and by the Prison Transparency Project. Québec's Public Safety Minister, Geneviève Guilbault, contested this by asking whether I had "actually seen human rights abuse," since she had sent emissaries as well as the Québec Ombudsman to the Leclerc prison, both of whom found little to nothing. This is surprising, since, as discussed earlier, in 2016—the year of the women's transfer to Leclerc—the Québec Ombudsman interceded following the deficient planning of the women's transfer, which spawned challenging prison conditions such as a lack of access to sanitary facilities for women (as a former men's prison, Leclerc had urinals), especially for women serving intermittent (weekend) sentences. Challenging prison conditions also included a lack of access to hygiene products and personal effects upon admission and release, low privacy spaces in which to perform strip searches, etc. (Québec Ombudsman, 2016).

It is also surprising, since in its 2019-2020 annual report (p. 96), the Québec Ombudsman demanded that the Ministry consider the needs of women, as provided for in the United Nations Rules for the Treatment of Women Prisoners and Non-custodial Measures for Women Offenders (Bangkok Rules) (United Nations, 2010). Such a demand suggests that women's prison conditions (at Leclerc and in other provincial prisons) still do not meet international standards.

Historically, in Canada, women prisoners have been what Canadian scholars Ellen Adelberg and Claudia Currie (1987) aptly characterized as "too few to count," that is, too few to justify the expense of dedicating sufficient correctional infrastructures to provide the women with local rather than centralized accommodation, as well as gender-sensitive programming and services. It remains to be seen whether the Ministry will choose to reactivate the dormant historical alternative proposed in *Creating Choices* to begin a process of trans-forming an antiquated, ill-adapted prisoning mode, or whether it will choose to walk the well-trodden path. The data analyzed in this book highlight the possibility that, in terms of corrections, women continue to be too few to matter.

Research shows that victimization and ensuing distress, as well as numerous forms of subjugation and marginalization, participate in women's criminalization in many cases (Turnbull and Hannah-Moffat, 2009; Balfour and Comack, 2014; Monchalin, 2016; Comack 2018). Research also shows that women tend to be found guilty of "survival" crimes: criminalized actions related to their marginalized status stem-ming from their poverty, modest educational assets, Indigenous descent, unsound residential situations, experiences of family violence, substance use, mental health issues, etc. (Sheehan and Trotter, 2018). For women, such vulnerabilities bring on social exclusion, which manifests itself in multifarious ways via social assistance cheques, homelessness, psychiatric hospitalizations, and imprisonment.

Senior managers and prison personnel have little choice but to admit, classify, and safely house the condemned sent to them by judges presiding in criminal courts. They offer correctional programs and organize daily prison regimes that they believe are best suited to pris-oners' characteristics and needs. However, they must do so within annual budgets allocated by governmental authorities. They must also do so within the confines of the prison as a secured institution meant to keep prisoners from escaping and, thus, grounded on security constraints, many of which prevent the implementation of prison reforms. In addition, senior managers may be constrained by a conscious or unconscious "call" to follow the main path of penal thinking and practices as if they had little leeway to engage in alternative paths.

I further inquired about the possibility for the Ministry to consider alternative options to women's incarceration, since the century-old scholarly literature concludes that women's criminalization profile seldom justifies imprisonment. As an example, women's incarceration profile shows that, in 2018-2019, the three most frequent crimes for which Québec women were declared guilty and sentenced to prison were possession of drugs for the purpose of trafficking, failure to comply with a probation order, and omission to comply with an undertaking. In 2018-2019, 2,025 women were incarcerated in Québec's provincial prisons, 71% of them serving short sentences of approximately 28 days. In general, single, undereducated, Inuit women and women living alone have significantly higher rates of incarceration. Most of the women serving a long sentence of approximately 133 days were housed at the Leclerc prison in 2018-2019 (Québec, 2020b). Although the Minister believes that ways could be imagined to avoid women's judicialization, especially since we know that most have suffered abuses in the past, she responded nonetheless that "a dedicated infrastructure is needed,"[1] as if, like Garud, Kumaraswany and Karnoe (2010: 763) suggest, "the past, the present and the future are intertwined, with [embedded actors engaged in] determining what portions of the past they would like to mobilize in support of their imagined futures."

By insisting on the "need" for a "dedicated infrastructure" for women prisoners, Ministry officials chose not to mobilize a particular portion of the Ministry's own recent past when Giroux and Frigon (2011: 9), in the Ministry's own 2007-2008 Women's Correctional Profile, argued for the necessity to rethink the need to incarcerate women in provincial prisons. Here again, the "need" for a "dedicated infrastructure" could entail that the Ministry 1) borrow essentially from the past by opting for a modern Auburn-style prison or a prison more in harmony with the principles of Creating Choices; 2) replicate the present by reproducing current prison conditions in the new prison; or 3) choose the future and imagine a "dedicated infrastructure" for women that is not a prison but either satellite apartments, abundant and

---

1.   Personal discussion with Québec Minister of Public Safety, Geneviève Guilbault, September 11, 2021.

well-appointed professional and community services, community treatment centres, multidisciplinary day centres, and the like. It could prove difficult for Québec correctional authorities to select the path ending with option #3, as evidenced by a report produced by a working committee under a partnership agreement between the Québec Ministry of Public Safety and the Société Elizabeth Fry du Québec—the well-established women-centred community organization. Two years after the women's transfer to the Leclerc prison, this committee tabled a 113-page report entitled *Une voix différente* (*A Different Voice*) (2018). I have been able to obtain only a heavily redacted version in which large portions of the report, as well as the names of all committee members and collaborators had been blacked out. Fortunately, these committee members' official professional titles and responsibilities had not been redacted, which made it possible to observe that four out of the five committee members (in addition to the coordinator of the committee) were affiliated with correctional services. Only one committee member came from the Société Elizabeth Fry du Québec. The same may be said of the eleven collaborators, all of whom appeared to be affiliated also with correctional services (e.g., Montréal Detention Centre, Correctional Services, Québec Detention Centre – Women's Unit, Correctional Professional Services Branch, Corrections' Research Division, Assistant Director General of the Montréal Correctional Network, Correctional Professional Services Branch – Female Clients).

Despite stating that "this uprooting [of imprisoned women from Maison Tanguay] has . . . set back, if not annihilated, the 'women's culture' in prison, greatly weakened what was developing within the organization, and raised significant concerns within civil society" (p. 17), the working committee promoted the development of an "innovative new prison infrastructure for women" (p. 33). Later in the report, this innovative infrastructure is promoted as an "intelligent prison" (p. 79), that is an empowering and rehabilitative prison that would use technologies like British Columbia where "nurses can respond to inmates by sending electronic messages. This reduces waste, improves accountability, reduces delays, allows for monitoring and reporting" (p. 79).

This "preliminary scenario" for the new carceral infrastructure (p. 76) would still comprise a security perimeter (Comité de travail, 2018: 77) despite long-standing evidence that a large majority of imprisoned women do not constitute a risk for the community. Based on this preliminary scenario, the new infrastructure would remain a prison, nonetheless. This assumption was confirmed when, in its 2021-2022 annual report, the Québec Ombudsman reiterated that the Leclerc prison was "dilapidated and inadequate" (p. 91), and recommended that the Minister of Public Safety make a "firm decision" (p. 92) before December 31, 2022, on the Québec government's intentions to build a new facility designated for women. On December 19, 2022, 12 days before the Ombudsman's deadline, the latest Public Safety Minister, François Bonnardel, confirmed in a press release that the Québec government would indeed build a "new prison infrastructure" to replace Maison Tanguay. The new prison will have 237 beds and cost nearly $400 million (Agence QMI, 2022). Completion is planned for the summer of 2029, but the prison will open only in 2030, according to the Ministry's projections (Radio-Canada, 2022). Since the decrepit Leclerc prison was to be a temporary solution to the decrepit Maison Tanguay, by the time the new prison opens in 2030, it will have been 14 years of "temporary." It appears that concrete remains the best of solutions, although $400 million is a significant amount of money that could propel a viable alternative to the prisoning of women. Although the press release specified that "the new facility [would be] truly adapted to the reality of incarcerated women" (Agence QMI, 2022), the fact remains that, by concretizing its "preliminary scenario," the Ministry of Public Safety is following the path already laid out. Thus, the "longue durée" through which the prison has been normalized will not have been cracked, doubted, or disputed.

There exists an assortment of veto spaces and moments in political decision-making configurations that provide clout to either foster or obstruct reforms. Prison has become established and standardized to the point where its interrogation may elude significant critical scrutiny, hence the persistence of the prison "becomes a normal state of affairs and diversions from it an odd curiosity" (Kronsell, 2016: 318).

Prison's future is not only meshed with portions of our correctional past, it is also attuned to the contemporary pulse of the population. Women prisoners are an invisible correctional population to which politicians and the public tend to be indifferent; thus, media images are critical in shaping people's understanding of this social issue. Local media analysis confirms a positive bias toward incarcerated women between 2010 and 2020, a bias that may have been borne out of *Unité 9*, a successful television series in 169 episodes broadcast between 2012 and 2019 by Radio-Canada and bought by TV5-Monde network starting in 2013. The series, which depicts the richness and complexity of the world of women in prison, drew average ratings of two million viewers weekly during season 2 (Numeris, 2015), which made it one of the most watched television programs in Québec. Threading away from the classic topics of Québécois television series such as the family, the woman playwright chose to tell an untold story on television after reading the Arbour Report of the Commission of Inquiry into Certain Events at the Prison for Women in Kingston (Caza, 2013).

The storyline revolves around the women prisoners, their loved ones, and the penitentiary staff. Prison conditions mirrored those of real women prisoners as close as possible (subjection, alienation, resistance), while taking into consideration television precepts on coherence, rhythm and tension, twists of the plot, etc. Despite a few improbabilities, the series is plausible. Because of its remarkable ratings, the series is important to the surrounding cultural mood in Québec. However, to fulfill broadcasting requirements to captivate and retain a large audience, the series tended to overrepresent manifestations of violence and abuse in prison, possibly nurturing public prejudice toward prisons.

Such public fascination with incarceration is borne and perpetuated in part by mainstream media. It shapes public opinion and can subdue public debate about some of the worst atrocities that take place in prisons (Jewkes, 2007). However, since *Unité 9* did not overuse stereo-typical depictions and had a strong human side, the series had the potential to become a public "pedagogical tool" (Cousineau and Frigon, 2016: 329) for awareness of lived experiences of detention and human-ization of detainees. With its transformative potential, it provided a voice for marginalized women and generated a capital of sympathy in the population toward imprisoned women. Such sympathy mounted precisely at the time the women were transferred from Maison Tanguay to the Leclerc prison, thus creating a temporal moment where such cultural influences on politics could sway actions and decisions away from a locked-in correctional path. Journalistic accounts analyzed in this book reflect such positive bias toward detained women during the 2010s. Although the broadcast of *Unité 9* ended in 2019, the effect lingers on in the media as headlines continue to condemn prison conditions and to pressure the government to shut down the Leclerc prison: "Pressure to close the Leclerc prison" (*Courriel Laval*, 2019); "The Leclerc prison case will be heard on an expedited basis" (*Métro*, 2019); "The Leclerc prison for women: a 'completely scrap' penitentiary" (*Le Journal de Montréal*, 2019); "Another woman commits suicide at the Leclerc prison in Laval" (*Le Devoir*, 2021); "Misery and contempt for women prisoners at the Leclerc prison" (*Le Devoir*, 2021); "The saga has gone on long enough at Leclerc prison" (*Le Devoir*, 2022).

As per the assumptions undergirding the concept of path dependence, it remains difficult to foresee whether the Québec Ministry of Public Safety will further entrench path stability and model its new prison designated for women on the Auburn prison model (and its derivatives), or whether it will introduce intermediate change, thus engaging in path departure. In December 2022, it became known that the Ministry would not venture into path cessation and further radical transformation of women's corrections as well as paradigmatic change. Ex post analyses will allow the tracing of the paths that the Ministry will consider, and that it will elect in the final instance.

Following Rubin's neo-institutional theory of formal penal change (2019a), to qualify as major penal change, idealized penal models such as the modern prison or *Creating Choices* must benefit from extensive espousal or diffusion. Rubin (2019a) makes it clear that the innovation of a model is insufficient for the model to qualify as major penal change: diffusion remains a crucial key. Yet, to achieve a comprehensive understanding of the significance of formal penal change, scholars must ask whether the model becomes institutionalized, which is what Rubin argues generates widespread diffusion. Diffusion has been documented to be slow, lagging over a few or several decades—notably in the case of adult reformatories (Pisciotta, 1994), probation (Cahalan, 1986) and supermax prisons (Reiter, 2012). Our brief rereading of the history of federal women's prisoning in Canada signals the extensive espousal and diffusion over one century of the Auburn-style modern prison as the preferred institutionalized model, with a short departure toward an alternative path (*Creating Choices*) and a swift return toward the trodden trail.

Provincial women's prisoning in Québec also signals an extensive espousal and diffusion of the Auburn-style modern prison, without any departure yet toward an alternative path. Following Rubin's neo-institutional theory of formal penal change (2019a), because of the paucity of its diffusion in the past three decades, *Creating Choices* cannot amount to a major penal change, since it has not been extensively institutionalized. Consequently, provincial correctional services like Québec's do not appear to have undergone notable pressure to adopt this model—or meet trials to its legitimacy—since it has not developed into an expected form of punishment. For the moment, it remains to be seen whether the 1990 *Creating Choices'* feminist correctional ideals will bear emulations in Québec, or whether prisons as a "regime of truth" that arose over time and dwarfed unconventional ways of socially reacting to women's criminalization will continue to appear as standard and innate, or at least inescapable.

One could argue that my argumentative amalgamation of women's federal and provincial prisons is ill fitted, and that the lack of adoption of the *Creating Choices* ideals by provinces ought not to be presumed to signal the non-institutionalization of *Creating Choices*. In fact, some provinces indeed followed suit and incorporated segments of the feminist and holistic ideals, or federal policies and practices borne out of *Creating Choices*. Following the publication of the *Creating Choices* report, the provincial government of Nova Scotia set up its own task force on women's imprisonment, whose report, *Blueprint for Change* (Nova Scotia, 1992), was modelled on the federal task force that bore *Creating Choices* and claimed the abolition of imprisonment for women serving a provincial sentence of less than two years. Although the Nova Scotia government accepted this recommendation to take sentenced women out of prison and house them in small community residences across the province, it has not been substantiated—quite the contrary. Recently, privacy breaches and the use of disparaging comments related to women imprisoned in one Nova Scotia provincial prison have been under investigation by the police, the Department of Justice and the Information and Privacy Review Officer (Donavan and Currie, 2021). The continued use of segregation, especially related to mental health issues, still fuels local human rights advocacy groups such as the Elizabeth Fry Society Mainland Nova Scotia and the East Coast Prison Justice Society (Jones and Bousquet, 2021).

Similarly, the Ontario provincial government established a Women's Issues Task Force, whose 49-page *Women's Voices, Women's Choices* report was published in 1995. The task force observed "the inappropriateness of incarceration for the majority of provincially sentenced women, the inadequacy of the physical facilities and the dearth of appropriate programs available to women" (Letter to Deputy Solicitor General, June 22, 1994: 1 enclosed in Ontario, 1995). Founding their recommendations on the principle that "incarceration is rarely, if ever, an appropriate placement for women in the provincial correctional system" (Ontario, 1995: 8), members of the task force centred most of their recommendations on the development of a cohesive network of community services for women "in conflict with the law" (Letter, p. 2). It essentially recommended that specific planning programs be implemented to "provide individualized community sentence planning for women who would otherwise be incarcerated" (Ontario, 1995: 15). Yet, at the time of writing, women are still incarcerated in Ontario correctional centres, detention centres, local jails, and correctional treatment centres.[2]

As a result of the above evidence, I would answer that the amalgamation of women's federal and provincial prisons that I sketch in my argument is not imprudent. In Canada, the separation between federal and provincial correctional services is a constitutional anomaly, since all instances build and manage prisons, detain prisoners, deliver correctional programs, and offer progressive release surveillance. As formal structures, prisons are not bound by constitutional dispositions; the 1835 Kingston Penitentiary designated for men was inspired by Auburn-style prisons from the United States, and the *Creating Choices* model was inspired, in part, by one particular prison designated for women in the United States (Bertrand, 1998).

The lack of conclusion of this book is an appeal to all peoples, communities, organizations, and institutions who respect humanity and aspire to see the complete reinstatement of human rights in correctional practices within prisons, or to question the common, uncontested assumption that the prisons—which "contain, and produce, pain" (Liebling, 2004: 462)—are necessary institutions in a safe, democratic

---

2.   https://www.cefso.ca/institutions.html, accessed December 15, 2022.

society. Might we need something like a "George Floyd effect" in corrections against prisoning?

Indeed, George Perry Floyd Jr. was a 46-year-old Black American man who, on May 25, 2020, died at the hands of Derek Chauvin, a Minneapolis, Minnesota, police officer during an arrest after a store clerk suspected Floyd may have used a counterfeit $20 bill. The arrest was captured on video showing Mr. Floyd being handcuffed and immobilized to the ground by Officer Chauvin's knee upon his neck for several minutes, eventually causing asphyxiation. The video generated months of nationwide protests against police brutality and systemic racism. Many believe such a nationwide racial justice movement had not been witnessed since the Civil Rights protests of the 1960s. The four police officers involved were fired and charged with crimes (New York Times, 2021). The so-called "George Floyd effect" is the joining by protestors and advocates of historic racism and social injustice to contemporary instances of police brutality (Buchanan, Quoctrung and Patel, 2020). Protests in this regard were documented in 2020 as well as in 2021. Following the one-year anniversary of George Floyd's murder, the incident had morphed into a year-long, countrywide movement showcasing the greatest mass protests in United States history (Burch et al., 2021).

I end this book by reiterating this essential question: might we need a "George Floyd effect" in corrections against prisoning, particularly women's prisoning?

References

Scholarly references

Acker, Joan (1990), "Hierarchies, jobs, bodies: A theory of gendered organizations," *Gender & Society*, vol. 4, no. 2, p. 139-158.

Adelberg, Ellen, and Claudia Currie (1987), *Too few to count: Canadian women in conflict with the law.* Press Gang Publishers.

Adelberg, Ellen, and Claudia Currie (1993), *In conflict with the law: Women and the Canadian justice system.* Press Gang Publishers.

Adelberg, Ellen, and Carol Laprairie (1985), *Répertoire canadien des programmes et des services destinés aux femmes ayant des démêlés avec la justice.* Ministère du Solliciteur général.

Alter-Justice (2016), "La FFQ et la LDL entendent mener une mission d'observation," https://www.alterjustice.org/dossiers/articles/160706-prison-leclerc.html, accessed 17 February, 2021.

Anonymous. (1977). *A summary of analysis of some major inquiries on corrections, 1938-1977.* Correctional Service Canada.

Aoki, Masahiko (2007), "Endogenizing institutions and institutional changes," *Journal of Institutional Economics*, vol. 3, no. 1, p. 1-31.

Arthur, W. Brian (1989), "Competing technologies, increasing returns, and lock-in by historical events," *Economic Journal*, vol. 99, p. 116-131.

Arthur, W. Brian (1994), *Increasing returns and path dependency in the economy.* University of Michigan Press.

Audesse, Alexandre, and Joane Martel (2020), "L'architecture singulière du populisme pénal," *Champ pénal/Penal Field*, vol. 19, doi.org/10.4000/champpenal.11931.

Balfour, Gillian, and Elizabeth Comack (eds.) (2014), *Criminalizing women: Gender and (in)justice in neo-liberal times*, second edition. Fernwood Publishing.

Balfour, Gillian, and Joane Martel (2018), "Critical prison research and university research ethics boards: Homogenization of inquiry and policing of knowledge," *Oñati Socio-Legal Series*, vol. 8, no. 2, p. 225-246.

Bandyopadhyay, Mahuya (2007), "Reform and everyday practice: Some issues of prison governance," *Contributions to Indian Sociology*, vol. 41, no. 3, p. 387-416.

Baron, James N., Michael T. Hannan, and Diane M. Burton (1999), "Building the iron cage: Determinants of managerial intensity in the early years of organizations," *American Sociological Review*, vol. 64, no. 4, p. 527-547.

Baron, James N., Michael T. Hannan, Greta Hsu, and Ozgecan Kocak (2007), "In the company of women: Gender inequality and the logic of bureaucracy in start-up firms," *Work and Occupations*, vol. 34, no. 1, p. 35-66.

Beckett, Katherine, Lindsey Beach, Emily Knaphus, and Anna Reosti (2018), "US criminal justice policy and practice in the twenty-first century: Toward the end of mass incarceration?" *Law & Policy*, vol. 40, no. 4, p. 321-345.

Beckett, Katherine, Anna Reosti, and Emily Knaphus (2016), "The end of an era? Understanding the contradictions of criminal justice reform," *ANNALS*, AAPSS, vol. 664, no. 1, p. 238-259.

Berger, Peter, and Thomas Luckmann (1967), *The social construction of reality. A treatise in the sociology of knowledge.* Anchor.

Berlant, Lauren (2010), "Cruel optimism," in Melissa Gregg and Gregory J. Seigworth (eds.), *The affect theory reader.* Duke University Press.

Bertrand, Marie-Andrée (1979), *La femme et le crime.* Les Éditions de l'Aurore.

Bertrand, Marie-Andrée (1998), *Prisons pour femmes.* Éditions du Méridien.

Berzins, Lorraine, and Renée Collette-Carrière (1979), "La femme en prison: un inconvénient social!," *Santé mentale au Québec*, vol. 4, no. 2, p. 87-103.

Beveridge, Fiona, and Jo Shaw (2002), "Introduction: Mainstreaming gender in European public policy," *Feminist Legal Studies*, vol. 10, no. 3-4, p. 209-212.

Beyer, Jürgen (2010), "The same or not the same: On the variety of mechanisms of path dependence," *International Journal of Humanities and Social Sciences*, vol. 4, no. 3, p. 186-196.

Boritch, Helen (1997), *Fallen women. Female crime and criminal justice in Canada.* Nelson.

Boritch, Helen (2001), "Women in prison," in John A. Winterdyk (ed.), *Corrections in Canada: Social reactions to crime.* Pearson Education Canada.

Boyer, Raymond (1966), *Les crimes et les châtiments au Canada Français du XVIIᵉ au XXᵉ siècle*. Cercle du Livre de France.

Brassard, Renée, and Joane Martel (2009), "Trajectoires sociocarcérales des femmes autochtones au Québec: effets de l'incarcération sur l'exclusion sociale," *Criminologie*, vol. 42, no. 2, p. 121-152.

Brodie, Janine (1995), *Politics on the margins: Restructuring and the Canadian women's movement*. Fernwood Publishing.

Brodie, Janine (2009), "Putting gender back in: Women and social policy reform in Canada," in Yasmeen Abu-Laban (ed.), *Gendering the nation-state: Canadian and comparative perspectives*. University of British Columbia Press.

Brunet, Lise (1989), "La situation à la prison Tanguay s'est améliorée mais beaucoup reste à faire," *Femmes et justice*, vol. 5 no. 2, p. 9.

Cadieux, Marie (Director) (2003), *Sentenced to life*, [Documentary: online video]. National Film Board of Canada, Catalogue Number NFB521875, https://www.nfb.ca/film/sentenced_to_life/, accessed March 29, 2022.

Cahalan, Margaret (1986), *Historical corrections statistics in the United States, 1850-1984*. Bureau of Justice Statistics.

Canada (1849), *Report of the Royal Commission to Investigate into the Conduct, Discipline, and Management of the Provincial Penitentiary* (Commissioner, George Brown), Journal of the Legislative Assembly, second session of the third provincial parliament of Canada, vol. 8, https://www.canadiana.ca/view/oocihm.9_00952_8/3?r=0&s=1, accessed April 27, 2021.

Canada (1914), *Report of the Royal Commission of Inquiry on Penitentiaries* (Commissioner, George Milnes MacDonnell). King's Printer.

Canada (1921), *Report on the state and management of the female prison at Kingston Penitentiary* (Commissioner, W.F. Nickle). King's Printer.

Canada (1938), *Report of the Royal Commission to Investigate the Penal System of Canada* (Commissioner, Joseph Archambault). King's Printer.

Canada (1947), *Report of General R.B. Gibson regarding the penitentiary system of Canada* (Commissioner, Ralph Burgess Gibson). King's Printer.

Canada (1956), *Report of a Committee Appointed to Inquire into the Principles and Procedures Followed in the Remission Service of the Department of Justice of Canada* (Chair, Gerald Fauteux). Queen's Printer.

Canada (1969), *Report of the Canadian Committee on Corrections* (Chair, Roger Ouimet). Queen's Printer.

Canada (1977a), *Report of the Sub-Committee on the Penitentiary System in Canada* (Chair, Mark MacGuigan). Queen's Printer.

Canada (1977b), *Report of the National Advisory Committee on the Female Offender* (Chair, Donna Clark). Ministry of the Solicitor General.

Canada (1978a), *Report of the National Planning Committee on the Female Offender* (Chair, Alan Needham). Queen's Printer.

Canada (1978b), *Report of Joint Committee to Study Alternatives for the Housing of the Federal Female Offender* (Chair, Doug Chinnery). Commissioner of Corrections.

Canada (1987), *Gestion des délinquants et programmes pour les délinquants*, Cahier documentaire préparé à l'intention du comité permanent de la justice et du Solliciteur général. Ministère des services correctionnels.

Canada (1988), *Taking responsibility. A report of the Standing Committee on Justice and Solicitor General on its review of sentencing, conditional release, and related aspects of corrections* (Chair, David Daubney). Queen's Printer.

Canada (1990), *Creating choices. Report of the Task Force on Federally Sentenced Women*. Correctional Service Canada.

Canada (1996), *Commission of Inquiry into Certain Events at the Prison for Women* (Commissioner, Hon. Louise Arbour). Public Works and Government Services.

Canada (2007), *Report of the Correctional Service Canada Review Panel. A roadmap to strenghtening public safety*, Catalogue No PS84-14/2007E. Public Works and Government Services.

Canadian Human Rights Commission (2003), *Protecting their rights: A systemic review of human rights in correctional services for federally sentenced women*. Canadian Human Rights Commission.

Capoccia, Giovanni, and R. Daniel Kelemen (2007), "The study of critical junctures: Theory, narrative and counterfactuals in historical institutionalism," *World Politics*, vol. 59, no. 3, p. 341-369.

Carlen, Pat (1983), *Women's imprisonment. A study in social control*. Routledge.

Caron-Labrecque, Mélissa (2017), *Prison des Patriotes-au-Pied-du-Courant. Vue générale*, Culture et communications Québec, https://www.patrimoine-culturel.gouv.qc.ca/rpcq/detail.do?methode=consulter&id=92595&type=bien, accessed March 17, 2021.

Centre de documentation sur l'éducation des adultes et la condition féminine (CDEACF) (2020), "Bulletin COVID #7: Lettre collective," *Centre de documentation sur l'éducation des adultes et la condition féminine*, Bulletin – spécial COVID: Prisons et COVID-19, http://cdeacf.ca/page/bulletin-covid-7-lettre-collective, accessed March 11, 2022.

Chan, Wendy, and George Rigakos (2002), "Risk, crime and gender," *British Journal of Criminology*, vol. 42, no. 4, p. 743-761.

Chartrand, Paul L.A.H. (1991), "'Terms of division': Problems of 'outside-naming' for Aboriginal people in Canada," *Journal of Indigenous Studies*, vol. 2, no. 2, p. 1-22.

Chen, Yu-Shu, Yung-Lien Lai, and Chien-Yang Lin (2013), "Dimensions and predictors of treatment needs for female inmates: An exploratory study in Taiwan," *International Journal of Comparative and Applied Criminal Justice*, vol. 37, no. 2, p. 119-142.

Chéné, Bernard (2020), *Analyse prospective de la population carcérale des établissements de détention du Québec, 2018-2019 à 2028-2029*. Québec, Services correctionnels, Ministère de la Sécurité publique.

Chéné, Bernard, and Eugénie Chouinard (2018), *Profil des femmes confiées aux Services correctionnels en 2015-2016*. Québec, Services correctionnels, Ministère de la Sécurité publique.

Collier, Ruth Berins, and David Collier (1991), *Shaping the political arena: Critical junctures, the labor movement and regime dynamics in Latin America*. Princeton University Press.

Comack, Elizabeth (2006), "The feminist engagement with criminology," in Gillian Balfour and Elizabeth Comack (eds.), *Criminalizing women*. Fernwood Publishing.

Comack, Elizabeth (2018), *Coming back to jail: Women, trauma and criminalization*. Fernwood Publishing.

Comité de travail formé dans le cadre de l'entente de partenariat entre le ministère de la Sécurité publique et la Société Elizabeth Fry du Québec (2018), *Une voix différente. Rapport pour une proposition d'un modèle innovateur en matière de gestion des services correctionnels pour la clientèle féminine*, http://www.elizabethfry.qc.ca/docs_pdf/Rapport_une_voix_differente.pdf, accessed October 21, 2022.

Commission des droits de la personne du Québec (1985), *Enquête de la Commission des droits de la personne à la prison Tanguay*. Commission des droits de la personne du Québec.

Cooper, Sheelagh Dunn (1987), "The evolution of the Women's Federal Prison," in Ellen Adelberg and Claudia Currie (eds.), *Too few to count: Canadian women in conflict with the law*. Press Gang.

Correctional Investigator Canada (2010), *Annual Report 2009-2010*, https://www.oci-bec.gc.ca/cnt/rpt/pdf/annrpt/annrpt20092010-eng.pdf, accessed February 23, 2021.

Correctional Investigator Canada (2014), "Reflections on conditions of confinement of federally sentenced women (FSW)," https://www.oci-bec.gc.ca/cnt/comm/presentations/presentations20140314-15-eng.aspx.%20Accessed%20May%2007, accessed May 7, 2021.

Correctional Investigator Canada (2019), *Annual Report 2018-2019*, https:// oci-bec.gc.ca/cnt/rpt/annrpt/annrpt20142015-eng.aspx#s10, accessed February 17, 2021.

Correctional Investigator Canada (2020), *Annual Report 2019-2020*, https:// www.oci-bec.gc.ca/cnt/rpt/pdf/annrpt/annrpt20192020-eng.pdf, accessed December 15, 2021.

Correctional Service Canada (1994), *Board of investigation: Major disturbance and other related Incidents – Prison for women from Friday April 22 to Tuesday April 26, 1994.* Correctional Service Canada.

Correctional Service Canada (2007), *Expert committee review of the Correctional Service of Canada's Ten-Year Status Report on Women's Corrections* (chair, Constance Glube). Public Works and Government Services Canada.

Correctional Service Canada (2018), *Quick facts: Women offenders*, https:// www.csc-scc.gc.ca/publications/092/005007-3012-en.pdf, accessed February 19, 2021.

Correctional Service Canada (n.d.), "Toward a Continuum of Care, Correctional Service Canada Mental Health Strategy," https://www. csc-scc.gc.ca/002/006/002006-2000-eng.shtml#_Toc267041277, accessed March 21, 2022.

Cousineau, Sophie, and Sylvie Frigon (2016), "Les femmes détenues d'*Unité 9*: entre espace fictionnel et réalité," *Criminologie*, vol. 49, no. 2, p. 323-347.

Cox, Robert (2004), "The path-dependency of an idea: Why Scandinavian welfare states remain distinct," *Social Policy and Administration*, vol. 38, no. 2, p. 204-219.

Coyle, Diane (2014), *GDP. A brief but affectionate history.* Princeton University Press.

Criminal Code, R.S.C. (1985) c. C-46.

David, Paul A. (1985), "Clio and the economics of QWERTY," *American Economic Review*, vol. 75, no. 2, p. 332-337.

de Vries, Michiel (2000), "The secret and cost of success: Institutional change and policy change," in Oscar Van Heffen, Walter J. M. Kickert and Jacques J.A. Thomassen (eds.), *Governance in modern society: Effects, change and formation of government institutions.* Kluwer.

Dickens, Charles (1874), *Pictures from Italy and American notes for general circulation.* G.W. Carleton & Co. Publishers.

Di Corleto, Julieta (2015), *Women in prison – Regional report: Argentina, Bolivia, Chile, Paraguay, Uruguay* (translation from Spanish by Mindy

Steinberg). Center for Justice and International Law (CEJIL), https://cejil.org/en/publications/women-in-prison-regional-report-argentina-bolivia-chile-paraguay-uruguay/, accessed October 10, 2022.

DiMaggio, Paul J., and Walter W. Powell (1983), "The iron cage revisited: Institutional isomorphism and collective rationality in organizational fields," *American Sociological Review*, vol. 48, no. 2, p. 147-160.

Dion, Mario (1999), *Final report of the Federal-Provincial/Territorial Policy Review*. Correctional Service Canada.

Drake, Deborah H. (2018), "Prisons and state-building: Promoting the 'fiasco of the prison' in a global context," *International Journal for Crime, Justice and Social Democracy*, vol. 7, no. 4, p. 1-15.

Driver, Felix (2004), *Power and pauperism: The workhouse system, 1834-1884*. Cambridge University Press.

Earle, Rod, and Coretta Phillips (2012), "Digesting men? Ethnicity, gender and food: Perspectives from a 'prison ethnography,'" *Theoretical Criminology*, vol. 16, no. 2, p. 141-156.

Ebbinghaus, Bernhard (2005), *Can path dependence explain institutional change? Two approaches applied to welfare state reform*, MPIfG Discussion paper no. 05/2. Max Planck Institute for the Study of Societies.

Edmison, John Alexander (1954), "The history of Kingston Penitentiary," in Kingston Historical Society (ed.) *Historic Kingston no. 3*. Kingston Historical Society, https://archive.org/details/historickingston03kinguoft/page/36/mode/2up?view=theater, accessed November 23, 2021.

Elliot, Liz, and Ruth Morris (1987), "Behind prison doors," in Ellen Adelberg and Claudia Currie (eds.), *Too few to count: Canadian women in conflict with the law*. Press Gang.

Elshtain, Jean Bethke (1995), *Women and war*, 2nd ed. Chicago University Press.

Faith, Karleen (1987), "Media, myths and masculinization: Images of women in prison," in Ellen Adelberg and Claudia Currie (eds.), *Too few to count: Canadian women in conflict with the law*. Press Gang.

Faludi, Susan (1991), *Backlash. The undeclared war against American women*. Crown Publishing Group.

Fecteau, Jean-Marie (1989), *Un nouvel ordre des choses: la pauvreté, le crime, l'État au Québec, de la fin du XVIIIe siècle à 1840*. VLB.

Fecteau, Jean-Marie, Marie-Josée Tremblay, and Jean Trépanier (1993), "La prison de Montréal de 1865 à 1913: évolution en longue période d'une population pénale," *Les Cahiers de Droit*, vol. 34, no. 1, p. 27-58.

Fournier, Jean-Pierre (1989), *Vision du bagne: la vie des forçats, de St-Martin-de-Ré à la Guyane*. Éditions du Pélican.

Fowler, Simon (2007), *The workhouse: The people, the places, the life behind closed doors*. Pen & Sword History.

Friesen, John W. (1995), "The changing public image of Doukhobors in Canada," *Canadian Ethnic Studies*, vol. 27, no. 3, p. 131-140.

Frigon, Sylvie (2001), "Femmes et emprisonnement: le marquage du corps et l'auto-mutilation," *Criminologie*, vol. 34, no. 2, p. 31-56.

Frigon, Sylvie (2002), "*La création de choix* pour les femmes incarcérées: sur les traces du groupe d'étude sur les femmes purgeant une peine fédérale et de ses conséquences," *Criminologie*, vol. 35, no. 2, p. 9-30.

Fyson, Donald (2006), *Magistrates, police, and people: Everyday criminal justice in Québec and Lower Canada, 1764-1837*. Osgoode Society for Canadian Legal History and University of Toronto Press.

Fyson, Donald (2017), "Crime and criminal justice history in Canada: Some thoughts on future developments," *Crime, Histoire & Sociétés*, vol. 21, no. 2, p. 173-182.

Garud, Raghu, Arun Kumaraswany, and Peter Karnoe (2010), "Path dependence or path creation?," *Journal of Management Studies*, vol. 47, no. 4, p. 760-774.

Giroux, Louise, and Sylvie Frigon (2011), *Profil correctionnel 2007-2008: les femmes confiées aux services correctionnels*. Québec, Services correctionnels, Ministère de la Sécurité publique.

Godderis, Rebecca (2006a), "Dining in: The symbolic power of food in prison," *Howard Journal of Criminal Justice*, vol. 45, no. 3, p. 255-267.

Godderis, Rebecca (2006b), "Food for thought: An analysis of power and identity in prison food narratives," *Berkeley Journal of Sociology*, vol. 50, p. 61-75.

Gormley, Rebecca, Sally Y. Lin, Allison Carter, Valerie Nicholson, Kath Webster, Ruth Elwood Martin, Michael John Milloy, Neora Pick, Terry Howard, Lu Wang, Alexandra de Pokomandy, Mona Loutfi, Angela Kaida, and CHIWOS Research Team (2020), "Social determinants of health and retention in HIV care among recently incarcerated women living with HIV in Canada," *AIDS and Behavior*, vol. 24, no. 4, p. 1212-1225.

Haggerty, Kevin (2004), "Ethics creep: Governing social science research in the name of ethics," *Qualitative Sociology*, vol. 27, no. 4, p. 391-414.

Hannah-Moffat, Kelly (1999), "Moral agent or actuarial subject: Risk and Canadian women's imprisonment," *Theoretical Criminology*, vol. 3, no. 1, p. 71-94.

Hannah-Moffat, Kelly (2001), *Punishment in disguise: Penal governance and Canadian women's imprisonment*. University of Toronto Press.

Hannah-Moffat, Kelly, and Margaret Shaw (2000a), "Introduction. Prisons for women – Theory, reform, ideals," in Kelly Hannah-Moffat and Margaret Shaw (eds.), *An ideal prison? Critical essays on women's imprisonment in Canada*. Fernwood Publishing.

Hannah-Moffat, Kelly, and Margaret Shaw (2000b), "Prisons that empower: Neo-liberal governance in Canadian women's prisons," *British Journal of Criminology*, vol. 40, no. 3, p. 510-531.

Hayman, Stephanie (2000), "Prison reform and incorporation: Lessons from Britain and Canada," in Kelly Hannah-Moffat and Margaret Shaw (eds.), *An ideal prison? Critical essays on women's imprisonment in Canada*. Fernwood Publishing.

Hayman, Stephanie (2006), *Imprisoning our sisters. The new federal women's prisons in Canada*. McGill-Queen's University Press.

Hennessy, Peter (1999), *Canada's big house. The dark history of the Kingston Penitentiary*. Dundurn Press.

Henry, Louise (2022), *Délivrez-nous de la prison Leclerc! Un témoignage de l'intérieur*, Collection Parcours. Éditions Écosociété.

Hinrichs, Karl (2000), "Elephants on the move: Patterns of public pension reform in OECD countries," *European Review*, vol. 8, no. 3, p. 353-378.

Howlett, Michael (2009), "Process sequencing policy dynamics: Beyond homeostasis and path dependency," *Journal of Public Policy*, vol. 29, no. 3, p. 241-262.

Jackson, Michael (1988), *Justice behind the walls. A report of the Canadian Bar Association Committee on Imprisonment and Release*. Canadian Bar Association.

Jackson, Michael, and Graham Stewart (2009), *A flawed compass: A human rights analysis of the Roadmap to Strengthening Public Safety*, https://commons.allard.ubc.ca/cgi/viewcontent.cgi?article=1029&context=emeritus_pubs, accessed June 13, 2021.

Jefferson, Andrew M. (2005) "Reforming Nigerian prisons: Rehabilitating a 'deviant' state," *British Journal of Criminology*, vol. 45, no. 4, p. 487-503.

Jeffries, Samantha, and Greg Newbold (2016), "Analysing trends in the imprisonment of women in Australia and New Zealand," *Psychiatry, Psychology and Law*, vol. 23, no. 2, p. 184-206.

Jewkes, Yvonne (2007), "Prisons and the media: The shaping of public opinion and penal policy in a mediated society," in Yvonne Jewkes (ed.), *Handbook on prisons*. Routledge.

Johnson, Dana (2015), "Architecture carcérale," in *Encyclopédie Canadienne*, https://www.thecanadianencyclopedia.ca/fr/article/architecture-carcerale, accessed April 20, 2021.

Jones, Daniel D., Sandra M. Bucerius, and Kevin D. Haggerty (2019), "Voices of remanded women in Western Canada: A qualitative analysis," *Journal of Community Safety and Well-Being*, vol. 4, no. 3, p. 44-53.

Karstedt, Susanne (2010), "New institutionalism in criminology: Approaches, theories and themes," in Eugene McLaughlin and Tim Newburn (eds.), *The Sage handbook of criminological theory*. Sage.

Kay, Adrian (2003), "Path dependency and the CAP," *Journal of European Public Policy*, vol. 10, no. 3, p. 405-420.

Kendall, Kathleen (2002), "Time to think again about cognitive behavioural programmes," in Pat Carlen (ed.), *Women and punishment: The struggle for justice*. Willan.

Kendall, Kathleen, and Soshana Pollack (2003), "Cognitive behaviouralism in women's prisons: A critical analysis of therapeutic assumptions and practice," in Barbara E. Bloom (ed.), *Gendered justice: Addressing female offenders*. Carolina Academic Press.

Kilty, Jennifer M. (2012), "'It's like they don't want you to get better': Psy control of women in the carceral context," *Feminism & Psychology*, vol. 22, no. 2, p. 162-182.

Kilty, Jennifer M., and Katarina Bogosavljevic (2019), "Emotional story-telling: Sensational media and the creation of the HIV sexual predator," *Crime, Media, Culture*, vol. 15, no. 2, p. 279-299.

Klein, Peter G. (1999), "New institutional economics," (entry 0530), in Boudewijn Bouckaert and Gerrit De Geest (eds.), *Encyclopedia of law and economics*. Edward Elgar.

Kronsell, Annica (2016), "Sexed bodies and military masculinities: Gender path dependence in EU's common security and defense policy," *Men and Masculinities*, vol. 19, no. 3, p. 311-336.

Krook, Mona Lena, and Fiona Mackay (2011), *Gender, politics and institutions: Towards a feminist institutionalism*. Palgrave Macmillan.

Kulawik, Teresa (2009), "Stacking the frame of a feminist discursive institutionalism," *Politics & Gender*, vol. 5, no. 2, p. 262-271.

Landreville, Pierre, and Ghislaine Julien (1976), "Les origines de la prison de Bordeaux dans l'emprisonnement au Québec," *Criminologie*, vol. 9, no. 1-2, p. 5-23.

Laplante, Jacques (1991), "Cent ans de prison: les conditions et les 'privilèges' des détenus hommes, femmes et enfants," *Criminologie*, vol. 24, no. 1, p. 11-32.

Larason Schneider, Anne (2006), "Patterns of change in the use of imprisonment in the American states: An integration of path dependence, punctuated equilibrium and policy design approaches," *Political Research Quarterly*, vol. 59, no. 3, p. 457-470.

Lasnier, Benoit, Michael Cantinotti, Louise Guyon, Anne Royer, Serge Brochu, and Lyne Chayer (2011), "Implementing an indoor smoking ban in prison: Enforcement issues and effects on tobacco use, exposure to second-hand smoke and health of inmates," *Canadian Journal of Public Health*, vol. 102, no. 4, p. 249-253.

Lawrence, Bonita (2004), *'Real' Indians and others: Mixed-blood urban Native peoples and Aboriginal nationhood*. University of British Columbia Press.

Levi, Margaret (1997), "A model, a method, and a map: Rational choice in comparative and historical analysis," in Mark I. Lichbach and Alan S. Zuckerman (eds.), *Comparative politics: Rationality, culture, and structure*. Cambridge University Press.

Liebling, Allison (2004), *Prisons and their moral performance. A study of values, quality, and prison life*. Oxford Clarendon Studies in Criminology, Oxford University Press.

Liebowitz, Stan J., and Stephen E. Margolis (1999), "Path dependence" (entry 0770 – Fundamental Concepts), in Boudewijn Bouckaert and Gerrit De Geest (eds.), *Encyclopedia of law and economics*. Edward Elgar.

Mahoney, James (2000), "Path dependence in historical sociology," *Theory and Society*, vol. 29, no. 4, p. 507-548.

Mahoney, James (2002), *The legacies of liberalism: Path dependence and political regimes in Central America*. Johns Hopkins University Press.

Manifeste des détenues contre l'austérité (2015), https://toutedetention estpolitique.wordpress.com/2015/12/31/manifeste-des-detenu-e-s-contre-lausterite/, accessed March 22, 2021.

Marques, Olga, and Lisa Monchalin (2020), "The mass incarceration of indigenous women in Canada: A colonial tactic of control and assimilation," in Lily George, Adele A. Norris, Antje Deckert and Juan Tauri (eds.), *Neo-colonial injustice and the mass incarceration of Indigenous women*, Palgrave Studies in Race, Ethnicity, Indigeneity and Criminal Justice. Palgrave Macmillan.

Martel, Joane (2006), "To be, one has to be somewhere: Spatio-temporality in prison segregation," *British Journal of Criminology*, vol. 46, no. 4, 587-612.

Martel, Joane, and Renée Brassard (2008), "Painting the prison 'red': Constructing and experiencing Indigenous identities in prison," *British Journal of Social Work*, vol. 38, no. 2, p. 340-361.

Martel, Joane, Renée Brassard, and Mylène Jaccoud (2011), "When two worlds collide: Aboriginal risk management in Canadian corrections," *British Journal of Criminology*, vol. 51, no. 2, p. 235-255.

Martel, Johane (1990), *L'intervention psychosociale au sein du pénal*, Première conférence internationale du Groupe de recherche sur l'étude de la production de l'ordre (GREPO), Annexe #2 Aperçu des pratiques au Canada, vol. IV. Département de criminologie, Université d'Ottawa.

Martel, Johane (1991), *La reconstruction de la criminalité à travers* La Presse *(1886-1989): l'image de la contrevenante et de la femme victime*, Master's thesis. Department of Criminology, University of Ottawa.

Martin, Ron, and Peter Sunley (2006), "Path dependence and regional economic evolution," *Journal of Economic Geography*, vol. 6, p. 395-437.

Martin, Tomas Max, Andrew M. Jefferson, and Mahuya Bandyopadhyay (2014), "Sensing prison climates: Governance, survival and transition," *Focaal: Journal of Global and Historical Anthropology*, vol. 68, no. 1, p. 3-17.

Mathieu, Edouard, Hannah Ritchie, Lucas Rodès-Guirao, Cameron Appel, Daniel Gravilov, Charlie Giattino, Joe Hassell, Bobbie MacDonald, Saloni Dattani, Diana Beltekian, Esteban Ortiz-Ospina, and Max Roser (2022), *Cumulative confirmed COVID-19 deaths per million people*, Our World in Data, https://ourworldindata.org/explorers/coronavirus-data-explorer, accessed March 11, 2022.

May, Trevor (1987), *An economic and social history of Britain 1760–1970*. Longman Publishing Group.

McEwen, Nicola (2006), *Nationalism and the state. Welfare and identity in Scotland and Québec.* Presses interuniversitaires européennes – Peter Lang.

McIvor, Gill (2010), "Women and crime: The rise in female imprisonment in Western jurisdictions," in Martine Herzog-Evans (ed.), *Transnational criminology manual (Volume 2)*. Wolf Publishing.

McKendry, Jennifer (1991), *William Coverdale and the architecture of Kingston from 1835 to 1865*, Doctoral thesis. Department of the History of Art, University of Toronto.

McLean, Julia (1995), "Prévenues et détenues logées à la même enseigne, l'exemple des prisons de Burnaby et de Tanguay," *Criminologie*, vol. 28, no. 2, p. 43-60.

McMahon, Maeve W. (1992), *The persistent prison? Rethinking decarceration and penal reform.* University of Toronto Press.

Milligan, Ronda-Jane, Glenn Waller and Bernice Andrews (2002), "Eating disturbances in female prisoners: The role of anger," *Eating Behaviors*, vol. 3, no. 2, p. 123-132.

Minaker, Joanne, and Laureen Snider (2006), "Husband abuse: Equality with a vengeance?," *Canadian Journal of Criminology & Criminal Justice*, vol. 48, no. 5, p. 753-780.

Ministère de la Justice (2016), *Établissements pénitentiaires disposant de quartiers femmes*. Direction de l'Administration Pénitentiaire, Service Communication, http://www.justice.gouv.fr/art_pix/Carte_quartiers_femmes_02_2016.pdf, accessed October 11, 2022.

Ministère de la Justice (2022), *Statistique des établissements et des personnes écrouées en France*. Direction de l'Administration Pénitentiaire, Bureau de la donnée (DAP/SDEX/EX3), http://www.justice.gouv.fr/art_pix/Statistique_etablissements_personnes_ecrouees_France_202209_.pdf, accessed October 11, 2022.

Monchalin, Lisa (2016), *The colonial problem: An Indigenous perspective on crime and injustice in Canada*. University of Toronto Press.

Neufeld, Roger (1998), "Cabals, quarrels, strikes, and impudence: Kingston Penitentiary, 1890-1914," *Histoire sociale/Social History*, vol. 31, no. 6, p. 95-125.

Noppen, Luc (1976), "La prison du Pied-au-Courant à Montréal: une étape dans l'évolution de l'architecture pénitentiaire au Bas-Canada et au Québec," *Revue d'art canadienne*, vol. 3, no. 1, p. 36-50.

Noppen, Luc, Hélène Jobidon, and Paul Trépanier (1990), *Québec monumental: 1890-1990*. Septentrion.

North, Douglass C. (1990), *Institutions, institutional change and economic performance*. Cambridge University Press.

North, Douglass C. (1993), *Economic performance through time*, Nobel Prize Lecture, https://www.nobelprize.org/prizes/economic-sciences/1993/north/lecture/, accessed February 26, 2021.

North, Douglass C. (2005), *Understanding the process of economic change*. Princeton University Press.

Nova Scotia (1992), *Blueprint for change. Report of the Solicitor General's Special Committee on Provincially Incarcerated Women*. Nova Scotia Correctional Services.

Numeris (2015), *Palmarès des émissions au Québec du 27 janvier au 02 février 2014*, https://assets.numeris.ca/Downloads/27%20janvier%20au%202%20f%C3%A9vrier%202014%20(Semaine%2023)-Québec.pdf, accessed July 7, 2021.

Observatoire international des prisons – section française (n.d), *Femmes détenues*, https://oip.org/decrypter/thematiques/femmes-detenues/, accessed October 11, 2022.

O'Malley, Pat (1999), "Volatile and contradictory punishment," *Theoretical Criminology*, vol. 3, no. 2, p. 175-196.

Ontario (1995), *Women's voices, women's choices: Report of the women's issues task force*. Ministry of the Solicitor General and Correctional Services.

Pace Law Review (2010), *Opening up a closed world: A sourcebook on prison oversight* (special issue), vol. 30, no. 5, p. 1383-1930.

Paci, Chris (2002), "Institutional representations of Aboriginal people," *Reviews in Anthropology*, vol. 31, no. 2, p. 165-183.

Padfield, Nicola, and Shadd Maruna (2006), "The revolving door at the prison gate: Exploring the dramatic increase in recalls to prison," *Criminology and Criminal Justice*, vol. 6, no. 3, p. 329-352.

Palier, Bruno (2000), "'Defrosting' the French welfare state," *West European Politics*, vol. 23, no. 3, p. 113-136.

Parole Board of Canada (2018), *Performance Monitoring Report, 2017-2018*. Parole Board of Canada.

Piché, Justin (2012), *The prison idea (un)interrupted: Penal infrastructure expansion, research and action in Canada*, Doctoral dissertation. Carleton University.

Pierson, Paul (1993), "When effect becomes cause: Policy feedback and political change," *World Politics*, vol. 45, no. 4, p. 595-628.

Pierson, Paul (2000), "Increasing returns, path dependence, and the study of politics," *American Political Science Review*, vol. 94, no. 2, p. 251-267.

Pierson, Paul (2004), *Politics in time. History, institutions and social analysis*. Princeton University Press.

Pisciotta, Alexander W. (1994), *Benevolent repression: Social control and the American reformatory-prison movement*. New York University Press.

Pollack, Shoshana (2005), "Taming the shrew: Regulating prisoners through women-centered mental health programming," *Critical Criminology*, vol. 13, no. 1, p. 71-87.

Porter, Theodore M. (1995), *Trust in numbers. The pursuit of objectivity in science and public life*. Princeton University Press.

Prado, Mariana Mota, and Michael J. Trebilcock (2009), "Path dependence, development and the dynamics of institutional reform," *University of Toronto Law Journal*, vol. 59, no. 3, p. 341-380.

Québec (2014), *Les services correctionnels du Québec. Document d'information*. Québec, Ministère de la Sécurité publique.

Québec (2015), *Transfert des femmes incarcérées de l'Établissement de détention Maison Tanguay et changement de vocation de l'Établissement de détention Leclerc de Laval*, Press release, September 24, 2015. Québec, Ministère de la Sécurité publique.

Québec (2018a), *Les infrastructures publiques du Québec. Plan québécois des infrastructures, 2018-2028*. Québec, Conseil du trésor.

Québec (2018b), *Plan stratégique 2017-2021*. Québec, Ministère de la Sécurité publique, https://cdn-contenu.quebec.ca/cdn-contenu/adm/min/securite-publique/publications-adm/plan-strategique/PL_strategique_MSP_2017_2021.pdf?1543587260, accessed October 14, 2022.

Québec (2020a), *Profil de la population carcérale en 2018-2019*. Québec, Ministère de la Sécurité publique, https://www.securitepublique.gouv.qc.ca/fileadmin/Documents/services_correctionnels/publications/profil_population_corr/profil_population_corr_2018-2019.pdf.pdf, accessed February 17, 2021.

Québec (2020b), *Profile of women referred to Correctional Services in 2018-2019*. Québec, Ministère de la Sécurité publique, https://cdn-contenu.quebec.ca/cdn-contenu/adm/min/securite-publique/publications-adm/publications-secteurs/services-correctionnels/profil-clientele-correctionnelle/profil_corr_femmes_2018-2019.pdf?1624307392, accessed February 28, 2022.

Québec (2021), *Plan stratégique 2019-2023*. Québec, Ministère de la Sécurité publique, https://cdn-contenu.quebec.ca/cdn-contenu/adm/min/securite-publique/publications-adm/plan-strategique/PL_strategique_MSP_2019-2023_maj_07-2021.pdf?1626456198, accessed October 14, 2022.

Québec Ombudsman (2014), *Annual report, 2013-2014*, https://publications.virtualpaper.com/protecteur-du-citoyen/en/rapport-annuel-2014/#50/, accessed June 22, 2021.

Québec Ombudsman (2016), *Annual Report, 2015-2016*, https://protecteurducitoyen.qc.ca/sites/default/files/pdf/rapports_annuels/rapport-annuel-2015-2016-protecteur.pdf, accessed December 15, 2021.

Québec Ombudsman (2017), *Annual Report, 2016-2017*, https://protecteurducitoyen.qc.ca/fr/enquetes/rapports-annuels/2016-2017, accessed April 4, 2022.

Québec Ombudsman (2018), *Les conséquences de l'augmentation des peines discontinues dans les établissements de détention du Québec (rapport spécial)*. Québec, Protecteur du citoyen.

Québec Ombudsman (2020), *Annual report, 2019-2020*, https://publications.virtualpaper.com/protecteur-citoyen/annual_report_2020/#76/, accessed November 30, 2021.

Québec Ombudsman (2022), *Annual report, 2021-2022*. Québec, Ombudsman Office.

Reitano, Julie (2017), "Adult correctional statistics in Canada, 2015-2016," *Juristat*, Catalog # 85-002-X. Statistics Canada.

Reiter, Kerameet (2012), *The most restrictive alternative: The origins, functions, control, and ethical implications of the Supermax Prison, 1976-2010*, PhD thesis. U.C. Berkeley.

Reiter, Kerameet (2014), "Making windows in walls: Strategies for prison research," *Qualitative Inquiry*, vol. 20, no. 4, p. 417-428.

Reynaud, Emmanuel (2000), *Social dialogue and pension reform: United Kingdom, United States, Germany, Japan, Sweden, Italy, Spain.* International Labour Office.

Rivard, Marguerite, and Mathieu Lavigne (2022), *Une fleur derrière les barreaux.* Éditions Novalis.

Rostaing, Corinne (2017), "L'invisibilisation des femmes dans les recherches sur la prison," *Les Cahiers de Framespa*, vol. 25, http://journals. openedition.org/framespa/4480, accessed October 11, 2022.

Roy, Shirley, Danielle Laberge, and Marie-Marthe Cousineau, (1992), "Les réincarcérations multiples: profil sexué d'un groupe de justiciables," *Criminologie*, vol. 25, no. 1, p. 101-117.

Rubin, Ashley T. (2019a), "Punishment's legal templates: A theory of formal penal change," *Law & Society Review*, vol. 53, no. 2, p. 518-553.

Rubin, Ashley T. (2019b), "The birth of the penal organization: Why prisons were born to fail," in Rosann Greenspan, Hadar Aviram and Jonathan Simon (eds.), *The legal process and the promise of justice: Studies inspired by the work of Malcolm Feeley.* Cambridge University Press.

Schreyögg, Georg, and Jörg Sydow (2011), "Organizational path dependence: A process view," *Organization Studies*, vol. 32, no. 3, p. 321-335.

Sheehan, Rosemary, and Chris Trotter (2018), *Women's transition from prison: The post-release experience.* Routledge, Taylor & Francis Group.

Skidmore, Rex A. (1948), "Penological pioneering in the Walnut Street Jail, 1789-1799," *Journal of Criminal Law and Criminology*, vol. 39, no. 2, p. 167-180.

Smith, Catrin (2002), "Punishment and pleasure: Women, food and the imprisoned body," *Sociological Review*, vol. 50, no. 2, p. 197-214.

Smoyer, Amy B. (2014a), "Feeding relationships: Food and social networks in a women's prison," *Affilia: Journal of Women and Social Work*, vol. 30, no. 1, p. 26-39.

Smoyer, Amy B. (2014b), "Good and healthy: Foodways and construction of identity in a women's prison," *The Howard Journal of Criminal Justice*, vol. 53, no. 5, p. 525-541.

Smoyer, Amy B. (2015), "Making fatty girl cakes: Food and resistance in a women's prison," *The Prison Journal*, vol. 96, no. 2, p. 191-209.

Smoyer, Amy B., and Kim M. Blankenship (2014), "Dealing food: Female drug users' narratives about food in a prison place and implications for their health," *International Journal of Drug Policy*, vol. 25, no. 3, p. 562-568.

Smoyer, Amy B., and Giza Lopes (2017), "Hungry on the inside: Prison food as a concrete and symbolic punishment in a women's prison," *Punishment & Society*, vol. 19, no. 2, p. 240-255.

Société Elizabeth Fry du Québec (2011), *La justice pénale et les femmes*. Éditions du Remue-ménage.

Statistics Canada (2022), "Indigenous population continues to grow and is much younger than the non-Indigenous population," *The Daily*, released September 21, 2022, https://www150.statcan.gc.ca/n1/en/daily-quotidien/220921/dq220921a-eng.pdf?st=HUY5MMY-, accessed November 22, 2022.

Strimelle, Véronique, and Sylvie Frigon (2011), "After prison: Experiences of women and employment in Québec, Canada," *Journal of Prisoners on Prisons*, vol. 20, no. 1, p. 108-137.

Struthers Montford, Kelly (2015), "Transforming choices: The marginalization of gender-specific policy making in Canadian approaches to women's federal imprisonment," *Canadian Journal of Women and the Law*, vol. 7, no. 2, p. 284-310.

Struthers Montford, Kelly (2022), "The embodiment of contempt: Ontario provincial prison food," *Social & Legal Studies*, vol. 32, no. 2, p. 237-256.

Thelen, Kathleen (1999), "Historical institutionalism and comparative politics," *Annual Review of Political Science*, vol. 2, no. 1, p. 369-404.

Thorpe, Rebecca U. (2015), "Perverse politics: The persistence of mass imprisonment in the twenty-first century," *Perspectives on Politics*, vol. 13, no. 3, p. 618-637.

Thrane, Sof, Steen Blaabjerg, and Rasmus Hanneman Møller (2010), "Innovative path dependence: Making sense of product and service innovation in path dependent innovation processes," *Research Policy*, vol 39, no. 7, p. 932-944.

Turnbull, Sarah, and Kelly Hannah-Moffat (2009), "Under these conditions: Gender, parole and the governance of reintegration," *British Journal of Criminology*, vol. 49, no. 4, p. 532-551.

Turnbull, Sarah, Joane Martel, Debra Parkes, and Dawn Moore (2018), "Introduction: Critical prison studies, carceral ethnography, and human rights – From lived experience to global action," *Oñati Socio-Legal Series*, vol. 8, no. 2, p. 174-182.

United Nations (2010), *Rules for the treatment of women prisoners and non-custodial measures for women offenders* (Bangkok Rules), https://www.unodc.org/documents/justice-and-prison reform/Bangkok_Rules_ENG_22032015.pdf, accessed April 12, 2022.

United Nations (2015), *Standard minimum rules for the treatment of prisoners* (Nelson Mandela Rules), https://www.un.org/en/events/mandeladay/mandela_rules.shtml, accessed December 9, 2021.

Van Hout, Marie-Claire, and Jakkie Wessels (2022), "Human rights and the invisible nature of incarcerated women in post-apartheid South Africa: Prison system progress in adopting the Bangkok Rules," *International Journal of Prisoner Health*, vol. 18 no. 3, p. 300-315.

Van Vugt, Marieke K., and Nico Broers (2016), "Self-reported stickiness of mind-wandering affects task performance," *Frontiers in Psychology*, vol. 7, p. 732.

Whittaker, Alison (2021), "No news is no news: COVID-19 and the opacity of Australian prisons," *Current Issues in Criminal Justice*, vol. 33, no. 1, p. 111-119.

Williamson, Oliver E. (1975), *Markets and hierarchies, analysis and antitrust implications: A study in the economics of internal organization.* University of Illinois at Urbana-Champaign's Academy for Entrepreneurial Leadership Historical Research Reference in Entrepreneurship.

Wolfe, David Allan, and Matthew Lucas (2005), *Global networks and local linkages: The paradox of cluster development in an open economy.* Published for the School of Policy Studies, Queen's University by McGill-Queen's University Press.

Zinger, Ivan (2021), "Vieillir et mourir en prison: enquête sur les expériences vécues par les personnes âgées sous garde fédérale," [paper presentation], Online conference *Les enjeux sociaux et de santé des personnes âgées judiciarisées*, March 31, 2021, CREGÉS-CAU en gérontologie sociale, https://www.youtube.com/watch?v=BsC2HlgXQXk.

Media references

Agence QMI (2022), "Québec confirme la construction d'une nouvelle prison pour femmes à Montréal," *Le Journal de Montréal*, December 19, 2022, https://www.journaldemontreal.com/2022/12/19/Québec-confirme-la-construction-dune-nouvelle-prison-pour-femmes-a-Montréal-1, accessed December 20, 2022.

Aile parlementaire de Québec solidaire (2019), "Alexandre Leduc invite Geneviève Guilbault à visiter la prison Leclerc avec lui," January 31, 2019, https://www.newswire.ca/fr/news-releases/alexandre-leduc-invite-genevieve-guilbault-de-visiter-la-prison-leclerc-avec-lui-899224925.html, accessed March 10, 2022.

Aubin, Erika (2020), "On a oublié les dossiers de 429 employés dans la prison," *Le Journal de Montréal*, December 20, 2020, https://www.journaldemontreal.com/2020/12/20/on-a-oublie-les-dossiers-de-429employes-dans-la-prison, accessed February 15, 2022.

Buchanan, Larry, Quoctrung Bui, and Jugal K. Patel (2020), "*Black Lives Matter* may be the largest movement in U.S. history," *The New York Times*, July 3, 2020, https://www.nytimes.com/interactive/2020/07/03/us/george-floyd-protests-crowd-size.html, accessed November 8, 2021.

Burch, Audra D. S., Amy Harmon, Sabrina Tavernise, and Emily Badger (2021), "The death of George Floyd reignited a movement. What happens now?," *The New York Times*, April 21, 2021, https://www.nytimes.com/2021/04/20/us/george-floyd-protests-police-reform.html, accessed November 8, 2021.

Caza, Pierre-Etienne (2013), "Danielle Trottier: derrière les barreaux d'*Unité 9*," *ActualitésUQAM*, April 15, 2013, https://www.actualites.uqam.ca/2013/danielle-trottier-derriere-les-barreaux-dunite-9, accessed February 21, 2021.

CBC News (2007), "Canada's only minimum-security women's prison to close," Canadian Broadcasting Corporation, February 20, 2007, https://www.cbc.ca/news/canada/ottawa/canada-s-only-minimum-security-women-s-prison-to-close-1.644209#:~:text=Canada's%20only%20federal%20facility%20forlow,.%2C%20the%20government%20said%20Monday, accessed March 21, 2022.

Dauphin-Johnson, Geneviève (2018), "Les conditions de détention à l'établissement Leclerc doivent être connues du public," Libre opinion, *Le Devoir*, June 22, 2018, https://www.ledevoir.com/opinion/libre-opinion/530940/les-conditions-de-detention-a-l-etablissement-leclerc-doivent-etre-connues-du-public, accessed March 1, 2022.

Donavan, Moira, and Brooklyn Currie (2021), "N.S. woman speaks out about 'dehumanizing' experience in correctional facility," Canadian Broadcasting Corporation, June 21, 2021, https://www.cbc.ca/news/canada/nova-scotia/health-segregation-privacy-breach-1.6073110, accessed November 8, 2021.

Drainville, Bernard (2020), "COVID-19: témoignage de Marie, détenue à la prison Leclerc," *Drainville PM*, 98.5 FM, https://www.985fm.ca/audio/305704/covid-19-temoignage-de-marie-detenue-a-la-prison-leclerc, accessed March 11, 2022.

Feith, Jesse (2018), "Rights activists, inmates decry 'nightmare' state of Leclerc prison," *Montreal Gazette*, December 21, 2018, https://montreal-gazette.com/news/local-news/rights-activists-inmates-decry-nightmare-state-of-leclerc-prison, accessed June 21, 2021.

Figarol, Noémie, and Catherine Descôteaux (2022), "La saga a assez duré à la prison Leclerc," *Le Devoir*, March 9, 2022, https://www.ledevoir.com/opinion/libre-opinion/683490/libre-opinion-la-saga-a-assez-dure-a-la-prison-leclerc, accessed March 10, 2022.

Fortier, Marco (2016), "Québec planifie une nouvelle prison pour femmes," *Le Devoir*, October 1, 2016, https://www.ledevoir.com/societe/481339/Québec-planifie-une-nouvelle-prison-pour-femmes, accessed February 16, 2021.

Gohier-Drolet, Alexis (2019), "Pression pour fermer la prison Leclerc," *Courrier Laval*, February 1, 2019, https://courrierlaval.com/pression-pour-fermer-la-prison-leclerc/, accessed March 15, 2022.

Groguhé, Marissa (2018), "Établissement Leclerc: la violence derrière les barreaux," *La Presse*, December 7, 2019, https://www.lapresse.ca/actualites/justice-et-faits-divers/201812/06/01-5206999-etablissement-leclerc-la-violence-derriere-les-barreaux.php, accessed March 11, 2022

Groguhé, Marissa (2019), "Établissement Leclerc: deux détenues déposent une demande d'injonction," *La Presse*, January 30, 2019, https://www.lapresse.ca/actualites/justice-et-faits-divers/actualites-judiciaires/201901/30/01-5212933-etablissement-leclerc-deux-detenues-deposent-une-demande-dinjonction.php, accessed February 28, 2022.

Guénette, Françoise (1983), "Comment vivent-elles en dedans? Mercredi à Tanguay," *La Vie en Rose. Magazine féministe d'actualité*, dossier "les femmes en prison," March 1983, no. 10, http://bv.cdeacf.ca/CF_PDF/LVR/1983/10mars/126095.pdf, accessed October 17, 2022.

Hébert, Vanessa (2019), "Prison Leclerc: la Cour supérieure propose une procédure accélérée," *Métro*, January 31, 2019, https://journalmetro.com/actualites/Montréal/2090490/prison-leclerc-la-cour-superieure-propose-une-procedure-acceleree/, accessed February 28, 2022.

Jetté, Élise (2019), "La prison Leclerc pour femmes: un pénitencier 'complète-ment scrap,'" *Le Journal de Montréal*, February 5, 2019, https://www.journaldemontreal.com/2019/02/05/la-prison-leclerc-pour-femmes-un-penitencier-completement-scrap, accessed June 22, 2022.

Jones, El, and Tim Bousquet (2021), "Vile video taken in Nova Scotia jail and posted to social media humiliates woman prisoner," *The Halifax Examiner*, April 2, 2021, https://www.halifaxexaminer.ca/featured/vile-video-taken-in-nova-scotia-jail-and-posted-to-social-media-humiliates-woman-prisoner/, accessed November 8, 2021.

La Presse canadienne (2019), "Québec solidaire met au défi la ministre Guilbault de visiter la prison Leclerc," *ICI Radio-Canada Nouvelles*, January 31, 2019, https://ici.radio-canada.ca/nouvelle/1150344/prison-leclerc-insalubrite-alexandre-leduc-denonciation, accessed March 10, 2022.

Lévesque, Lia (2016), "Femmes détenues à Leclerc: des groupes demandent à Couillard d'intercéder," *Le Devoir*, June 7, 2016, https://www.ledevoir. com/politique/Québec/472802/femmes-detenues-a-leclerc-des-groupes-demandent-a-couillard-d-interceder, accessed February 17, 2021.

Messier, François (2016), "Le sort de femmes détenues à Leclerc 'extrêmement' préoccupant," *Radio-Canada*, June 7, 2016, https://ici.radio-canada. ca/nouvelle/785922/etablissement-leclerc-mission-observation-ffq-ldl-coiteux-couillard, accessed February 15, 2022.

Nadeau, Jean-François (2016a), "Les détenues paient le prix de l'austérité," *Le Devoir*, February 20, 2016, https://www.ledevoir.com/societe/ justice/463507/les-detenues-paient-le-prix-de-l-austerite, accessed June 10, 2016.

Nadeau, Jean-François (2016b), "Détention difficile au temps de l'austérité," *Le Devoir*, March 10, 2016, https://www.ledevoir.com/politique/ Québec/465087/prisonnier-au-temps-de-l-austerite#, accessed June 25, 2016.

Nadeau, Jean-François (2016c), "Thériault a sa part de responsabilité, dénonce le PQ," *Le Devoir*, March 11, 2016, https://www.ledevoir.com/ societe/465275/femmes-en-prison-theriault-a-sa-part-de-responsabilite-denonce-le-pq, accessed January 25, 2021.

Nadeau, Jean-François (2016d), "À la défense des détenues de Leclerc," *Le Devoir*, April 28, 2016, https://www.ledevoir.com/societe/469341/les-conditions-de-vie-des-detenues-denoncees, accessed March 5, 2019.

Nadeau, Jean-François (2016e), "Prison Leclerc – Le ministère de la Sécurité publique étudie les demandes," *Le Devoir*, April 29, 2016, https://www. ledevoir.com/societe/469563/prison-leclerc-le-Ministere-de-la-securite-publique-etudie-les-demandes, accessed June 22, 2019.

Nadeau, Jean-François (2016f), "Les religieuses se mobilisent en faveur des prisonnières," *Le Devoir*, May 3, 2016, https://www.ledevoir.com/ societe/469797/les-religieuses-se-mobilisent-en-faveur-des-prisonnieres, accessed September 20, 2021.

Nadeau, Jean-François (2016g), "La prison Leclerc interdite d'accès," *Le Devoir*, June 8, 2016, https://www.ledevoir.com/societe/472821/pas-de-mission-d-observation-en-prison-decrete-le-ministre-coiteux, accessed March 4, 2019.

Nadeau, Jean-François (2016h), "La prison Leclerc bientôt visitée par l'ONU?," *Le Devoir,* June 9, 2016, https://www.ledevoir.com/ societe/472988/conditions-de-detention-la-prison-leclerc-bientot-visitee-par-l-onu, accessed March 4, 2019.

Nadeau, Jean-François (2018), "Mauvaises conditions de détention des femmes à la prison Leclerc," *Le Devoir*, December 5, 2018, https://www.ledevoir.com/societe/542857/mauvaises-conditions-de-detention-des-femmes-a-la-prison-leclerc, accessed August 13, 2021.

Nadeau, Jean-François (2019), "Mauvaises conditions de détention des femmes à la prison Leclerc," *Le Devoir*, February 1, 2019, https://www.ledevoir.com/societe/546810/mauvaises-conditions-de-detention-pour-les-femmes-a-la-prison-leclerc, accessed January 12, 2022.

Nadeau, Jean-François (2021a), "Misère et mépris pour les femmes détenues à la prison Leclerc," *Le Devoir*, March 31, 2021, https://www.ledevoir.com/societe/597902/leclerc-degradation-des-conditions-de-detention-pour-les-femmes, accessed March 31, 2021.

Nadeau, Jean-François (2021b), "Une autre femme se suicide à la prison Leclerc à Laval," *Le Devoir*, May 3, 2021, https://www.ledevoir.com/societe/599941/prison-une-autre-femme-se-suicide-a-la-prison-leclerc, accessed January 12, 2022.

Nadeau, Jean-François (2022), "Une nouvelle prison pour femmes bientôt?," *Le Devoir*, December 1, 2022, https://www.ledevoir.com/societe/773060/justice-une-nouvelle-prison-pour-femmes-bientot, accessed December 20, 2022.

New York Times (2021), "How George Floyd died, and what happened next," November 1, 2021, https://www.nytimes.com/article/george-floyd.html, accessed November 8, 2021.

Pelletier, Francine (1983), "L'histoire de Danielle D.," *La Vie en Rose. Magazine féministe d'actualité*, dossier "les femmes en prison," March 1983, no. 10, http://bv.cdeacf.ca/CF_PDF/LVR/1983/10mars/126095.pdf, accessed October 17, 2022.

Plante, Caroline (2019), "QS invite la ministre Guilbault à visiter la prison Leclerc," *La Presse*, January 31, 2019, https://www.lapresse.ca/actualites/politique/politique-quebecoise/201901/31/01-5213101-qs-invite-la-ministre-guilbault-a-visiter-la-prison-leclerc.php, accessed March 10, 2022.

Radio-Canada (2019), "Pas d'injonction pour améliorer les conditions de détention à la prison Leclerc," *ICI Radio-Canada Nouvelles*, January 31, 2019, https://ici.radio-canada.ca/nouvelle/1150163/prison-leclerc-conditions-detention-tribunaux-injonction, accessed August 13, 2021.

Radio-Canada (2022), "Encore sept ans d'attente avant une nouvelle prison pour femmes à Montréal," *ICI Radio-Canada Nouvelles*, December 20, 2022, https://ici.radio-canada.ca/nouvelle/1942826/femmes-detention-prison-construction, accessed February 15, 2023.

Rédaction Laval (2020a), "La LDL dénonce les conditions de détention à la prison Leclerc," *Courrier Laval*, March 8, 2020, https://courrierlaval. com/la-ldl-denonce-les-conditions-de-detention-a-la-prison-leclerc/, accessed March 10, 2022.

Rédaction Laval (2020b), "La LDL veut contenir la propagation dans les lieux de détention," *Courrier Laval*, March 22, 2020, https://courrierlaval.com/ la-ldl-veut-contenir-la-propagation-dans-les-lieux-de-detention/, accessed March 11, 2022.

Tanner, Adrienne (1996), "Shut it down – Bill Smith," *Edmonton Journal*, May 2, 1996, p. B1.

TVA Nouvelles (2012), "Le pénitencier Leclerc sera fermé," April 19, 2012, TVA Nouvelles, https://www.tvanouvelles.ca/2012/04/19/letablissement-leclerc-sera-ferme, accessed November 23, 2021.

TVA Nouvelles (2018), "Prison Leclerc: une coalition interpelle l'ONU," December 5, 2018, TVA Nouvelles, https://www.tvanouvelles. ca/2018/12/05/prison-leclerc-une-coalition-interpelle-lonu, accessed March 1, 2022.

Glossary

Adaptive expectation: Process by which institutions or organizations form expectations about what will happen in the future based on what has happened in the past. They adapt their reasoning, decisions, and activities to fit options expected to generate broad acceptance.

Bandwagon effect: Phenomenon whereby institutions or organizations do something essentially because other institutions or organizations are doing it, while ignoring or overriding their own beliefs.

Cognitive stickiness: Modes of reasoning or lines of thought from which it is laborious to disengage. They drive decisions in the same direction across many, even decentralized, institutional and organizational settings.

Critical juncture: Within the discipline of economics, critical junctures are short-term periods of institutional flux when new conditions sporadically disrupt or overwhelm an ongoing institutional trajectory and may initiate either a process of lock-in to a path or a bifurcation toward a different path. Within political science, critical junctures are political conflicts and power relations whereby collective actors institute new rules during a window of opportunity for action. Also referred to as choice point, triggering event, tipping point.

Exogenous shock: A shock or a force that is external to the institution or organization, such as major changes in the economy, depression, war, the COVID-19 pandemic, etc.

Formation phase: In the path dependence process, period which begins with a critical juncture and where a once unspecified logic of action begins to transform into an emerging dominant action pattern.

Gender path dependence: Process by which historical gender roles become persistent and resilient.

Increasing returns: Economic term for the process by which the benefits of engaging in certain institutional or organizational activities increase over time as more and more people devote time and money to a given way of doing things. As a result, the relative cost of exploring alternative avenues steadily grows.

Learning effect: Phenomenon by which institutional or organizational gains grow as familiarity with an activity increases.

Lock-in phase: In the path dependence process, period during which an institution or organization's reasoning, decisions, and activities are further contracted into a dominant path that will crystallize. Decision processes and established practices continue to produce the same outcomes even when faced with more efficient alternatives.

Network effect: Phenomenon whereby increasing the number of institutions, organizations, people that adopt a choice, a decision, an activity improves the "value" of such choice, decision, activity. The more people use a mode of functioning, of consuming, of reasoning, the greater the benefit for others to also embrace them.

Path cessation: Process by which the self-reinforcement mechanisms of an institution or organization end, which may open the way to a new institution or organization to replace the established one.

Path departure: Process by which intermediate change or gradual adaptation is achieved through partial rejuvenation of institutional or organizational long-standing arrangements. Limited rerouting of the institution or organization's core principles.

Path dependence: Process by which the strengthening of a given set of arrangements in social processes over time increases the cost of changing them. Institutions and organizations are said to be on a path-dependent process when they become locked into a trajectory from which they can only depart with the involvement of exogenous forces of shocks such as major changes in the economy, depression, or war.

Path stabilization: Process by which institutions or organizations achieve negligible adaptation to environmental changes. Little or no altering of the institution or organization's core principles.

Positive feedback mechanisms: Mechanisms that entrench particular standards and norms into institutions' or organizations' choices and habits and insulate them from change. Network and bandwagon effects are examples of positive feedback mechanisms.

Preformation phase: In the path dependence process, period of open access to a wide range of possible actions and alternatives within an organization.

Self-reinforcing process: Political term for "increasing returns." Social mechanism underlying the process by which one institutional or organizational alternative takes the lead over others.

Printed by Imprimerie Gauvin
Gatineau, Québec